The Way to Write Radio Drama

WILLIAM ASH

reversed.

Elm Tree Books · London

ELM TREE BOOKS

Published by the Penguin Group
Penguin Books Ltd, 27 Wrights Lane, London W8 5TZ, England
Penguin Books USA Inc., 375 Hudson Street, New York, New York 10014, USA
Penguin Books Australia Ltd, Ringwood, Victoria, Australia
Penguin Books Canada Ltd, 10 Alcorn Avenue, Toronto, Ontario, Canada M4V 3B2
Penguin Books (NZ) Ltd, 182–190 Wairau Road, Auckland 10, New Zealand

Penguin Books Ltd, Registered Offices: Harmondsworth, Middlesex, England

First published in Great Britain 1985 by
Elm Tree Books/Hamish Hamilton Ltd

5 7 9 10 8 6 4

A CIP catalogue record for this book is available from the British Library

ISBN 0–241–11446–2 Pbk

Printed in England by Clays Ltd, St Ives plc

Contents

Ken Whitmore; *Beach Games* by Derek Coltman; *Made in Heaven* by Andrew Sachs; *Taybridge* by Gerry Jones; *The What on the Landing* by Alan Plater; *Trouble on the Line* by Jennifer Phillips; *When the Music Stops* by David Marshall; *Vienna ABC* by David Marshall; *Cloth Caps, Mufflers and Ill-fitting Suits* by Tony Allen; *The Day Willy Put His Ear to the Wall* by David Fitzsimmons.

Acknowledgements

I wish to thank those authors who have permitted use of excerpts from their plays in this book — not only for the right of quotation but, much more, for the pleasure and excitement their work for radio has given to me and to many thousands of other listeners.

I wish also to thank the BBC Radio Drama Department for being such good colleagues, for teaching me so much during the years I worked among them and for realising, as all sections of the BBC should, that good broadcasting depends on recognising and encouraging the creative talents of outside artists — particularly the writers who in lonely toil perfect fine radio plays in all their engaging variety. I am indebted to Richard Imison, Radio Drama Script Editor, for the 'Reports on Plays', issued as guidance to radio drama editors.

I would like to express my appreciation of the efforts of Tony Cornish, of Capital Radio, and Michael Bartlett, of County Sound, to name but two of those who have concerned themselves with the broadcasting of radio drama by commercial stations.

Foreword

The writing of a radio play, I have always thought, was rather like the riding of a bicycle. Wonderfully simple, if only you knew how, but impossible if you didn't: and the learning process better left somewhere way back in the past, with its vague memories of blood, sweat, tears, scrapes, bruises and parental reproaches. Until suddenly there you are, as if by magic, in the heady company of those you most admire and respect, actually doing it, riding a bike! Writing a play! All that other stuff, the not riding of the bicycle, the not writing of plays, forgotten. Wheeling and dealing and look no hands! And the ahs and the oohs of those around changing suddenly to smirks of derision, I told you so's, as you push your luck too far, and oops, there you are, come a cropper, on your nose! Look, not enough hands! Oh yes, riding a bike, writing a play!

And as to writing a book on how to write a radio play — as tricky, surely, as writing one on how to ride a bicycle! And imagine the difficulty of that! A proper book, that is — not the kind usually written, on markets and techniques, and how long, and how to present Mss, those running obsessions of the would-be playwright, which serve well enough, I daresay, to mask the sheer terror he or she feels at the prospect of creativity (and rightly feels, for does not the dramatist usurp God, tread on His toes, inventing a world He never thought of, characters He never suggested? Such activities simply aren't allowed in, say, Islam . . .) but, as I say, a proper book, not just on the how but the *why* of radio drama! And of the very, very few people in the world fitted to write it, who better to do so, and succeed, than William Ash, one of the Little Fathers of Radio Drama through the sixties and the seventies, its nurturer through a joyous childhood (it being out of its infancy by then) and through a tumultuous adolescence; into what, I fear, now he is retiring, may become a somewhat maturely complacent form. But that early training will have its long-term effect: no-one should worry: some mid-life crisis or other will presently send it energetically bounding off again into hitherto unthought-of and miraculous realms. Early conditioning, as we know, always has its effect.

It is the capacity of fiction — of novels, stories, plays — to change our view of the world, and with our view of it, the world itself. And fiction requires two — the writer who invents; the reader (listener, viewer) who accepts the invention. Both are artists: the first acknowledged as such, the latter rarely so. Both are supremely important. *Under Milk Wood*, on the radio, one evening, accepted and understood, civilises us more than any mere change in the Abortion Laws. Or so I would argue.

And these two require, the world being a practical place, and some bridge between reality and imagination needs, a third. They require a magician, a producer, who stands in one world with his eyes on the other; it is he who makes the crossing possible: who conceives, understands and orchestrates the new forms of fiction as they come along: who yanks us up painfully — writers, readers, listeners, all — by our short creative hairs, as we drop our head and yawn and lapse back into hack-ish slumber, and reminds us of what we are, what we can be, what we used to be and will be again. Such a one is William Ash, born in Dallas, Texas in 1917, wartime fighter pilot, then fighter for the interests of writers of radio drama, overseeing its transition from the evening activity it used to be, losing its battle for a time to the more instantly gratifying forms of drama then provided by the television playwrights, to an afternoon celebration (at its best) of life and living.

We take so much for granted in the new worlds of radio and TV drama. It begins to seem to us now that these forms have always existed as they are, but of course they have not. They started as little vague sparks of animation and interest, and were breathed, blown, cherished, nurtured into self-sustaining life by a very particular kind of man and woman, working modestly, with a great deal of power and very little glory, at the BBC. Our debt to these unsung heroes and heroines is very great, as will no doubt, after the manner of these things, be properly recognised by future generations if not by us. In the meantime we have Bill Ash and 'The Way to Write Radio Drama', which is, of course, far more than a manual of mere instruction, but an essay on the nature of those powerful alternative realities blithely referred to as radio plays. In the same way that a book on 'How to Ride a Bicycle' has to be about more than just how to put your foot on the pedals, but about freedom, power, speed, wind, self-determination, life, death, sheer exhilaration.

Fay Weldon
September 1984

Introduction

SO you want to write radio drama. It puts you in the company of writers who began their careers as dramatists by writing for radio — like Harold Pinter, Robert Bolt, Joe Orton or Tom Stoppard. You will be writing for a medium which has attracted the talents of well-established writers in other fields — like Samuel Beckett, Richard Hughes, Fay Weldon or John Arden. And it is also by way of radio drama, as broadcast by the BBC, that some sixty to seventy new writers every year, who have never had anything published or performed before, first gain a public for their work.

Perhaps you, too, are just beginning as both writer and radio dramatist and, in addition to mastering the techniques of writing radio drama, will also have to acquire the discipline of turning blank sheets of paper into purposeful writing of any kind at all. But you will learn from the start to work in this new dramatic medium which uses sound alone to achieve all its effects.

Or perhaps you have tried your hand at writing radio drama already but have not been particularly successful in satisfying either yourself or some radio script editor with the results. It may be that a deeper knowledge of the nature of radio drama, of the limitations that have to be overcome and of the peculiar freedoms it allows the playwright, will enable you to write more effectively or even suggest better stories to tell in this dramatic form.

Or perhaps you have written other things — novels, short stories or poetry — and want to try your hand now at radio drama. An understanding of the difference between narrative and dramatic form, of visual and aural drama and an appreciation of the language of the radio play will help you make the transition.

In any case, this book is dedicated to you, the radio drama writer, seeking to express yourself in this new medium — new, that is, in the sense that the radio play has been with us only sixty years, even though it is made up of dramatic and narrative elements that are as old as human civilisation. The book is written in the hope that it will help you to write radio drama, to write it better and to increase your appreciation of this interesting art form which has now come to stay as part of our contemporary culture.

Chapter One

A Short History of the Radio Play

THE RADIO PLAY can be defined quite simply as a story told in dramatic form by means of sound alone. Depending on the wireless transmission and reception of sound without appreciable loss of quality the radio play is a child of the media and its birth only goes back about sixty years.

It is not often that we can date the beginning of a new art form precisely by citing the first work in that form to be produced. In 1924 Richard Hughes, well known as the author of such books as "A High Wind in Jamaica", undertook to write a play which could be put out on the air by the BBC. He completed it in one night; and *Danger*, the first radio play, was duly broadcast.

The first radio play equivalent to a full-length stage play, *The White Chateau* by Reginald Berkeley, was set during the First World War and was broadcast on Armistice Night, 1925. At the end of the 1920s Tyrone Guthrie, the distinguished theatre director, was attracted to the radio medium and wrote such plays as *The Flowers Are Not for You to Pick* and *Matrimonial News*. By 1931 the BBC was broadcasting fifty full-length plays a year; but many of these were adaptations from stage or novel and not original dramatic works written specifically for the sound medium.

Technological experiments in radio drama production at Savoy Hill, the BBC's first home, made it possible to plan studios elaborately equipped for different acoustic effects and cubicles with highly sophisticated control panels which were the very core of the design of the new Broadcasting House opened in 1932.

During the Second World War, when people were forced to spend most of their nights at home, there was a great increase in the audiences for radio drama. By 1951 the number of radio plays broadcast each year had risen to over 300. In 1955, just before television viewing began to have serious consequences for radio listening, the audiences for radio drama reached their maximum size. 'Curtain Up' on the Light Programme had an audience of seven and a half million; 'Saturday Night Theatre' on the Home Service six and three-quarter million, and, also on Home, 'World Theatre' one and a quarter million and 'The Monday Play', then as now the

1

main spot for original radio dramatic writing, two and three-quarter million.

But even with audiences for radio drama of this size not nearly enough radio plays of the requisite quality could be found in the middle '50s to fill the drama spots. Donald McWhinnie, one of the great radio drama producers, in his book, 'The Art of Radio', published in 1958, says that the BBC's Drama Department 'could not meet the enormous demands made on it without recourse to non-radio material'. Stage plays by such dramatists as Ugo Betti, Kleist and Anouilh, as well as the works of British dramatists, were adapted for radio; and there were many adaptations of novels, including Barbara Bray's excellent version of 'Le Grand Meaulnes' and Donald McWhinnie's own adaptation of James Hanley's 'The Ocean'.

Many of the best known works written specifically for radio — Louis MacNeice's *The Dark Tower,* Henry Reed's *Streets of Pompeii* or Geoffrey Bridson's *March of the Forty-Five* — were not radio drama but dramatic features, depending on the affective qualities of sound to 'paint' thematic pictures rather than on the narrative capabilities of sound. We'll be dealing with dramatic features later. Poets were more to the fore than dramatists and every British entry for the Italia Prize, a yearly award established by Italian Radio after the War for excellence in radio production, came from Lawrence Gilliam's Feature Department rather than from Val Gielgud's Drama Department right up to 1955.

Good radio plays were being written at this period. James Forsyth's *Trog* was a reflective play about the Second World War with the same country house setting as that first full-length play about war, *The White Chateau.* Frederick Bradnum's *Private Dreams and Public Nightmares* was interesting for its use of *musique concrète* and its distorting of the human voice to achieve special effects. Robert Bolt's *The Drunken Sailor* made use for narrative purpose of the poetic sound shorthand the creators of dramatic features had been developing. Clever storytellers like Francis Durbridge were discovering how most effectively to deploy their planted clues and twists of plot in the sound medium.

Probably the writer who did most for the radio play at this stage of its development was Giles Cooper. He was, artistically speaking, born in, matured in and remarkably flourished in the field of the radio play. It is fitting that the plays included in an annual anthology of the Best Radio Plays year by year beginning with 1978 win for their authors the distinction of a Giles Cooper Award.

In *The Disagreeable Oyster* and *Under the Loofah Tree,* to name but two, he explored with humour and insight radio drama's wonderful capacity for witty, economical storytelling. *Without the Grail* and a number of other full-scale plays show Giles Cooper so at home in the medium that we lose all sense of participating in a new art form as he invites us into his radio theatre of contemporary man, blundering about in a world too changed to suit him any more, but still clutching about him odds and ends of values left over from the past. While Giles Cooper was not, in any overt sense, a political writer, his plays show a humane understanding of the prejudice and hypocrisy which had been part of the imperialist dream and which the English had better shed.

Mention must be made of the creative editorship of Barbara Bray who, as Script Editor during the most formative period of the development of the radio play, did so much to discover the talent of new writers for the medium, including Harold Pinter, and to attract to the field of radio drama writers already established in other fields, including Samuel Beckett.

Beckett's fine play for radio *All that Fall* shows how wonderfully such a mastery of words takes to the air waves. Donald McWhinnie's efforts to realise the author's intentions in this play by the use of subjective sound effects, that is, sounds as we imagine the fictive characters in the play would hear them rather than as mere mechanical reproduction of natural sounds, gave rise to the radiophonic workshop which has been at the disposal of creative drama producers ever since.

Harold Pinter's play *A Slight Ache* can be considered something of a landmark in demonstrating what radio can do so much better than any other dramatic medium. Listening to this play we have no difficulty in accepting that the old match-seller is not only a figment of the husband's and wife's imagination but also that this same fantastic creature is, at once, the shabby, menacing figure that threatens to replace the man and the sexually attractive figure that appeals to the woman; and furthermore, that man and woman have called this shadowy being into monstrous life by digging, under the most civil and urbane surface, into each other's and their own subconscious. Such a creature, the product of the author's, the characters' and our own imagination, all in dramatic relationship with each other, cannot be adequately reproduced in any other medium — as attempts to stage this play have shown.

From the middle of the '50s and right through the '60s television viewing grew at the expense of radio listening until the radio audience dwindled to a relatively small minority. In the United States and other countries where there was no public service broadcasting, the audience for radio plays became much too small to interest advertisers and the radio play disappeared altogether. In

Britain the radio play survived but the traumatic experience of having its audiences reduced from many millions to a few hundred thousands made it think about itself as never before. It had to decide what it could still do better than any other dramatic medium and what it ought to surrender as better done elsewhere.

By this process of self-consciously assessing its proper role the radio play held on to the audience still left to it and began to recruit new listeners on a selective basis. It was never again going to claim mass audiences; it could not compete at peak viewing times with the popular shows on television; but in the early afternoon, for instance, it could provide dramatic entertainment which, unlike any form of visual drama, could be combined with other activities like driving a car, cleaning a room, cooking a meal or hiking across country. Indeed, a band of radio drama was established at this time of day on Radio 4 running right through the week.

It was not during the period of huge audiences that the radio play could be said to have come into its own, but during the period of self-realisation and artistic specialisation when it was fighting for its life. It is within the last fifteen to twenty years that the radio play has developed to the point where it depends less for its artistic credit on single outstanding works often written by distinguished interlopers from other areas of dramatic writing and more on the continuing level of excellence of a whole corpus of accomplished works written specifically for the medium and broadcast to an expectant and loyal audience of a million or more. The great radio plays, instead of being exotic importations or strange sports, have become the upper reaches of an amply based pyramid of radio drama.

Now every week on Radio 4 alone there are two ninety minute plays, three plays of an hour or less and a thirty minute play. Together with repeats of successful plays of the past and plays on Radio 3 it all adds up to some 500 plays originally written for radio broadcast every year. The BBC Radio Drama Department is the biggest sponsor of new dramatic talent in the country; it has stimulated regional play writing, the names of such northern writers as Henry Livings or Alan Plater coming to mind, and it has attracted many women from the afternoon theatre audience in which women predominate to write excitingly, penetratingly and most dramatically of their own problems for a general listenership or of everybody's problems from their own point of view.

In Britain we have enjoyed the cultural advantage of broadcasting's having been initiated by a public service corporation. As commercial television and then commercial radio developed they came on to a scene already dominated by public service standards. Just as commercial television has produced plays and serialisations of a comparable quality with the BBC, so commercial radio in London, Leeds, Liverpool and so on have begun to broadcast radio drama — though on nothing like the quantitative scale of the BBC.

To give some idea of the size of the regular audience for radio drama: the average audience for the Saturday Night Theatre play with its repeat on Monday afternoon is about a million and a quarter, and for the Monday Play, often more serious and demanding, with its repeat on the following Sunday afternoon, some three quarters of a million. It must be remembered that these audiences for the radio play represent people who have tuned in to make the extra effort required to follow a radio play and are consciously and selectively listening, not just letting sounds and pictures wash over them.

This, then, is the audience you are writing for when you take up radio dramatic writing. To appreciate better what it means, you have only to consider that a play would have to attract packed houses every night for two years at the National Theatre to reach the same number of people.

Chapter Two

Narrative and Dramatic Form

WE have defined radio drama as stories told in dramatic form by means of sound alone. There are two elements in this definition: the narrative element, the plot or storyline, and the dramatic form which imposes a particular shape on the way the plot or storyline develops.

In the broadest sense narration is telling us about something that has happened. Drama is the acting out of the happening itself. The very word 'drama' is the Greek word for deed, action. Drama is active and immediate while narrative is the more passive recounting of past action.

Both forms, narrative and dramatic, go back in their origins to our ancient tribal beginnings. With the recounting to those sitting around a campfire by storyteller or bard of creation myths or the adventures of tribal leaders of the past or moral tales in which animals and gods and spirits all might intermingle with men and women on a more or less equal footing, narrative form was born. It developed into such elaborate oral constructions as epic poems and came in time to take the literate guise of novel or short story. Narrative form is like a thread strung out in time along which there are discrete events like beads which we tell over successively until the storyline is completed.

Dramatic form has a different origin. It was born out of the ritual actions performed by the tribe. These might be a hunt or a harvest in which the various stages were mimed in dance rhythm, or initiation and marriage rites, or, later, religious ceremonies like the mystery cults of Greece or the Christian mass. In all of these enactments there is one point toward which everything moves — the slaying of the animal the tribe depends on for food or the harvesting of a crop; the assumption of maturity and tribal membership of a boy or the exchange of vows uniting man and woman as one; the partaking of the body of a god for the spiritual uplift of the communicants. This is the basic shape of drama — action rising to a climax and then subsiding to a new level. Some conflict breaks out within an organic unity, between man and nature, or man and man, or man and god, and tension grows to the point at which a more or less violent resolution takes place, like the flash of lightning between oppositely charged poles, and a new unity is restored for the process to begin all over.

Narrative form trails out loosely, the story gradually evolving until we get to know the characters and their fates through an accumulation of descriptive detail. It often takes the form of the picaresque — a series of adventures held together simply by the fact that they befall the same character. The things that happen to Odysseus on his return to Ithaca can be told as separate stories and one or more incidents can be left out entirely without much altering the main thrust of the storyline.

Dramatic form is much tighter in construction. Instead of meandering through time it, as it were, grows on the spot, drawing into itself external conflicts and generating inner contradictions which reach a climactic pitch and explode, bringing about a new balance of forces. The unities of time and place and a limited cast which Aristotle speaks of as essential to drama are the means preventing the kind of loose dissipation of energy characteristic of narrative form in order to build up the charged dramatic situation in which the tension of the climax in the moment before resolution can be almost unbearable. Dramatic form, with its tightening and relaxing of tension, its ebb and flow of energy and passion tends always toward the cyclical.

Narrative form is evolutionary, the gradual unfolding across time of a storyline. Dramatic form is revolutionary, the climactic change that suddenly occurs making things different from what they were before.

Of course, these two elements do not exist in a pure form as isolates. All narrative has dramatic aspects. It may be episodic in a very rambling sort of way but each episode can have dramatic shape. The narrator's voice can suddenly take on a dramatic quality of immediacy and his language change from past descriptive to historic present. The novelist Henry James, who failed to achieve his great ambition of writing a successful stage play, nevertheless wrote novels containing such strong dramatic scenes that others have made excellent stage adaptations of his books.

And all drama tells a story. However much the narrative element may be compressed at the moment of climax, however time, the essence of storytelling, may seem to stop, the movement through rising action to resolution tells a story. It tells a dramatic story of change, of people who in their relationships and situation will never be the same again as a result of what we have seen them do — to each other and to themselves.

The radio play is the heir in a distinctive way of both the narrative and dramatic tradition. It has in common with that old storyteller spinning tales to listeners around a camp fire the fact that it, too, involves only one sense, the sense of sound. Just as the storyteller by the vividness of his descriptive powers prompts the listener to supply imaginatively the visual aspects of the story he is telling, so the radio dramatist stimulates the listener to imagine what the characters look like, how they are dressed, what kind of setting they are in, at what period in time and so forth.

Storytelling and radio play writing are 'blind'. The listeners in both cases see nothing; but they imagine that they do. The art of good storytelling and good radio play writing is never to forget that the audience is blind without ever making them feel for a moment that they are. When Richard Hughes wrote that first radio play, he chose as the setting a coal mine in which an explosion had occurred, snuffing out the miners' lamps and making the characters in the play as blind as the listeners. R. C. Scriven, who contributed to the development of radio drama, wrote his first play, *The Single Taper*, about an eye operation like that which failed to save his own sight, and went on to write other radio plays in which he introduced listeners, without any sense of loss or panic, into the world of visual imagination which had become permanent for him.

The way the radio play came into being was that the narrator became split up into the characters of any particular story, acting out in the present what had formerly been recounted as happening to them in the past. But even though the characters had now become actors in a drama, they still kept their narrative role of supplying 'visual' information — and without seeming to be doing anything but playing their parts in a dramatic situation.

We shall have to deal at length with this complicated task the dialogue in radio drama has to perform. For the moment what we have to consider is what happens when the transition of the radio play from a form that is predominantly narrative to a form that is predominantly dramatic is incomplete.

One of the commonest faults in the radio drama written by those new to this medium is simply that it is not dramatic enough. There may be quite a good story or plot-line and some interestingly conceived characters but it fails to make dramatic capital out of the possibilities of conflict and confrontation implicit in the play. Indeed, one of the most frequent criticisms of the Afternoon Theatre plays, which form a major part of the BBC's radio drama output, is that they are too bland, too unexciting — that is, too undramatic.

It is all too easy in radio drama for the actors, whom we cannot see, to turn back into narrators and start telling us about what has happened instead of acting it out for us. The injunction to all dramatists, 'Don't tell us; show us', must be addressed with an even greater cogency to radio dramatists.

Writers who are new to the field of radio drama often complain that they were looking forward to writing up some big scene such as, for example, the confrontation between husband and wife when he realises that if she has a lover it has to be the man on whom his own political career depends; and yet the scene comes and is almost over and very little has taken place beyond a few angry exchanges.

What has happened is that instead of developing the scene dramatically, letting the conflict draw into itself past resentments and future anxieties on each side until it reaches some changeful climax, the writer has allowed the actors to tell each other and us about their seething passions and thus to skate narratively over the surface of the scene.

The writer, from his knowledge of dramatic form, must stop them in their tracks and plumb the depths of each character. Is the husband angrier over his wife's possible infidelity or the fact that he can only do anything about it at the cost of his career? Is the wife, out of resentment that he would even suspect her, concealing the fact that she is innocent or has she, perhaps, embarked on the affair out of contempt for her husband's crawling to the other man for advancement? If he agrees to forgive her, will that merely increase her contempt? And is there not somewhere deep down a guttering mutual love that may, if they find the right words and acts, still be rekindled? And so on. The writer must ask if all this subtle and violent interplay is there in what the two characters are saying and doing to each other.

Something like the same procedure must be applied to the unexciting households of suburbia portrayed by actors reciting bland lines and giving rise to the soporific sound known as 'Afternoon Theatre hum'. Probing under the surface can reveal that the Parkinsons of Number Two, The Willows, are not all that different, in suppressed intent and its consequences, from the House of Atreus.

The same deep analysis and dramatic expression can distinguish the simplest action. A man condescendingly greeting the window cleaner in his block of flats and receiving as patronising a 'Mornin', Guv' in reply, may remind us of generations of fraught class relations and bring even two minor characters to momentary life.

In a sense narrative and dramatic writing work from opposite ends. The loose, strung-out, somewhat meandering course of the novel, say, lends itself to the writer's simply starting at the beginning and, without too concise a notion of all the characters to be encountered on the way or of exactly how it is all to come out in the end, proceeding from chapter to chapter until the story is told. Drama is different. Once it is known what the crux of the play is, the dramatist tends to work backward from it to the beginning, eliminating what is non-essential to the rising tension and, by withholding a piece of information here or putting in an ambiguous reference there, heightening the impact of the climax. Compared with the relaxed, sprawling character of narrative form dramatic form is taut and economical. Whole episodes can be left out of a long narrative which, while missed, do not damage the overall picture the writer is cumulatively developing. Any scene that can be spared from a play ought not to be there anyway.

The effect the dramatist is always trying to achieve, whether the resolution of the play results for the audience in laughter or tears, is a feeling of surprise followed more or less immediately by a sense that it is exactly what one ought to have expected. To get this kind of double-take at the end of a play, the dramatist, in his conquest of the audience, plans his plot and deploys his characters with all the skill of an army commander.

Not only does the dramatist aim for this combination of wonder and contentment at the end of the play; each scene and each act ought to be structured in such a way as to yield minor anticipations all along of the big surprise and final sense of satisfaction at the conclusion. In setting up expectations in the audience and then not satisfying them for some time or satisfying them in some different manner than the audience could have anticipated, the dramatist is involved in a slower-paced, broader-stroked version of the teasing game the music composer plays with his audience, constantly setting up dissonances and unresolved chords to be dealt with tantalisingly along the course of a melodic line.

Indeed, the play script is not unlike a musical score, requiring performance for its proper enjoyment. The author of a narrative work in reading it over before publication is experiencing it in the same way as the potential readership. The dramatist is far less sure until the play is performed by actors under the guidance of a director just how successful the work is in terms of its impact on an audience.

Chapter Three

The Nature of Radio Drama Compared with Visual Drama

ALL FORMS of visual drama, stage play, film or television, start with a varied scene more or less peopled which, just by itself, before anything begins to happen, is of some interest to the spectator. Then that spectator is directed by the playwright to eliminate much of what can be seen in order to concentrate on those elements which begin to be invested with a narrative function. The telephone in the drawing-room setting rings, a maid answers it and supplies some necessary details about the household one-sidedly. Or a film-maker in a pan shot around the room comes back to a close-up of a door knob and we know that it will play a significant part in the beginning of the story.

Radio drama, however, begins with nothing at all, with absolute silence. It is like the primordial void before the generative word is spoken. To this utter emptiness the playwright, bit by bit, using only sounds, adds setting, period, characters and everything else needed to tell a dramatic story. Where the visual medium is abstractive and the playwright is constantly having us dispose of what is not to the purpose, the aural medium is additive, the playwright building up the structure and substance of the play by the various kinds of sounds he keeps adding.

The author of a radio play does not have to and, indeed, should not add the least element not needed for the particular dramatic story being told. The radio play is one of the most economical of the arts. At its best nothing is superfluous, every word, every sound playing its part. A radio play script is like a musical score in which everything the listener is to hear performed, down to a single micro-note or instant rest, is part of the composer's overall design.

It is the visible setting and characters, shared by all the people in a theatre or in a cinema or even all the people in the same room watching television, that make visual drama a collective experience. In radio drama the playwright prompts the listener to supply imaginatively the setting and the look of the characters. With the first sound the listener hears, be it word or effect or a snatch of music, the playwright and the listener together begin to create a 'visual' world based on the dramatist's words and the listener's imagination. Radio drama is a private rather than a collective experience.

Since, under the stimulus of the author's language, the radio play is cast by each listener from his or her own mind, the characters in the play will differ from listener to listener and may be very like, to 'look' at, the first woman any particular male listener ever loved or the first man any particular female listener ever kissed or his or her best friend or worst enemy. A drama in which these familiar figures are appearing can have a deeper and richer emotional impact.

It is perfectly possible in a radio play about the Trojan War, say, to have as one of the characters the most beautiful woman in the world without a single listener demurring that it is not *his* idea of supreme beauty. In radio, absolutes and abstractions can be clothed in flesh and blood to walk and talk among us.

Because there is no geographical distancing in a purely audible dramatic medium, no stage or ground over there at a specific distance from the audience where it is all happening, because instead there is an imaginary place common to playwright and listener, providing the ideal context in which the characters move about and have their being, the listener is much more at the centre of the dramatic action. By sharing in the maintenance of that imaginary world where the play is being acted out and in the visualisation of the characters' very appearance, the listener comes to have something of the close feeling for them an author has for his or her own creatures.

The suppression of geographical distancing and the more intimate relationship with the characters in the radio play — and remember that these characters are never any farther away from the listener than the actors are from the microphone — mean that asides, soliloquies and interior monologues have their full subjective intention and do seem to be murmured into the ear of the listener alone, unheard by the other characters. What so often, even when magnificently written, seems clumsy and implausible on the stage, has its proper privacy in radio. Shakespearian plays lend themselves admirably to radio because of this, and also because his poetic scene-setting for a relatively bare Elizabethan stage works wonderfully well for the blind listener — as of course does his descriptive character-drawing in lively verse.

Because radio drama takes place in the mind of the listener it is possible for the listener, as in no other form of drama, to enter into the minds of the characters — to have the sense of thinking their thoughts and feeling their feelings.

Hegel has said that freedom is the consciousness of necessity. Understanding the limitations inherent in an art form transmutes them into the freedoms the conscious artist enjoys in that particular form. The limitation of radio drama to sound alone seems at first thought a heavy restriction; but properly understood and used by the playwright it turns into a kind of liberation. We often close our eyes to allow imagination free play. The radio play in, figuratively, closing our eyes, gives the imagination free play. Indeed, it relies and depends on the free imaginative response of the listener as no other dramatic medium does. Radio drama has the freedom and also the privacy of daydreaming — at the playwright's suggestion.

Once the listener is responding imaginatively to the playwright's prompting, the playwright can whisk that listener anywhere with the speed of thought — to a star in some far galaxy, to an ancient city long since crumbled to dust or, most dramatically significant of all, right inside the minds of the characters of the play. That is why radio drama has been called by Martin Esslin, Val Gielgud's successor as Head of BBC Radio Drama, the Theatre of the Mind.

The earliest radio playwrights began very quickly to exploit this characteristic of the radio play whereby, because it takes place in our minds, it is easy for us to enter into the minds of its characters. These playwrights realised that because, at the author's bidding, we have shared in the imaginative creation of the characters, with our mind's eye costuming them and adding this or that personal touch to their appearance, we have made them our creatures, too, and experience their dramatic fate with a peculiar poignance.

Tyrone Guthrie, very much a man of the theatre, found himself, as a writer, drawn to this theatre of the mind. At the end of the '20s he wrote a number of radio plays, including *The Flowers Are Not for You to Pick,* which takes place in the mind of a young clergyman who has fallen overboard and who, in the moments before drowning, relives scenes from the past showing us how he came to be floundering there.

The same idea was used in a wartime play, *He Had a Date,* by Louis MacNeice, which takes us into the mind of a young lieutenant just before a torpedo strikes his ship and lets us 'see' the influences in his life putting him in that spot at that particular moment in time.

This is something the radio play has continued to do beautifully and powerfully. One of the most successful radio plays of 1977, *Blossom,* by Rose Tremain, takes place for the most part in the mind of a middle-aged woman whose brief passionate affair with a younger man long after her husband's death sets up disturbing emotional contradictions which can only be resolved for her by her husband's compassionate voice speaking to her, as voices in the mind always do, as though he were alive and with her.

In *Variations on the Snow Queen*, by Valerie Windsor, broadcast in the early '80s, Kay Patrick, who had produced *Blossom* several years before, used a new radiophonic technique to pull the listener right inside the mind of a woman in a psychiatric ward. We share her deep wish to commit suicide because we have come to understand that, for her, life really is too painful for us to want her to continue in it. We think her thoughts, feel her feelings and hear the outer world and other people just as she hears them.

There is constant drama going on in our minds as we revise our judgments of people we have known and rewrite our own emotional history with each new romantic attachment; and the radio play is the ideal theatre in which all these voices of the past and present can come together in spirited colloquy without any sense of strain or oddness because, of course, the setting of this dramatic skiamachy is of the same shadowy imaginative stuff as the characters themselves and the whole, by the radio playwright's art, has been transformed into a world more real while the play holds us than the ordinary one of sight and touch.

That is not to suggest that all, or even most radio plays take place largely in the minds of the characters. We shall have occasion to consider the special qualifications radio drama has for handling perfectly ordinary comedy, thrillers, horror plays and dramatic encounters in which our only clue to what the characters are thinking is what they say and do. But this intimate theatre within the minds of certain characters is a dramatic dimension which the radio play by its nature is uniquely qualified to explore.

The fact that the radio play is directed to an audience of discrete individual listeners rather than to a collective audience influences the way the playwright handles dramatic material. In writing comedy the playwright cannot expect to enjoy the benefit of the infectious quality of laughter which can soon have a whole theatre convulsed over a farce that heard individually would not strike many as all that funny. Nor can the radio playwright achieve the rousing communal effect of having an entire theatre audience come to its feet with a roar of sympathetic indignation or a vow of rectificatory dedication — not that we have had much powerful writing for the stage of that kind lately. On the other hand, the radio playwright can speak into the ear of a unique captive audience of one most affectingly, most insinuatingly, most wittily, making up in depth and subtlety and perceptiveness what the medium lacks in the way of mass response.

This closeness, this intimacy has another important consequence. Insincerity, falseness, pretentiousness are very soon exposed when the playwright cannot cloak them in plausible garb and give them a splendid setting some distance away from the audience. The dramatic media which, by making use of a powerful magnifying agent, camera or microphone, have given us the close-up, have called for a different style of acting and directing than the broad gestures and projected voice of the large theatre. In films, television or radio, stage technique comes over as 'staginess' and has to be replaced with another scale of expressiveness. And radio drama provides the ultimate in close-ups, that of being inside the character's mind.

But the creative collaboration of author and listener which makes the radio play such an intimate and involving experience has to be paid for. Listening to a radio play, compared with watching any form of visual drama, is hard work — particularly during the first few minutes. The listener has to attach the various characters to the sounds of their voices and pick up from clues in the dialogue what their relationship with each other is.

'Who's that, then? Oh yes, that's the uncle who's spent so much time in Australia that he's acquired something of a down-under accent. But who's the one referred to as Bert? Is Bert Arthur's brother-in-law, the one who couldn't possibly have taken the pearls because he was with Mabel all day?' Yes, it can be tough going, those first three or four minutes. And, not only is it a question of sorting out the dramatis personae from scraps of conversation alone: the listener has also to be alert to hints and suggestions telling, not too obtrusively, what has to be known about the place, the period, the time and even what kind of a play it is anyway — comedy, thriller, domestic drama or what.

There are ways we shall have to study of making this early burden on the radio drama listener as light as possible; but the radio playwright has to remember that however well the beginning of the play is written, considerable demands are made on the listener. The radio playwright has to remember that while people are not likely to walk out of the theatre or cinema if they find the first few minutes of play or film confusing or in any way objectionable, it is the easiest thing in the world for the listener to a radio play to decide it is not worth the effort and switch off. That is the challenge the radio dramatist has to accept at the outset.

But the effort required of the radio play listener can become an advantage if the playwright does, in fact, succeed in holding the audience at the start. We tend to remember things to the extent that we have been actively involved in acquiring our knowledge of them. Radio plays are often a more memorable experience than other forms of drama because the listener has been more actively involved in the imaginative process of its realisation.

People who have enjoyed a varied diet of dramatic presentations over a year usually find that the radio plays they have listened to with pleasure or excitement stand out in their memories with peculiar vividness. What they are, in part, recalling is all that making-up and costuming of characters, all that stage-setting and scene-shifting which they did in their own minds while the play was on.

****

These first three chapters have provided in very compressed form the history and essential nature of the radio play to give us a context in which to begin writing radio drama. Many of the points raised we shall have to come back to and develop in a much more detailed and practical way.

Certain guiding principles for the radio playwright can be drawn from this introductory material; but only when we have become involved in the actual process of thinking of a suitable idea for a radio play, getting the dialogue down on paper and then knocking it all into the best possible dramatic shape will the significance of these apothegms begin to be clear to us.

The radio play is at once the hardest form of drama to become involved in and the easiest to turn off.

The radio play is the most absorbing form of drama while at the same time being the only form of drama which can be enjoyed while doing something else.

The radio playwright must never forget that the audience is blind without ever making them feel for a moment that they are.

The dialogue of a radio play has to set the stage, provide all the props, describe and costume the characters, change the scenes and ring down the final curtain without ever seeming to do anything but advance a dramatic story.

The rein by which the radio playwright holds the listener's imagination in check is the storyline.

The radio play starts with silence, emptiness, nothing — the primordial void. Radio playwrights need not and should not introduce into this void one word or one sound that does not help them tell their dramatic story.

Chapter Four

Beginning the Radio Play

SO FAR we have been talking *about* radio drama. Now we are going to get down to the business of writing a radio play. From a narrative account of how the radio play came into being and what it has developed into we are going over to the more dramatic task of making a radio play ourselves. In this practice of actually doing something called radio dramatic writing we shall test such theories about radio plays as those at the end of the last chapter and see whether or not they are useful guides for our creative work in this medium.

First we have to decide what we are going to write. This really breaks down into two questions — what is the play going to be about, that is to say, what is its theme; and how are we going to exemplify, illustrate and dramatically develop this theme or, in other words, what is the plot going to be?

Theme and Plot

The theme is simply what, in the broadest sense, the play is about. It may be some very general subject like 'man's inhumanity to man', or 'the unifying effect on people of common danger' or 'the self-defeating tendency of an obsessive search for pleasure'. Folk wisdom may provide the theme — 'love is blind', or 'blood is thicker than water' or 'you can't teach an old dog new tricks'. The theme may be taken from the way a particular society works or is supposed to work — 'look after the pennies and the pounds will look after themselves', or 'a labourer is worthy of his hire' or 'crime does not pay'. Any religion, of course, is full of moral sayings which can be a play's basic subject.

The play need not exemplify the truth of whatever popular wisdom or moral rules are taken up as themes. This or that saying may be challenged or, indeed, it may be considered that times are so changed that all previous laws of conduct no longer apply — and then that very lack of validity of the morality of the past becomes the theme. In any case, most folk wisdom states both sides of any

17

approach to the problems of life, as 'look before you leap' and 'he who hesitates is lost'. For all the slogans and mottoes drawn from the way our society is supposed to work there are counter-assertions like 'property is theft' or 'money rules'.

The point we are making is that one way of thinking of something to write about is to go over these expressions which encapsulate some aspect of human experience and see if, in thinking about the kind of situations which would test their validity, one or other of them does not give us our theme.

Some of you may be thinking that you are not really very concerned with this question of theme. You have an exciting or moving story to tell about spies or about human relationships and you want to get on with it. You are just going to concentrate on your plot.

But every play says something about life and our attitude toward it, about the way we live or ought to live, over and above the specific story we are telling. That is the theme, whether we are aware of what it is we are saying in that sense or not.

Furthermore, our audience expects it. They are saying to themselves: 'This is an interesting or exciting play; pretty soon I'll know what the playwright means me to get out of it.' And even if we can imagine a writer really believing that he is not saying anything at all in a particular play because he is only interested in the money he is going to get, then he has made a very pertinent if damning statement about the way we live now.

If we are not clear on this question of theme, then we may find that we are saying something in this larger sense that we did not intend to or may be saying something in such a confused or self-contradictory way that it will leave the audience puzzled and dissatisfied, however neatly our plot seems to work. Or it may be that we feel so strongly about some current issue that our theme is set for us from the start and all we have to do is to find the right plot to contain our passionate conviction. But there are dangers for us here. People do not, on the whole, like didactic plays; and if the playwright is not careful, all those who disagree with the stand taken on a controversial question will have switched off leaving only an audience of the converted. Thinking of a compellingly interesting plot and letting the other side have some good arguments too will get the best hearing for such a theme.

If we are fully aware of what our play in this broad sense is about, of the general point we are making about people and the way they live in the dramatic story we are telling, then it becomes a kind of leitmotif giving the whole play depth, cohesion and resonance.

In the attitude we take toward the theme we determine the kind of play we are going to write — comedy, tragedy, farce or what. Let us take, for example, 'crime does not pay'. Countless cops-and-robbers or courts of justice plays are written which, by assuming that crime does not pay and that justice will be done, not only tell good stories but also serve to strengthen people's faith in their own social institutions. These plays may be comedies, both in the sense of being funny or of coming out happy in the end, or they may be tragedies in which a policeman or judge, through some personal flaw or mischance, is brought to a fatal end while still upholding what is legally or judicially right.

Or suppose our attitude toward this theme is one of scepticism or downright disbelief. Our society may seem to us so corrupt that we are not at all sure that crime does not pay. The police may be bribable and the courts rigged; and our cops-and-robbers or courts of justice play may turn into farce or black comedy. Or the state itself may be seen as the villain — in Nazi Germany, say — so that the heroes and heroines have to be rebels or outlaws. It would be difficult to write any play in such circumstances without an underlying political theme.

Once we know our theme and the broad category into which our play is going to fall we can start thinking of an appropriate plot, of the right storyline to express as dramatically as possible whatever it is we want to say.

It is at this point that we must be critically aware that the plot we are thinking of is for a *radio* play. We want a storyline which works for a medium depending on sound alone.

This means that wherever possible we want the incidents in our story to involve interesting or even definitive sounds. If our play is about the effect of competition on human relationships, why not have the story about contestants for a prize for young musicians? Or why not let our triangle of emotionally entangled lovers be a string trio rehearsing for a concert with the music they make commenting wittily or sentimentally on their plight? Or why should our play about a tempestuous marriage not involve opera singers, buskers or pop stars?

As means for advancing our plot, let us try to replace letters, telegrams and diaries with telephone calls, automatic listener services and tape recordings.

If we are thinking out the plot of a whodunnit, instead of visible clues like footprints, let us have audible ones like voice-prints. Not nearly enough use has been made of such devices as letting listeners recognise that the voice telling the threatened heroine that he will stay with her for her protection is one of the voices already heard plotting to do away with her.

In a science fiction play, instead of superpowerful laser beams, let the story revolve around the fatal effects of certain sound frequencies. A very interesting little radio play was written recently in which the listeners gradually realise that the peculiar combination of sonic and ultrasonic frequencies which is destroying the mind of one of the characters is the same sound they are hearing themselves! All sorts of subtle, comic or horrifying effects can be achieved by the use of soundful story-telling devices in a sound medium which puts listeners in the shoes of the characters in a way no visual medium ever can.

Sometimes just to think of a situation for a play which both makes interesting noises and is potentially dramatic, like riveters on a skyscraper under construction, or bidders in an auction at a cattle market or at Sotheby's, is to be halfway toward thinking of a workable plot.

But there are also negative rules to be aware of in plot construction for a sound medium.

Quite obviously our story cannot involve too many principal characters because it simply is not possible for listeners to a radio play to distinguish and get to know more than four or five major personages. Furthermore the characters in a radio play have to be introduced to the listeners in very small groups indeed, with single additions as the play progresses. Not for the radio playwright that first noisy scene at a cocktail party or sporting event or public meeting when the camera pans around the scene picking out the various individuals who are to be featured in the play.

Radio playwrights have to avoid painting themselves into a corner where a single character on the stage has to explain to the listeners in a highly contrived piece of interior monologue how he has managed to shin up a drainpipe, pry open a window and, having stealthily tiptoed across the room, is just about to employ the extremely sensitive balls of his fingers to discover the combination of the safe in which the priceless pearl necklace is to be found.

Interior monologue can be used in radio drama very effectively, more effectively indeed than is ever the case with visual drama, but not for the purpose of simply conveying information to a 'blind' audience. The plot will have to be altered to include a catburglar's mate, whispered conversations with whom will convey to listeners what is happening, or the scene can be left out and we can hear the solo cracksman describing to a friend in a pub afterwards how the burglary went.

There are other types of situations to be avoided because they are going to create difficulties for the listener. It must be remembered that the BBC's more popular radio dramatic output during the afternoon is intended for listeners who may be doing something else at the same time. Therefore, plot clues and hinges cannot be too subtle. They have to be perfectly clear without being obviously contrived.

What is necessary in terms of plot to exploit the rich possibilities of this medium and to avoid pitfalls is to be able to think and work directly in sound and not to have to work out a plot that would suit a visual medium like stage or screen and then translate it into sound terms. It is like the difference between an artist's drawing a sketch and then applying paint afterwards, or being able to work from the start in oils, getting all the visual excitement from subtle gradations of tone and laying bright colours side by side. The radio playwright has to think out a plot in terms of the sound 'pictures' it makes as it unfolds.

It is most important of all to remember that warning to playwrights about radio drama being the hardest to become involved in and the easiest to turn off. The plot must be devised in such a way that as soon as possible the listener is caught up in an interesting story and wants to know what is going to happen next. Any plot that requires the passing on to the listener of a good deal of information before the action can begin needs radical rethinking. *In medias res* Horace advised all narrative poets — start in the middle when something is already happening. That applies with even greater force to someone beginning to write a radio play. We shall see when we deal with dialogue how easy it is to give the listener whatever information is needed as the scene progresses instead of providing it in narrative form before the dramatic action gets underway.

The logical order of starting to write a radio play is to think of a theme, decide the kind of treatment it ought to have — tragic, comic, satirical or what — and then work out an appropriate plot. But the actual sequence may be quite different. The playwright may think of a good dramatic scene or a potentially dramatic relationship between two characters, then proceed to construct a plot around these isolated dramatic constituents and then finally decide, when the play is beginning to take firm shape, what it is really about. But however the process of writing radio drama has, in this instance or that, been sparked off, it can be analysed into these two distinguishable but inseparable elements — theme and plot. The perfect marriage of these elements, the ideal harmony between what the playwright is saying about some aspects of life and how, dramatically, it is being said in terms of the sound medium, is the fundamental basis for a good radio play.

It need hardly be said that no one is going to come up with a new plot in the sense of thinking of something people have never done to each other before or something people have never felt about each other before. The problem of all writing is to give to what has happened or been felt billions of times already a freshness and wonder that makes us feel as if we are encountering it for the first time.

This is largely a question of perspective. The same things go on happening but we see them in a different light because we are looking at them from a different point of view. Women dramatists, for example, have found radio drama a particularly appropriate medium and have been giving us fine plays with a different slant on things. The dramatic writings of people of other lands and very different backgrounds are more freely available than ever before, providing us with a whole new variety of perspectives which can have the effect of making us see things differently too.

Ultimately, because all of us are unique individuals, no two of us exactly alike, we each have a peculiar perspective from which these all too commonplace human actions and feelings look slightly different from the way they look to anybody else. This is what gives us the right to tell all the old dramatic stories over again. This is the personal vision that determines our style. It is the source of the themes we are going to write about and it indicates the most suitable genre for us to write in. It provides the viewpoint from which to continue our search for suitable ideas for radio plays.

Thinking of ideas for radio plays

We have already touched on the possibility of starting with a piece of a plot, some tiny scene or hint of a relationship which seems to have dramatic possibilities. It might be something we see or some snatch of conversation we overhear. A man reaches down to pick up a woman's dropped handbag for her and she screams that she is being mugged. A woman in the seat in front of us says to her neighbour: 'Well, I put it all down to the fact that her first husband was eaten by a shark, you know.'

If our ears are listening out for such fragments of radio plays, not only will we frequently catch sound of them, we will also begin imagining the people around us saying the kind of thing we are looking for to start us off building an entire play around some little part of one. We should have about us a notebook in which these provocative scraps can be jotted down, whether we think of them on the way to and from work, while performing household chores or in the middle of the night.

We can add to our collection of jigsaw pieces for which the rest of the puzzle can be invented by taking quite arbitrary lines of dialogue and imagining the circumstances in which they might be said. 'What the devil are you doing here?' or 'Then you must be my step-father!' or 'No, Bert is the one with the tattoo; I'm the one with the gold earring.' When we have thought about what could have led up to that line and what comes after it, we are beginning to have an idea for a play.

To have a keen ear for dialogue, to be able, once certain people have been thought of in a particular situation, to imagine what they are going to say to each other and exactly how they are going to say it, is for the radio playwright to have practically solved the problem of plots. The shorter radio plays of Harold Pinter are a good example.

Another way to approach this matter of thinking of ideas is to divide the radio plays we expect to write into those in which we find the extraordinary in the ordinary and those in which we find the ordinary in the extraordinary.

In the first case, we take some situation which is thoroughly familiar to us because we encounter it every day of our lives. And then we give it some sort of twist which suddenly transforms the utterly trite into the strange, puzzling or horrifying — all the more disturbing because of the very ordinariness of everything leading up to it.

We come down to breakfast and say to wife or husband just as we have for the last fifteen years, 'Sleep well, darling?', only to have wife or husband say, 'You know perfectly well that I got up, dressed and left the house at 2.30 a.m., and didn't get back until four. Why are you pretending you don't know that?' Or, we go to the building where we work, as we have done ever since our firm moved there, enter our office and sit down at our desk to look at the morning post. But the letters are all addressed to someone else. We get up, go over and open the door and find that someone else's name is on it.

In working out what the explanation could be for something unusual in the fixed pattern of our daily lives, we have our plot for a radio play.

The advantage of this approach is that having chosen such a familiar situation we know how everybody talks and behaves. There is going to be no difficulty about achieving authenticity; and we must never forget that in a sound medium we have only the spoken dialogue to make the characters believable. Furthermore, the setting will be just as familiar to a large|number of listeners. They are going to find it very easy to identify with the characters in our play and are going to experience whatever it is that has suddenly pushed the pattern askew with a particular dramatic shock.

Or take the other case, the completely strange situation in which we begin to find some familiar pattern after all. Perhaps in our writing we want to get right away from the boring sequence of events that makes up our everyday life. We are going to whisk our listeners off to life on one of Neptune's satellites or in the depths of a rain forest or some 200 years from now — and, of course, radio makes such exotic scenes easy to realise. But once we have made our escape from the ordinary we are going to have to begin discovering ordinary actions and feelings in the new setting. Otherwise there will be no point of contact to enable the listener to become involved.

Perhaps we have arrived somehow or other on an inhabited planet of Arcturus only to discover that one of the space gods, Vardon the Red, is mobilising his army of automated mastodons to attack the daemon of darkness, Marbane the Moog, for daring, when passing through the intergalactic computer pool, to make a play for the same luscious female Vardon has had his eye on himself.

Of course, the reason science fiction was such a useful genre for American writers in the McCarthy era was that it enabled them to comment on the contemporary scene in a way that did not get them blacklisted. We can get an idea for a play by thinking of analogous historical or mythological settings to make a comment about present times.

Certainly no medium serves so well as radio drama the writer of science fiction or about fabulous places and creatures or time travel. It is no harder, if as hard, for the radio playwright to prompt the listener to imagine the interior of a space rocket on the way to Mars or the Emerald City or a Victorian poorhouse than the front room of a Surbiton semi-detached. When television drama cannot afford costume plays, radio drama can accoutre all the knights of the Round Table at the cost of a recording of some metallic jingling. James Saunders, in *Random Moments in a May Garden,* has shown how in radio drama one time can be superimposed on another in a poignant double-exposure.

Or we might approach the problem of finding an idea for a radio play by looking for it in a place which by its very nature has dramatic potential — like a courtroom or the House of Commons.

We have described drama as being dialectical in nature, capitalising on the pros and cons into which any statement about life tends to split. In drama, conflict, opposition between individual and society, between different individuals or even within one individual grows until there is such tension that a climactic resolution has to take place. Everything that happens in a courtroom

24

or in Parliament takes this dramatic form. There is prosecution and defence or government and opposition; there is growing tension as the argument over guilt or innocence or over the correctness or incorrectness of a line of policy is fought out and there is the climax of verdict or vote. Indeed, it is not surprising that the two countries in which drama has developed most strongly, ancient Athens and Elizabethan England, should also be countries with the most precocious political and judicial development.

Thinking about court cases or Parliamentary debates may well spark off ideas for plays. And since in both arenas the result may depend almost as much on the persuasiveness of the spoken word as on the actual facts, they are ideal locations for radio plays.

We must never forget that conflict, opposition, is the essence of drama and our plots must never avoid the big dramatic scenes to be played with all the stops out. There are reasons why, in a visual dramatic medium like stage plays, much of the action may have to take place in the wings. This is certainly not true of radio drama which can take us into the centre of a raging battle or the midst of a howling mob. A play like *Coriolanus,* where one of the main characters is the Roman citizenry, comes alive on radio as it never quite can on the stage.

There are ways in which radio lets us think big in dramatic terms and ways in which it allows us to whisper seductively. We must learn to appreciate this enormous range of possibilities in order to devise the most compelling plots.

Plot has even greater importance in radio drama than in visual drama. It is the storyline that the 'blind' listener holds on to like a thread through a labyrinth. The trailed storyline is what the listener first grabs in order to become involved in the play and it leads that listener through a succession of scenes to the play's climax.

In visual drama there are many things incidental to the plot to interest or beguile the spectator — ingenious stage settings, magnificent natural scenery, splendid costumes or the detailed faithfulness to life of more ordinary locations. Spectacle or stage business may not only flesh out the plot line: they may take on a silent narrative function like mimed exchanges in a farce or like the elaborate wedding scene or bleak scaffold which tells us all we need to know about the end of a play. Radio drama can call up such scenes in the listener's mind by twitches the radio playwright gives to the storyline: but they cannot usurp the role of the plot as it comes out of the mouths of the characters.

Chapter Five
Characters

AS we have shown, the way the narrative line of storytelling is transformed into the dramatic shape of radio drama is that the narrator is split up into the various characters of a particular story who then act out in the present what was formerly said about them in the past. Of course, we do not follow this sequential transformation of narrative into drama when writing a radio play. We do not first think of a piece of straight storytelling and then dramatise it. We start off writing creatively in dramatic form. But the narrative nature of what the storyteller said about the characters is preserved in dialogue which still performs an informative role while seeming only to contribute to the play's dramatic development.

So far we have been thinking about the radio play we are going to write in terms of theme, what we really want to say about people, and plot, what actually happens to the characters in this particular play. We could have approached this same question of what we are going to write by thinking of our play in terms of the characters who are going to be in it.

Thematic and illustrative characters

Our whole idea for a radio play may have been suggested by the conception of a particular character, so villainous or so heroic or such an interesting combination of the two, that his nature and his effect on those around him determine the nature of the play. Or it may be that the development of a particular character, from her victimisation by a brutal husband to her realisation of herself as a person in her own right with her own contribution to make, gives the play its shape. Such characters can be considered as thematic. What we want to say in our play is bound up with and derives from the principal characters we have conceived.

Or, having thought of an interesting or exciting plot, we may begin thinking of the characters who will be needed to enable us to tell our dramatic story. In this case the characters are illustrative, derived from the storyline instead of determinative of it.

Considering radio plays from the point of view of these two conceptions of the role of characters gives us two broad categories of plays — those about what is going on internally in our characters' minds and hearts and those about what is happening to our characters externally.

Most plays which simply tell a rollicking good yarn belong to the latter category. Exciting things happen to a character or to a group of characters and our interest is maintained by our concern with how they will cope with and surmount the obstacles and dangers they encounter.

Such adventures befalling our characters may be made more dramatic by using the unities of time and place and a strictly limited cast to heighten tension — passengers in a ditched aircraft which can only stay afloat a certain time, hostages being held by a gang of bank robbers who are going to start killing them off if their demands are not met within an hour, a country house murder mystery where it is imperative for the amateur sleuth to know who the murderer is to prevent another crime before the police arrive.

In the other broad category of plays are all those in which what is going on in the hearts and minds of the characters brings about dramatic changes in a pattern of human relationships, or perhaps it is dramatic change within a single character that provides the climax of our play.

Because, in these plays, what is going on subjectively inside people is more important than what is happening objectively in the outside world, they may seem relatively 'quieter'; but, dramatically speaking, such is not the case. We may be overhearing two old tramps talking together on a park bench and nothing could 'look' more tranquil; but the movement in their relationship, through self-contempt to mutual hatred and from the edge of violence to some kind of understanding of each other which enables each to accept himself, may make a big dramatic noise indeed.

Radio drama is a good medium for this sort of dramatic movement because by keeping us closer to the characters involved it makes our own involvement with them more intimate. The interplay of their thoughts and words fills our whole conscious world with passionate rhetoric and pregnant pauses.

In fact, neither type of play has a better story to tell than the other — only a different story told in a different way. Nor should we think of these two categories of plays as being mutually exclusive. A play about what happens objectively to a group of people will be all the more gripping if the characters are real people who are changed by the experience and not simply stereotypes. The play about internal developments in characters will make all the more impact if some inner change becomes objectified in overt action which becomes an external force for the other characters.

Importance of identification

We have considered and will have to go on considering that challenge to the radio playwright: radio drama is the hardest to become involved in and the easiest to turn off. We have noted that one way to keep the listener's attention during those particularly difficult first few minutes of a radio play is to start telling a buttonholing story at once. There is another way, one that involves the characters the listener begins to meet in our radio play.

Let us imagine those listeners coming on to the scene blind, groping about for clues as to where they are and cocking their ears for a familiar voice to help them find their way. If quite soon they hear the voice of someone with whom it is possible to identify, a person who is likeable or, at least, understandable or in a situation they can easily imagine being in themselves, then they have acquired a guide who will lead them around the blacked-out stage without barking their shins, introduce them to the other characters and, as it were, 'put them in the picture'.

Of course, this identification with one or more of the characters which holds the listener's attention through those first difficult moments of a radio play also involves that listener intimately in the twists and turns of the plot so that everything which overtakes the character or characters with whom the listener has acquired this exclusive relationship seems almost to be happening to the listener. It is that blind reliance on a sympathetic guide or guides as one's best way into the play which tells their story that makes the experience of radio drama so powerful and moving — once we have been persuaded by the playwright to commit ourselves, sightless, to the care of certain of his creatures.

This does not mean, of course, that within the first few minutes of a radio play we will have to have met, for our fullest enjoyment, a good or nice man or woman. Likeable rogues or not all-bad villains may do perfectly well, as long as they are interesting. What it does mean is that if we begin a radio play with a number of characters who all seem pretty repellent to most of our listeners we are soon going to have very few listeners.

Visual drama may begin with a stage full of mindless louts or depraved criminals or completely demoralised youths and in due course we may realise that some of them are redeemable after all or that it is society that has made them like that and they could have been quite different. But the listener to a radio play, who is having to work quite hard to take it all in anyway, may simply feel that these unattractive, unpleasant people, addressing each other in the foulest language, are not worth the effort being asked.

This is an important aspect of the special relationship that obtains between radio playwright and listener. The writer of a radio play makes such demands on the listener's attention, and expects so much creative co-operation in terms of the listener's imagining what the setting and characters look like, that special consideration for that listener is called for. Insulting the intelligence of the audience to put them in a combative mood to receive a message or telling them sharply not to wallow in emotional responses to the plight of the characters but *think* how they got that way are not likely to be very successful approaches to the listeners of a radio play — certainly not within the first five or ten minutes in any case. The listener's response to any alienation technique early in a play can all too easily be to switch off.

Casting the radio play

We have already considered the difficulty for the audience of a radio play in sorting out the voices of the characters at the beginning. To make it as easy as possible to distinguish these voices the characters should be presented at first in twos or threes and additional characters — not too many — should be introduced singly. We can also help the listener in the task of identifying characters by making the voices as distinctive as possible. Scenes between men and women, young and old, natives and those not so familiar with the English language present no problems. We should avoid if we can situations where all the voices are likely to be the same sex and age with the same regional and social background. Idle, Yorkshire, and Ugley, Cambridgeshire, might be good places to set a radio play, but having the plot concern the affairs of the Idle Working Men's Club or the Ugley Women's Voluntary Service could present serious problems in distinguishing the speakers.

This would be equally true of a play about an officers' training course or a Girl Guide troop. And the latter raises another question about casting — the use of children. Speaking parts for children should only be included if they are absolutely essential to the play. It is possible to get quite good performances from children if their parts are suitably written but it takes time and there are various regulations about the employment of children which have to be observed. Some actresses are very good at children's voices but it would be risky to have the crux of a play depend on the successful mimicry of a child's voice.

Characters can be distinguished by giving them different regional accents; but unless the parts are also characterised regionally and given the right regional turns of phrase and even vocabulary it will begin to sound like one of those jokes about a Scotsman, an Irishman, a Welshman and an Englishman.

In a multi-racial society like Britain, Indian or West Indian actors should sometimes be cast as nurses, clerks, solicitors, traffic wardens or bus conductors — not because the play is about a racist theme but simply because a proportion of people belonging to settler communities are to be found in these jobs. No Peter Sellers-type accents are to be tolerated.

Insofar as we think of a radio play in terms of contrasting scenes each with easily distinguishable characters as, for example, a duet for young lovers or a trio for the angry voices of a sexual triangle or a quartet of married couples occupying the two halves of a semi-detached house, we are approaching the problem of players almost as we would deal with the casting of an opera. An interesting pattern of voice sounds, male and female, high and low, young and old, of accents vulgar or refined, native or exotic, of staccato or slowly paced speech, can help to fight off that awful fate which always threatens to overtake the radio writer — monotony.

Characterisation in radio drama

The greatest demand which the radio dramatic medium makes on the writer is the creation of interesting, believable characters solely out of what they say or what is said about them within a few minutes of their 'appearance' in a radio play.

In a visual dramatic medium we can take in at a glance a good deal of information about characters — whether they are good-looking, plain or ugly, old, middle-aged or young, well or shabbily dressed and so on. In a narrative medium like the novel the author has all the time in the world to pile up descriptive detail about a character. Indeed, we may have begun learning about the hero or heroine from the hour of birth.

In a radio play not only do we not see the character who has just been introduced, but that character has at once to begin playing a characteristic part in the unfolding drama.

In beginning to make the characters come to life the radio

playwright has the help of the listener's imagination. As we have already pointed out, at the prompting of the playwright the audience may cast the characters out of the repertory company of acquaintances, friends and relations in their own lives, past and present. The radio playwright has the advantage that the tough employer, doting aunt, beloved young man or woman or kindly grandfather are not only given a general 'appearance' by the listener, drawing on his or her own experience, but also the listener already dislikes that employer who 'looks' like his own boss or is already half in love with the man or woman who has the face of the listener's first love, and so on.

Sometimes the playwright may let minor characters discuss a major character not yet 'on stage', so that when the character does appear, the audience already has a pretty good idea of what to expect. Any actual descriptive phrases used, like 'golden hair' or 'broad shoulders', must come at the image-forming stage in the listener's mind. It can be disconcerting for a listener to hear something later on about a character's appearance which conflicts with the image already formed.

The really crucial part of characterisation is simply the speeches the character utters — particularly those at first appearance. The playwright, having written what the character says as a participant in that particular dramatic story, then has to test the rightness of every word of the speech from the point of view of characterising the speaker in some depth. Is that the way a bishop, a shipbuilding worker, a matron in a hospital, a housewife in Surbiton would express that idea? In the situation described, exactly what would that character feel and would that feeling give rise to a flip or measured or hypocritical observation? One wrong expletive can so damage the image of a major character beginning to form in the listener's mind that the play itself is ruined.

What has to be remembered is that in visual drama everything a character says is qualified by that character's general presence and by facial expression and gesture. A misjudged epithet is not going to change our attitude completely toward a visible character whose overall appearance has not changed. But speech in the radio play is absolute. It determines the way the character 'looks' to us. 'Looks' never modify speech. It is this absolute quality of dialogue in a radio play that makes uncharacteristic remarks irredeemably destructive of the character the playwright is trying to establish in the listener's mind.

In order to give real depth of character and hint at some of the hidden or complicated motives which may barely break surface, the playwright may have to devise a scene ostensibly for carrying the plot forward but actually to show us something of a character's inner contradictions. The radio playwright has to be very clear about the characters in order to establish them for us in all their depth and solidity.

Furthermore, he has to remember that, hard as it was to plant the characters there four-square before us, those characters have a tendency to disappear when not speaking. In a scene with three or more characters, if one of them does not say anything for a long time, the listener may forget all about him and experience a puzzled shock when he speaks again.

But if the creation of in-depth characters presents problems for the playwright, the radio medium also has its advantages. We have mentioned that the characters may carry a higher affective charge for being more closely associated with the dramatis personae of a listener's own life than is the case with other media. Also the economy of radio playwriting may work for the author when it comes to characters personifying a particular vice or virtue or caricaturing some human foible. Visual drama gives us such characters looking very much like the other characters except for some particular exaggeration of feature or dress. Radio drama can create in our minds the very figure of greed, self-love, sentimentality or insensate fury having no lineaments but those of the conceptualised creature the author wants us to imagine for some dramatic purpose.

For reasons of not making too heavy demands on the listener's ability to distinguish and on the budget for actors of the radio play, characters should be kept to the minimum necessary for the telling of a particular dramatic story. Those minor characters that are required should be brought to individual life and not treated simply as props. Remember the wonderfully vital minor characters in Shakespeare or Dickens or Rembrandt's sketch books and try to bring alive the people you need for your plot with a few telling strokes.

Something else to be borne in mind in connection with radio drama characterisation is that the microphone acts as a powerful magnifying agent bringing the actors in the play as close to the listeners as the actors in the studio are to the microphone. Radio acting is always in close-up and any speech that is pretentious or does not quite ring true is going to be exposed. The kind of rhetoric or inflated sentiments that may sound all right at the back of the stalls are going to sound 'stagy' and 'theatrical' when the actor is practically in the living room with us.

On the other hand, this magnification makes possible subtler and more delicate nuances of character delineation than would be possible in the theatre.

Although the magnifying agent of camera or microphone makes those forms of drama based on technological advance like radio, television and film unsuitable for the kind of voice and emotion projection characteristic of the stage, the radio play, sparing us the larger-than-life facial expression or gesture and exploiting sophisticated recording equipment which can handle a wide range of sound without distortion, can probably accommodate bravura performances which would seem out of place on film or television. Certainly most Shakespeare takes to radio better than to the small screen.

Characterisation is simply dramatic storytelling from the point of view of the people the story is about instead of what happens to them. But from whichever point of view we approach the writing of a particular radio play, good characterisation is inseparable from good plotting.

Chapter Six

Dialogue

RADIO drama *is* dialogue. Through dialogue the plot develops. Through dialogue the characters become known to us. Dialogue may be the most important element in a stage play: it is the *sine qua non* of a radio play.

The radio play makes use of sound effects and music but only as adjuncts to dialogue. To tell a story in dramatic form and at the same time to direct the traffic of the audience's imagination toward providing a visual accompaniment to that story in sound, the radio playwright is completely dependent on the spoken word, on dialogue. In no other dramatic medium does the word in its full range of denotation and connotation, the word with all its associated ideas in train, the word unqualified by any gesture or facial expression, the word freed from any visible context whatsoever come more richly and significantly into its own — creating opportunities for the writer by means of dialogue alone to scale the dramatic heights and show us our world stretched out below, or, by dialogue misused, to tumble into some bathetic pitfall.

Narrative function of radio dialogue

We have seen how the radio play comes into being by the splitting up of the narrator of a story about people into those people themselves, acting out their story in the present instead of their story's being told to us as something that happened in the past. But these characters in what has now become a radio play retain something of the narrative function of the storyteller when it comes to providing us with information necessary to follow the dramatic action.

This narrative function is particularly important in a blind medium like radio which cannot show us at a glance what characters look like, how they are dressed or against what sort of interior or exterior background they are acting out their parts. Radio drama shares with other dramatic media dialogue that has both a narrative and dramatic function, but radio dialogue has to work a lot harder at its narrative function — and without appearing to sacrifice its dramatic role. If the characters in a radio play begin providing us with information at the expense of getting on dramatically with the action of the play, the play will begin to turn back into a narrated story and the characters will be in danger of coalescing into that old storyteller.

One kind of information that dramatic dialogue in general has to get across is telling us what has been happening to the various characters before this play about them begins. In keeping with the unities of time and place the drama has started when the relations of the characters are about to take a dramatic turn and it may be important for us to know how the characters' relations with each other got to the point at which they are when the curtain rises.

This might be done by economical references to the past in what the characters are saying to each other now. For example: 'That's what you say every time this argument comes up between us,' or 'I know she did, but she wasn't in love with him then,' or 'That's not true, what he said about the Normandy landings. He wasn't there. He wasn't even in the army. Some physical disabilty, I think.'

But it may be that something in the past is so crucial for dramatic development that, instead of mere oblique references, an actual staging in the present of that earlier incident is required. Such flashbacks are much easier in the recorded dramatic media, like films, television and radio, than on the stage where the switch of scenes may take time and lower the dramatic tension considerably. But it is easiest of all in radio where, because visual location is in the mind of the listener, changes of time and place can be managed with the utterance of a few words. If a character in a radio play says: 'I can hear now the very words she used when she told me about it,' we will have no difficulty in identifying the next words we hear as her actual speech whenever and wherever she made it. This facility enables radio drama to strike the best possible compromise between providing necessary information about the past and maintaining dramatic impetus in the present.

Informative dialogue in the visual dramatic media, particularly stage plays, may be used to cover some dramatic event it would be impossible or prohibitively expensive to stage visibly — like the cowardice of the villain as his town is demolished by an earthquake or the courage of the hero as his battleship goes down with all hands on board. Scenes of this kind present no difficulty for radio, and radio playwrights must exploit the capabilities of a sound medium for giving us extraordinary opportunities for dramatic dialogue.

Radio dialogue performs certain other functions as discreetly as the unseen person who raises and lowers the stage curtain — functions like ending or beginning a scene, changing from one scene to another or indicating lapses in time. A snatch of dialogue like: 'All right. Meet you in half an hour, then, at the Dog and Duck' is all that is necessary to tell us where we are when the next scene begins, how much time has elapsed meanwhile and who the two main characters in the scene are.

Listen to a radio play with your ears tuned for them and you will hear many examples of dialogue doing this job of ringing down curtains and starting up or changing scenes — which, if playwrights know their business, usually go completely unremarked. 'Thank you, Jamison. I don't think we can take this matter any further for the present.' (*Fade out*). Or, (*Fade up*) 'You're at your desk early, Charles. You don't usually get in before ten.' Or, 'When we've finished our meal, I'm going around to the hospital to see her.' (*Fade down. Fade up*) 'Hello, Rosemary. How are you feeling now?'

This scene setting and scene shifting can be accompanied by appropriate sound effects. The last bit of dialogue might have had the sounds of a restaurant being faded down to be replaced with the sounds of a hospital. But sound effects by themselves are rarely adequate for scene setting. They are too ambiguous, a trolley with food on it sounding much like a trolley with medicines, and almost always have to be pointed by dialogue.

Indeed, in radio plays, the dialogue constantly and unobtrusively sets up little signposts to keep listeners moving along with the drama, unworried about whether they have blindly taken the wrong road.

In addition to its narrative function and its use for characterisation, dialogue in the radio play has to prompt the listener's imagination to provide the visual aspects of the drama. The appearance of the characters, the kind of clothes they are wearing, the sight of mountains or the sea in the distance, or the furnishings of a sitting room and what they indicate about the means of the people whose house it is, even whether it is day or night — all of this wealth of 'visible' detail, which may have a very important bearing on the unfolding of the dramatic story, is brought to pictorial life in the listener's mind by carefully planted verbal stimuli in the dialogue.

This may be done directly by the comment of two characters about a third or about their present surroundings. 'Well, you've got to admit that he's good looking, even if he *is* a bit of a scoundrel,' or, 'Don't you feel insignificant out under the stars like this?' Or hints about the looks of things may be dropped in indirect references: 'I always feel so out of place at a party like this — like a clumsily wrapped parcel left at the wrong address. But, of course, *you* couldn't know what it's *like* to be plain and know it.' Or, 'No, I'm fine, sitting on this lumpy chintz cushion. It's probably good for me, not to be able to relax too completely.'

Dialogue as part of its narrative function also makes the listener aware of all stage business — like the serving of tea or drinks, the opening and shutting of doors or windows, the fondling of lovers or the fisticuffs of enemies.

Since in the radio play the dialectic of playwright's stimulus and listener's imaginative response takes place with the speed of thought in an imaginary aether where no visible material objects impose a natural order of space and time, events like the uncorking of bottles or the eating of a meal or the typing of a letter can have the pace required by the emotional exigencies of the drama rather than the time they would normally take as physical actions. Because of this subjective nature of time in radio plays they run much more quickly than would a similar amount of dramatic material acted out on the stage. A ninety minute radio play has about the same amount of dialogue as a full three act stage play running over two hours.

Once listeners are involved in a radio play, their imagination at the playwright's disposal, they are enormously suggestible and the merest nudge in the dialogue is all that is required to make them 'see' what is necessary. It is usually a mistake to try to be too specific about the visual experience you want your listeners to have. Let their imaginations have a freer play while making sure that a strong storyline corrals their images and keeps them from straying.

Radio dialogue has to perform all these narrative functions without seeming to do anything but advance the dramatic action. Handled properly the purely informative aspect of radio dialogue is a supreme example of *ars celare artem est.*

What happens when radio dialogue fails to do its narrative job in a completely unremarkable way has been delightfully demonstrated by Timothy West in a classic parody of the radio play: *This Gun That I Hold in My Right Hand is Loaded.* It can be considered as an actor's revenge on radio playwrights for all the obviously informative lines they have expected him to say quite naturally. It abounds in such speeches as: 'Whisky, eh? That's a strange drink for an attractive auburn-haired woman of 29 to be having,' or, 'You're my wife, Laura. You can tell me. I'm your husband,' or, 'Ah, missed! The bullet must have been deflected by that steel flange just above my head. Now to raise to eye level the pistol I took away from the man I knocked down earlier this afternoon, and sighting carefully along the barrel, let him have it!'

The play is full of radio tricks like: 'A letter for me, you say.

Damn, I've left my glasses at the office. Read it out for me, will you?'
The characters not only address each other obsessively by name
but, for identification purposes, all tend to have broad Scots, Welsh
or Germanic accents. In short, it is a laughable compendium of the
faults of radio dialogue at its worst — and does not sound all that
different from old recordings of early popular radio theatre at its
most self-conscious!

Dramatic function of radio dialogue

We have so far been considering the narrative, informative aspect
of radio dialogue; but this is subsidiary to its main dramatic task of
involving us in the lives of a particular cast of characters, of sweeping
us up to a climax in their fortunes which resolves certain
contradictions and leaves us with a satisfied feeling that we have
participated in something that makes the world a marginally
different place from what it was before.

To think in some detail about how radio dialogue achieves this
dramatic result we have to remember what is distinctive about
listening to a radio play. Radio play enjoyment is almost as private
an experience as daydreaming — indeed, it *is* a kind of author-
directed daydreaming. It is a much more private experience than
television play viewing, even though the latter is intended for the
home rather than the public gallery and is, to that extent, different
from stage or film. It is possible for a small group of people watching
a television play to comment among themselves about the casting of
the play or whether they are enjoying it or not without destroying
the visible world on the screen which is their common point of
reference: such interchanges among people listening to a radio play
temporarily dissipate the dramatic universe each shares with the
playwright and make it necessary to reconstruct that universe as
attention returns to the play. Many people prefer listening to radio
plays through earphones, not only for the improved quality of the
sound but also for the purpose of cutting themselves off from others
— even from those who may be listening to the same play in the
same room.

This intimacy, this closeness, this uniqueness of the relationship
between radio playwright and radio play listener provide that
playwright with special dramatic opportunities — and also hazards!

The degree of listener involvement in radio drama, deriving both
from the imaginative contribution the listener makes and from the
absolutist quality of the feelings and impressions of someone
listening as a completely isolated individual, means that the

emotional effect can be much greater. But the closeness, the intimacy of the medium also means that insincerity, falseness or pretentiousness are going to be very quickly exposed. The playwright might get away with dialogue that is phoney in this respect or that when the speeches written for the actors can be delivered with a masterly technique in a commanding voice that can be heard clearly all the way up in the gods. Spoken into the ear of the listener, radio dialogue has to ring true. The radio play is a terrible test of an author's integrity.

The success of a radio play depends on the responsiveness of the listener's imagination to the writer's prompting; but how can the writer prevent the imagination of the audience from being over-stimulated and going far beyond what this particular play requires? The scene of a loving couple fondly embracing each other can summon up an image of debauchery or a naughty child being slapped one of vicious sadism.

This is all the more likely to happen at a time when the cultural field has been so pervaded by the near-pornographic and the gratuitously violent. The tendency for so much theatre, cinema and television to turn audiences from involved sympathetic spectators into detached voyeurs creates a climate in which the radio playwright has to write very careful dialogue using exactly the right words for precisely the nuances of feelings to be evoked in order to make sure that listeners have not drifted off into some other play than the one intended.

But, of course, as has been pointed out before, it is dialogue under the control of a good strong storyline that will be able to control, in turn, the imaginations of the listeners.

The intimacy of the medium means that the radio play is on a somewhat smaller scale than other forms of drama. This is not to say that the emotional impact is less. To the contrary, we have seen why that impact may be very powerful indeed. It is just that radio drama creates that powerful impact by somewhat subtler, quieter and more precise means. The instant rapport between playwright and listener means that dialogue can achieve quicker, more fleeting effects. More delicate shades of feelings can be expressed. A more rapid dialectic of action and reaction between one character and another or between playwright and listener can be effected.

The things we laugh at and the way we laugh are different if we are reading an amusing book on our own or watching a sex farce at the Whitehall Theatre with our charabanc party. The laughter provoked by a radio play is more like the chuckle in the former case and less like the outburst of hearty guffaws in the latter. The writing of radio humour, like any other variety of dramatic writing, has to be mindful of that audience of one, listening all alone. The dialogue accordingly should avoid anything in the nature of loud rhetorical bombast, broad rib-nudging bawdiness or heavy teutonic sentimentality and, instead, with lighter, quicker, defter strokes share with that lone listener the whole range of dramatic possibilities somewhat scaled down.

We have mentioned that in radio drama the spoken word comes into its own, freed of any visual context to create new universes of sound for the mutual exploration of playwright and listener. But this very freedom from being pinned down to the visible, this very realisation of the imaginative potency of the spoken word, can tempt a writer into verbal indulgence, into an intoxication with the sound of words and the effects the technical staff can create to go with those words which ceases to have any narrative line at all. There is no reason why we should not have an interesting thematic sound collage — as long as it does not pretend to be a play.

Some radiophonic works on German radio or on Radio 3 have this kind of linguistic exhibitionism which expects a great deal from the listener without providing that listener very much in return but a humble appreciation of how clever the writer is. But, ironically, the radio play, which, by its great verbal freedom, can lure a writer into verbose display, obfuscating sound patterns and empty rhetoric, by its equally great intimacy of involvement, shows up insincerity and pretentiousness.

Strong language in radio drama

The question of the use of strong language in radio drama has been blown up out of all proportion to its real importance, both by those who protest vociferously at every instance of its use and those who campaign vigorously for greater freedom to use it.

On the one hand, any stronger language in BBC drama than one might hear at a vicarage tea party is regarded as bringing the country to the verge of moral collapse; and on the other, the use of certain four-letter words is considered to be evidence of a great social advance toward a more egalitarian society and to be allowed to use them in radio plays is to smuggle revolution into people's homes.

Neither party seems to be all that aware or concerned about whether the themes of plays, what the plays are really saying, are life-enhancing or demoralising, supportive of some moral system or degenerate and corrupting — rather like the old Hays Code for Hollywood films, which laid down specific rules about what could not be shown, like the inside of a woman's thigh, without touching on the question of whether or not these films were spreading false values all over the world.

Certainly many taboos about strong, vulgar or obscene language have been swept aside and there is considerable freedom in the use of such language in films and on the stage. However, there is an obvious difference in the use of strong language in a cinema or theatre that people go out of their homes to attend, having first been alerted in various ways of what to expect, and the use of strong language in radio or television plays which, with no warning, come into homes at times when children may be about.

It is generally accepted by the BBC that strong language — or at least stronger than usual language — is justifiable for purposes of characterisation and of indicating a dramatic situation of great stress or strain. 'Heavens above!' would be a pretty implausible expletive from a tough criminal and 'Fiddlesticks!' is hardly the kind of expression we would expect to be wrenched out of a man on the rack.

In fact, language that is completely appropriate to characters once they have become established or to difficult situations once we know the people involved in them is so much what we expect to hear that we are hardly aware that it *is* strong. The trouble usually comes when strong language occurs early in a play when the listener has not yet become involved in the story and is still getting to know the characters. It is a matter of record that there are many more complaints about strong language in a play that fails to grip people's imagination and leaves them for long moments bored and critical than in one that involves their interest quickly and holds it.

But there is a special reason why particular care has to be exercised about the use of strong language in radio drama. In a visual dramatic medium like theatre or film we can see from the dismissive expressions of the characters whether the strong language is being used in a casual 'throw away' sort of manner. In radio drama there is not the same equivalent of 'throwaway' lines spoken out of habit. Unqualified by expression or gesture the strong word or phrase fills the sound universe of that play while it is in the course of being uttered.

Often a repetitive use of certain words or expressions is intended to reproduce the actual speech of, say, workers on a building site or soldiers in barracks. But, of course, the point about such purely habitual speech is that those uttering and those hearing these words and expressions are not aware of them at all. This is hardly going to be the case when they are spoken by actors pretending to be building workers or soldiers on stage, screen or the air. In any case,

41

for dialogue to work well it has to avoid all language so threadbare that it does not really say anything anymore.

Sparingly used at exactly the right time and place, like one word in Harold Pinter's radio piece *Landscape,* strong language can have its full dramatic force restored. The absolute importance of the word in radio drama means that it is neither in the interest of writer nor listener that there should be the kind of linguistic inflation that has lowered the value of language in other media.

Insofar as the repetition of certain words like, for example, the ubiquitous 'bloody', represents laziness on the part of the writer, that writer should be pulled up and made to think about other ways of making a strong impact on the listener than constantly drawing on a vocabulary of tired words and phrases. That this can be done is shown by the fact that often when a play has contained a strong scene, the kind of listeners who consider themselves the custodians of propriety in speech will complain about strong language although none has been used — simply because the well-written scene *felt* that it had such language in it.

Writers who have something they want very much to say to an audience in dramatic terms ought not to risk losing a lot of listeners through the gratuitous use of offensive language. Otherwise they will be like the unfortunate playwright whose play condemning the British occupation of Northern Ireland by comparing it with the Roman occupation of Britain was hardly discussed at all except in terms of a bit of stage business by no means essential to the theme.

Naturalism and radio dialogue

We have just been noting that the use of a steady flow of habitual 'bad' language to achieve naturalness in radio dialogue does not work. In fact, for a number of reasons the mere imitation or reproduction of any actual speech, as overheard on buses, at places of work or of amusement, does not work well for drama in general and even less for radio drama in particular. What is required is very carefully wrought dialogue which contrives to *sound* natural.

We have seen how hard dramatic dialogue has to work to provide information and perform a narrative function without seeming to do so. Ordinary speech is always too loose, repetitive and imprecise to carry out this task efficiently and self-effacingly. This is even truer, of course, of radio drama dialogue which has the additional job of prompting listeners to supply imaginatively all the visual aspects of a play. The heavy responsibility of radio drama dialogue in its double role of enabling a blind audience to follow a storyline and at the same time to become dramatically involved in the actions of the characters, can hardly ever be discharged by the kind of speech to be met with in ordinary life.

Not only does radio dramatic dialogue have to work too hard to be able to pick up much that is useful in the speech heard all about, it also works much faster and more economically. In the radio play time is subjective, not bound to the movements of physical bodies in material space, and the action moves more quickly. Ordinary speech thus seems slow and lags behind the dramatic movement reflected in the listener's imagination. We have often considered the economy of the radio play, the author not being required to put in one word or one sound that does not help realise the dramatic purpose of the piece. Ordinary dialogue is much too verbose and periphrastic to work in such a medium.

What distinguishes the language of all forms of drama is that it is heightened language. Dramatic dialogue is not necessarily poetic or rhetorical language. It is certainly not florid or stilted. It is not even particularly grammatical. Passion can play havoc with syntax, and people whose normal speech may depart radically from standard English can be made to speak in a powerfully dramatic and, at the same time, perfectly credible way.

What is this heightened language of drama, then? What distinguishes it from ordinary speech? One clue to it was given when we mentioned the fact that in Beckett's play *All That Fall,* natural sound effects did not seem to work and had to be replaced with sound specially created to accompany Mrs Rooney to the railway station and fit in with her reflections on the way. If we were ending a play with the sound of an iron door clanging shut on a young man who has been condemned to life imprisonment, no ordinary spot effect of a closing door would work. What is required is a sound like the slamming shut of the gates of Paradise behind our guilty first parents reverberating on and on down the ages. It is what is called a subjective sound effect — the way we imagine something would sound to a person in a particular state of mind.

The heightened language of drama is subjective language. In writing a dramatic scene the playwright makes each speech not only express the feelings of the speaker but also sound the way we imagine it would sound to the other person hearing that speech in the frame of mind he or she is in. Then the same thing happens with the interlocutor's reply — and so on right through the scene. The effect on the audience is that they are|constantly being pulled inside one or the other of the characters to hear each speech as it falls on the ears of a terrified, deeply grieving, spitefully vengeful or hilariously amused person. It is the writer's ability to put this dialectic interplay of impassioned perspective into dialogue that makes us, as spectators or listeners, feel that what is happening emotionally to those players is happening to us.

The basic shape of drama — rising tension, climax and resolution — is repeated not only in each scene but even in each major speech. The heightened language of drama not only sets before us the contradiction out of which the tension comes but pulls us inside the characters involved in that contradiction.

When we analyse something like writing radio drama dialogue, it begins to seem very complicated and we may even begin to wonder how it ever gets written at all — rather like the way analysing our perception of the world around us can sometimes make us question whether we really know the external world at all. This is because analysis lays bare the whole history of a development like drama and shows us how, over generation after generation, it got to be what it is now. In writing a play we certainly do not have to go through the same age-long process, but knowing what dramatic dialogue is and how it got that way can help us to write better, that is, more dramatic dialogue and avoid the flatness and triteness that can kill any dramatic scene.

What we have learned about the nature of radio drama helps us to understand why it is a particularly unsuitable medium for naturalistic dialogue. With its limitation to the single sense of hearing, radio drama cannot present us with reality, not even the approximation to reality of visual drama. It gives us instead the shared creation of an illusion of reality into which pure naturalism does not fit. Since both the context of radio play and the characters themselves are largely imagined, completely realistic, unimaginative speech does not come across as real but seems to strike a false note.

Two radio playwrights who often collaborate in a kind of documentary drama about working class life prepared themselves for one of their earliest plays, about deep sea fishing, by shipping on a trawler and recording on a tape machine the actual speech of trawlermen on and off work. Many of these speeches they incorporated verbatim in their play — and they sounded phoney! The art of writing good radio play dialogue, for characters of any walk of life, in any situation, is to get inside those characters and make them say what they need to say for the purpose of the drama in a way that strikes us as fitting. Real-life speech no more gives us such language gratis than history ever provides us with a complete historical play.

A radio playwright like Gilly Fraser or Barrie Keeffe, with this gift of getting inside characters with backgrounds so well known to them, can make people who are naturally somewhat inarticulate speak their thoughts and feelings comprehensibly and movingly without sounding at all forced or artificial. Another playwright, writing about the same sort of characters because plays about them are 'in', and imitating their speech from outside, by picking up particular words or turns of phrase, will always come across as patronising. Their plays will not ring true.

So we see how in the radio play, whose very substance is so much a matter of imagination, any mechanical reflection of reality has even less place than in other art forms. Recorded natural speech cannot be accommodated in the texture of a radio play and even recorded natural sound effects, except for casual background noise, often have to be turned into subjective effects by the skill of technical staff before they can fit into the imaginative fabric of a play. In a sense the world of the radio play is not so much a real as a *sur*real world.

Chapter Seven
Sound Effects and Music

JUST as radio drama dialogue performs both a narrative and a dramatic function, so the adjuncts to dialogue, sound effects and music, may assist words in providing information or in heightening dramatic impact.

Sound effects

We have already considered what are called subjective sound effects, effects which have been doctored in some way to make them sound as we would imagine them sounding to characters in some particular emotional state. We shall have more to say about the dramatic use of sound effects, but first let us look at them in their narrative, informational role.

Simple effects accompanying the actions of the characters in the play, sounds of the opening and closing of doors, pouring of drinks, striking matches, breaking china and so forth, are usually made in the studio by an assistant using a number of gimmicks and gadgets for the purpose. The susurrus of the heroine's formal gown may be obtained by the actual wearing of taffeta or the crumpling of taffeta cloth by the prop person. Slaps and blows can be managed by the same person.

The playwright need not write into the script most effects of this kind. A bit of dialogue like 'Drink? Thanks,' or 'Do you mind if I smoke?', or 'Close the door as you go out, will you? There's a bit of a draught in here' will alert the producer to what is required in terms of accompanying sound. Incidental effects like footsteps, sinking into a chair, lying on a bed, and so forth, are best left to the producer who will put them in or leave them out according to the needs of that particular play.

There is certainly no need to illustrate every exit with appropriate effects, as: 'Well, I'm off.' (*Walks over to door, turns handle, opens door, steps out of room, closes door behind.*) On the other hand, if one of the characters is leaving the room angrily, the playwright may put in such stage directions as: 'Well, it's the last time I'll ever come *here.*' (*Goes out, slamming door.*) And if the exit is an absolutely crucial point in the play a subjective effect may be called for, as: 'Goodbye, and may you rot in hell!' (*Door slams with the reverberant sound of the crack of doom.*)

More complicated effects, usually recorded, can be used to set scenes and tell the listener where we are — background sounds of hospital, restaurant, concert hall, busy street corner, and so forth. As was said before, such sound effects are often inadequate in themselves to place the listener unmistakably in the right scene and usually need a bit of designative dialogue, as 'Dr Thorpe will be doing his round at ten o'clock and you can ask him then,' or 'My bill, please,' or 'We'll be able to hear very well in these seats,' or 'Mind that taxi. I think he's pulling out.'

Often a single sound will tell us a good deal about a setting. A grandfather clock or a crackling fire in a fireplace or a wind chime on a veranda, or drops in a bucket from a leaking roof or jangly bedsprings all tell us not only that we are in a room in a house but also something about the means of the inhabitants.

Out of doors a seagull tells us that we are at the coast, a curlew that we are on a lonely stretch of marsh, an owl that it is night and a wood pigeon that it is a hot summer's day. These are all useful shorthand devices for establishing settings or the time of day or year. We never have to worry about such natural sounds becoming clichés. Clichés are turns of phrase or figures of speech which once had the freshness of invention but have now become trite with over-use. But seagulls, not even the original BBC seagull which has been taking listeners to Brighton or Dover or Skegness for over 60 years now, having never tried to sound any different from the way they always do, never strike us as boringly affected.

There are plenty of recordings in sound effects libraries of animals or other natural sounds like storms, floods and so forth. Sometimes better than recordings of a dog or cat may be a live performance by a good animal impersonator — like Percy Edwards. People have been known to take their pets back to the shop because they did not sound like Percy Edwards.

Some situations are difficult to establish in terms of sound, like the interior of a motor car in motion which poses the problem of the right balance between the engine heard from inside and the conversation of the passengers. Other sound settings which may be interestingly noisy, like an iron foundry or an underground train, become increasingly hard listening for an audience having to strain to hear the dialogue. One device is to establish the sound of such a noisy environment and then gradually fade down the effects to make the conversation easier to hear.

Certain scenes creating problems for visual drama — like erupting volcanoes, travel in outer space or the great tank battles in World War II when whole armoured Nazi armies were smashed — present no problem for radio while, ironically, some simple action like moving around a room looking for a dropped collar stud may be hard to do. Characters only a few feet away from us may turn into howling wolves or squeaking bats while we cannot easily follow two people talking as they leave one room, go upstairs and enter another.

The reason for this is that radio drama space is for the most part made up of relative distances from a stationary microphone. There is no simple way for the microphone, which is normally the centre of the sound universe, to move about the way a mobile camera does through a fixed visible world.

New technological developments, which we shall be considering in a later chapter, have solved some of these problems of radio drama — and created others. The radio playwright will learn through the experience of having plays produced just how to exploit in terms of sound effects the freedoms and avoid the limitations of the sound medium. In the meanwhile, it is largely a question of common sense helped by the assurance that some producer will help the writer of a good radio play deal with the problems of sound drama.

The main rule governing the use of sound effects is that old principle of the economy of radio dramatic writing — only put it in if it helps tell the dramatic story.

Music

Why a rising sequence of quick notes should be jolly while a descending sequence should have a sad dying fall is the same kind of mystery as how certain sounds came to have meanings attached to them. In any case music, as a kind of language of the emotions, could not but have a place in drama. Indeed, choric dances were a feature of drama's earliest phase and the musical comedy is one of the most popular forms of theatre today.

Not only can a bit of music help to set the right emotional tone for a scene: it can be very informative as well. If a young man and woman are in a nightclub and the band is playing in strict tempo 'A Nightingale Sang in Berkeley Square' or if over the radio is coming Vera Lynn singing 'The White Cliffs of Dover', we know we are somewhere in England during World War II. In the same way, by appropriate music we could help set our scene in the court of Queen Elizabeth I, at the Café Royal during the Mauve Decade, in a Welsh mining village during the depression or in a southern United States Black Baptist church during the Civil Rights Movement. The advantage of using music for setting date and place is that the information comes freighted with nostalgic sentiment which, as well as telling the listener when and where the play is taking place, also puts that listener in the right mood for the play.

Useful musical quotes for informational purposes or for helping to establish a particular mood can be included by setting scenes where the music required is likely to be encountered — a nightclub, a hotel tea salon, a Wigmore Hall recital. Or it might be possible through casting the play with music students, piano tuners, instrumentalists with the LPO or a visiting musician from India to introduce some music quite naturally. In *Venus at the Seaside,* Jennifer Phillips made her loving but constantly quarrelling married couple both opera singers. Their matrimonial ups and downs are played out humorously to the contrapuntal effect of a running commentary of snatches from *La Belle Hélène* to the *liebestod* music.

What does not work so well in a sound medium, fortunately, is the Hollywood heavenly choir in the background, accompanying Shirley Temple in her ascension to her place among the angels. Radio listeners would be wondering where all those people have suddenly come from! As dialogue has become less and less important in films they have become more and more drenched in the syrup of sentimental music or set to the unendingly relentless pace of pop rhythm.

We have seen that radio drama begins with silence. That means that our noisy world of competing sounds, of a confused mush of noise, has to be hushed before the radio play can begin. Then a new world can be created of selective sound, of just those words and sounds and music the playwright needs to tell a dramatic story. In this world music has a role, an important but subsidiary one. Its role is to enhance the words, to give them a stronger emotional tone or a lighter melodic touch. But it must never begin to seep through the whole play or large parts of it. Radio drama needs silence, against which the dialogue can achieve subtle effects, quick twists of plot and delicate nuances of feeling. It needs silence in which the words, which are its essence, can reverberate and take on a richer significance. The beats and pauses of good radio dialogue, momentarily recalling that primordial silence before the beginning, must not be cluttered up with extraneous background noise and music.

A radio play by Gwen Cherrell, *Interior,* pursues with great ingenuity the idea, so admirably suited to a sound medium, of the extent to which we are all plagued in our modern world by noise. Edward thinks of silence as of the hole in Henry Moore's sculpture — not just a nothingness in the middle but that which gives meaning to the somethingness all around it. He collects silences — the silence in an empty lift, the silence just before the penalty kick in a drawn football match, and, most profound of all, when he has done something about a talkative, never-quiet spouse, the silence just before a jury announces its verdict.

Fashions in radio drama production change. At one time, when radio drama was still not too sure of itself as a viable medium, much more lavish use was made of sound effects and music. Since then there has been a move toward sparer, more economic production and, as producers have realised how responsive radio audiences can be, productions have been taken at a much quicker pace.

Sometimes this trend has gone to the other extreme — productions too severely shorn of illustrative sounds and music and romping along at too fast a pace to give dramatic developments their full weight — as if the way to keep listeners from feeling boredom were to rush them along too quickly for them to have time to think about whether they are enjoying the play or not.

It is for the playwright to think about the use of adjuncts to the dialogue and decide whether the play should be slowed up at this place or that, to make full use of them in emphasising or colouring the drama. Usually the way the play or a scene of it is written will tell the producer how it ought to be done. The sound effects or the music the playwright thinks necessary can be called for quite specifically or the kind of thing wanted can be indicated and the producer can decide how best to realise the writer's wishes.

The thing to remember is that producer and technicians have half a century of experience behind them now in helping writers create sound universes in which the listener can take up habitation and live and breathe and feel while the play lasts. Producer and technicians have a vast library of sound effects and recorded music to draw upon and a radiophonic workshop which can create new synthetic sound to order. They like to be challenged to join with the writer in the co-operative creation of one of those new universes, pictured by descriptive sound and moving to the music of its spheres. Call upon them imaginatively to get the effect you need in launching your dramatic world.

Chapter Eight

Radio Drama Construction

WE HAVE decided on the theme we are going to write about and know how we are going to treat our play — as comedy, tragedy, satire or what. We have roughed out a storyline and have a vague idea of what the climax of our story is. Now, how do we set about constructing our play?

Making it easy for the listener at the beginning

We have talked a lot about the demands radio drama makes on the listener. The imaginative collaboration the listener enters into with the playwright, actively participative rather than passively acceptive, is the means by which subjective elements in the radio play, the passage of time, the affective impact of words and the purely sound-evoked 'look' of things become objectified through the suppression, while the play holds writer and listener together in·this exclusive relationship, of all frames of reference other than that heard and imagined realm of their joint creation. The radio play draws the listener inside the dramatic situation by recreating the situation inside the listener's own head. In other words, radio drama provides the very intimacy of involvement which is a necessary condition for the participatory demands it makes.

We have also considered the precise means by which radio |drama persuades the listener to submit to his involvement to begin with. In the first place it begins at once to tell that listener a good story that arouses an eager expectancy of what is going to happen next. In the second place it assures that listener that one or other of the characters is sufficiently sympathetic or the situation sufficiently recognisable for some kind of identification to make the listener stay with that story once begun.

So that tells us just how to write the opening scene. We have to get started with the story as soon as possible. Let us suppose the story is about a chief inspector of police who can only clear himself of a corruption charge by exposing his wife's affair with a czar of the

Soho vice rackets. Obviously we do not want to start at any point except one at which this particular story is dramatically under way. It might be the police commissioner's informing the chief inspector that evidence of a bribery charge is so strong that the case is to be handed over to the Public Prosecutor; or it might be the chief inspector's telling his wife that he has known about her affair for some time and hoped she would get over it but now it looks as if it might all come out; or it might be the wife telling the Soho racketeer what has happened to her husband and how this is likely to affect their relationship.

Now any of these possible openings will raise questions in the listener's mind about what has gone before. The art of good dramatic storytelling is to be able to deal with these questions as the scene progresses, in such a way that they spur the listener on to get the answers instead of discouraging the listener with a feeling of not knowing enough to follow the story.

Which scene we start with depends on whom we intend to be the most sympathetic character in the play — the chief inspector or the wife, or, it may be, the vice czar. Perhaps it is husband and wife equally, in which case we should probably begin with a scene between the two of them. If it is none of them and we are supposed to recognise that they are all simply what a society like ours makes of people, then we are going to have the problem of keeping listeners interested in what happens to automata.

Let us say that we are now clear enough about an opening scene and what it is going to contain to rough it out in dialogue. We know what shape it ought to have. A play is made up of scenes and each scene is like a playlet, having the same statement, counter-statement, rising tension, climax and resolution that is the basic pattern of all drama. This first scene has to sweep up to a conclusion that represents some dramatic development, points ahead to the next scene and makes the listener want to go on to hear it.

At this point the playwright might wonder if, as the process goes on like this of planting one scene after another, there is any assurance of keeping in the right dramatic direction? Might it not be like putting one stone after another to cross a stream to a climax on the opposite shore and then finding that you have curved away downstream from it?

Working backward from the climax

In considering the difference between narrative and dramatic writing we observed that while the loose, strung-out-in-time structure

52

of narrative lends itself to the writer's simply starting at the beginning and keeping on to the end, the tighter construction of drama, with everything playing its part in building up to a climax, could better be written by starting at that crucial point of the play and working backwards. Since, as we have also observed, the play combines both narrative and dramatic elements, what this really means is that the playwright's creative imagination has to work both backwards and forwards. Having thought the storyline forward to the climax, the playwright now works dramatically backward from the climax to make sure that all the elements making for maximum tension converge at this crucial point and that anything in the way of characters or scenes not really needed for the strongest possible climax is eliminated.

To work backwards in this way means that we have to be absolutely clear about what the climax of our play is. In the example we have been considering there are a number of implicit conflicts. There is the conflict between society, represented by the chief inspector, and the criminal racketeer; there is the conflict between chief inspector as husband and racketeer as wife's lover; there is the conflict between husband and wife and, probably, between wife and lover as well; there is the conflict inside the chief inspector between his duty as a police officer and his love for his wife, and so on. We have to decide which is the main conflict in our play, which is also a decision about the theme of our play. What is this play really about?

Once we know that we can carry on with laying down our stepping stones, the individual scenes, from both ends, thinking both narratively and dramatically as we go. Working backward from the climax we will consider ways of imparting or withholding information so as to create little surprises along the slope of rising tension leading up to the big surprise. The playwright can think of the process of doling out information about the characters to make the maximum dramatic impact as a kind of game played with the listeners. The rules of the game are that, on the one hand, the listeners must never feel wilfully or clumsily excluded from knowledge needed to understand what is going on and, on the other, they must never feel that it is clear how the play is going to end now and that there are unlikely to be any more surprises. The justification of the game is that the playwright is teasing and tantalising the listeners for their own greater enjoyment of the play.

Start each scene knowing just how far you want to advance the story and in just what way you can do that dramatically by giving another turn to the screw of the main contradiction within the limits of the scene. Make sure that all the characters needed for that scene

53

are established and, particularly important for radio drama, do not let minor characters 'disappear' by having nothing to say for long stretches. See to it that the dialogue ending the scene both concludes one piece of action, giving it dramatic unity, and at the same time leads on naturally to the next. Constantly keep in mind the climax you are working toward so that you weight each twist and turn of the plot with dramatic promise and eliminate minor characters or any bits of the scene which do not seem to be playing their proper part in the build-up.

Avoid monotony in radio drama scenes

The very word 'scene', coming from the word for the tent which served the ancient Greeks as a stage, has to mean for radio drama, not something seen, but something imagined. It makes striking one scene and setting up another the easiest thing in the world for the playwright to do. All that is needed is to say the right words and, hey presto!, a new scene appears in the minds of the listeners.

This is very fortunate. What continuously haunts the radio playwright, working with one sense alone, is the worry that the sounds being woven into a play will become monotonous and the listeners will begin to nod off. One remedy for this is to use the facility of quick-as-thought scene changing which radio drama enjoys. Let a scene with an indoor acoustic be followed by one out of doors, or a noisy scene at a fairground by a quiet one in somebody's study, or let a scene viewed from inside the mind of one of the characters be followed by a perfectly objective scene from the author's point of view in the next. In other words, take full advantage of the fact that radio drama offers, by its nature, the kind of variety that no visual drama could ever manage.

Variety can also be achieved by following a noisy angry scene with a tender quiet one, a funny scene with a sad one, and so forth. Of course, the ultimate weapon against monotony and boredom is simply good strong dramatic writing which not only in each scene but even in every major speech holds in delicate suspension the contradictory elements which are finally to explode in the climax.

Other forms of radio dramatic development

So far we have considered radio dramatic construction based on the traditional form of the stage play with dialogue raising and lowering the curtain on a succession of imagined settings all organised in the shape of statement and counter-statement, rising tension, climax and resolution.

But radio drama offers other dramatic possibilities. New technical developments can give the listener the sensation of hearing exactly what one of the characters hears and even, through interior monologue, of seeming to feel and think that character's very feelings and thoughts. A binaural microphone effects a far closer identification with a character than a hand-held movie camera can and it makes possible on tape the same flowing sequence as film which seems to have been shot continuously without being broken up into scenes.

By this technique a dramatic story can be told in the stream of consciousness method developed by novelists like Virginia Woolf. Of course, it still has the dramatic shape of building to a climax which will take the form of some dramatic happening to the character with whom we identify, or some dramatic change which other people bring about in that character.

Arthur Kopit's *Wings*, in which we begin the play inside the head of a woman who is just regaining consciousness in hospital after an air crash, is a good example of this kind of radio theatre of the mind. The play was subsequently transferred to the stage but never worked as movingly in a visual form as when we enjoyed the kind of intimate relationship only radio can make possible.

There are various patterns of dramatic form which the radio play may take. Instead of one plot strand of the play leading up to climax and resolution, there might be two or more plot strands which meet at the crucial point — or the strands of major plot and subplot may run in parallel, counterpointing each other.

Instead of the climax coming at a particular point in the play, it may be spread over a pattern of gradual change, as when we start with rich villain lording it over poor hero and then by a series of gradual changes we end up with rich hero and poor villain. Jill Hyem's play, *Equal Terms,* which has been broadcast all over the world and frequently adapted for visual dramatic presentation, is an excellent example. A voluntary social worker calls to help a woman whose life is in a mess and it is gradually realised that the social worker herself is in a far worse plight, stating dramatically the simple truth that people cannot help others if they are unable to recognise and accept their own need for help.

The cyclical nature of drama, building up to a climax and resolving it so that the process can begin all over again, may suggest a circular pattern for a play. A character in a particular dilemma may take various steps to get out of it and after a whole series of adventures find himself or herself right back in the same dilemma, perhaps even using the same line of despondent dialogue with which the play began. Such a shape for a play is also saying something about life — that human beings cannot escape their fate, that history does not introduce real change, that there is no novelty in the world, and the same old cycles go on revolving. That is certainly the feeling one often gets with television situation comedy series whose episodes take this form.

What has to be remembered about constructing a radio play, particularly the popular plays of about an hour in length broadcast in the afternoon, is that the listener is very likely to be doing something else. The play must be constructed with this in mind, so that it is particularly absorbing and easy for the 'blind' listener to follow.

Chapter Nine

The Script of Your Radio Play and What Happens To It

YOU HAVE completed your radio play, either in manuscript or roughly typed out. Now you are ready to make a fair typed copy for submission.

There are certain obvious rules that apply to the submission of any written material. Always keep a copy, either by making one or more carbon copies as you type or by photocopying the completed script. Always give yourself every chance of acceptance by providing a legible, clearly set out text that is very easy to read. Do not forget to put your present correct address somewhere on the first page, probably in the lower right-hand corner. Before you try to get one more script from that used-up ribbon, think of some reader or script editor who has already ploughed through dozens of submissions and is looking about for one more to glance at before calling it a day. Will your typescript invite his tired eyes to choose it rather than something else to see if at least one play with promise cannot be found before going home?

On the first page of the script, with the title of your play and your name, it is helpful to give the cast of your characters in the order of appearance with approximate ages for the major characters. It will tell the script editor at a glance whether the cast is a manageable size or not and will help sort out the characters for a first reading. It may also remind *you* that your cast is too large and make you think of eliminating some characters or suggesting ways in which minor parts can be doubled — that is, several smaller roles to be played by the same actor.

For guidance in script layout two pages of a BBC dramatic production are reproduced here. The main two points to bear in mind are: (1) Keep a wide margin on the left in which nothing appears but the names of the characters who are speaking, so that anyone reading the script always knows who the speaker is, and (2) distinguish clearly between the words which the listener is to hear and all 'stage' directions, suggestions to actors, sound effects, and so

57

1.	LOCKWOOD: (continued)	On that bleak hill-top the earth was hard with a black frost, the air made me shiver through every limb and the first feathery flakes of a snow shower were falling. I knocked on the door and, receiving no answer, went on knocking till my knuckles tingled.
	F/X	EXTERIOR OF WUTHERING HEIGHTS. SOUND OF KNOCKING AGAINST BACKGROUND OF WIND.
2.	LOCKWOOD:	Wretched inmates! What churlish inhospitality.
3.	JOSEPH:	(from the barn) What are ye for? The master's down in the field if you want to speak to him.
4.	LOCKWOOD:	Is there nobody inside to open the door?
5.	JOSEPH:	They's nobbut the missis; and she'll not open.
6.	LOCKWOOD:	Why ever not? Can't you tell her who I am?
7.	JOSEPH:	Not me.
8.	HARETON:	(COMING UP BEHIND LOCKWOOD) Come with me.
	F/X	DOOR OPENS. BRING IN CLOCK: FIRE. LOSE WIND AS DOOR CLOSES. INTERIOR PARLOUR WUTHERING HEIGHTS.
9.	LOCKWOOD:	Ah that fire! (to the young woman sitting there) It's snowing heavily outside now. I'm afraid, Mrs Heathcliff, I may have left the mark of my knuckles on the front door, the consequence of your servants failing to open to me.

1.	HARETON:	Sit down. He'll be in soon.
	F/X	LOW GROWL FROM THE BITCH.
2.	LOCKWOOD:	(SITTING NEAR FIRE) We've met before, haven't we? A beautiful animal. Do you intend parting with the little ones, madam?
3.	CATHERINE:	(unamiably) They are not mine.
4.	LOCKWOOD:	Perhaps your favourites are among those over here.
5.	CATHERINE:	A strange choice of favourites — dead rabbits.
6.	LOCKWOOD:	Oh, I thought they were cats.
7.	CATHERINE:	(not sympathetically) You should not have come out in this weather.
	F/X	DIP BACKGROUND UNDER FOLLOWING.
8.	LOCKWOOD: (narrating)	She was slender and scarcely past girlhood: an admirable form and the most exquisite little face that I have ever had the pleasure of beholding: small features, very fair, golden ringlets hanging loose on her delicate neck, and eyes — had they been agreeable in expression her eyes would have been irresistible. Fortunately for my susceptible heart, the only sentiment they evinced hovered between scorn and a kind of desperation.
	F/X	PEAK BACKGROUND TO NORMAL

She reached for a canister on a shelf near the chimney-piece.

forth. Here, UNDERLINED CAPITALS are used for 'stage' directions, like PEAK BACKGROUND TO NORMAL or sound effects like LOW GROWL FROM THE BITCH and (underlined lower case in brackets) for instructions to actors, like (to the young woman sitting there) or (unamiably).

A point about the last bracket. Usually it is not necessary to tell the actor how to say a line. The line should be written in such a way that *it* tells the actor how to say it. We do not want to be like Shaw who was notoriously suspicious of what actors might get up to and, therefore, might include an instruction like '(tenderly) I love you.' But this is Catherine's first appearance and there is nothing in this short line as written to indicate the disagreeableness which is going to be Lockwood's first impression. A playwright might have a good dramatic reason for wanting a speech spoken against the way it would normally be said or for having some patriotic or highly moral expression sent up and in such cases a word or so of instruction to the actor (in brackets) may be necessary.

There is no need to number speeches on the page. That is simply a device for the ease of reference of producers and actors in, for example, going back to a particular point for a retake.

It is worth noting how an exterior and an interior setting are etched in by sound. Also how the interior background of the room is 'dipped' down for a purely descriptive piece from the narrator to enable us to see Catherine with our mind's eye.

The Script Unit of the BBC

Let us suppose you have submitted the clearly typed script of your play to the BBC. (We are taking the BBC Radio Drama Department as the model for what happens to scripts of radio plays because, although commercial radio does some radio drama, the amount of it is still very small compared with the BBC.) Your script will go by way of the play library, where it will be noted if you have ever submitted anything before and if anything of yours has ever been broadcast, to the office of the Script Editor who will then send it to a reader for a report or he might send it straight to the editor of the spot your script would seem to fit.

You might have said, in your letter to the BBC Radio Drama Department accompanying the script, that you wrote it as an 'Afternoon Theatre Play' or a 'Saturday Night Theatre Play'. Because, of course, you had some particular spot in mind when you decided on the play you were going to write. How else would you have known how long it was to be? There would not be much point in writing an excellent little fifteen minute play when the 'Just Before Midnight' slot for plays of that length disappeared several years ago.

Also it was through listening to the kind of plays broadcast at different times on Radio 4 or Radio 3 that you knew that the play you had in mind to write, in theme and treatment, suited this placing or that. Anyone interested in writing radio plays must be a fairly regular listener to them; and a person who sent in a script with a letter saying, in effect, 'I never listen to radio drama myself but thought the attached might work well somewhere on radio' is not going to get the most enthusiastic response.

The main weekly radio play spots on Radio 4 are:

The ninety minute Monday Play (with a repeat on Sunday) —
    the main full-length original radio play spot on radio.

Thirty Minute Theatre (Tuesday, repeat on Saturday) —
    the shortest play in the regular schedule. A good spot for a first play but, with a built-in repeat fee, an attractive spot for professional writers too.

Afternoon Theatre (usually three a week at one hour or under) —
    the established spot for popular theatre. Worth writing for because suitable scripts are used up at such a rate.

The ninety minute Saturday Night Theatre (with a repeat on Monday) —
    intended for family listening. Probably very few families actually gather around the radio of a Saturday night as they did during the war but if they did this is the sort of dramatic entertainment they might enjoy together.

If you feel that the necessarily idiosyncratic way you have dealt with some extremely challenging and unusual subject demands a certain length play whether such a spot exists or not, and calls for a certain kind of attentiveness on the part of the audience, then you may be writing for Radio 3 where more leeway in duration is allowed.

There is only one reliable way of estimating the length of your script — read it as you think it ought to be performed and time yourself. It is better to err on the side of writing a little over the desired time than under, as many producers like to have a bit of time in hand to tighten up speeches, cut out unnecessary bits of dialogue, and so forth.

So now your script is in the hands of a reader, or a spot editor. You can appreciate our repeated insistence on the importance of the first few minutes of a radio play and how hard the playwright has to work to make the beginning of the play involving. The same steps taken to try to make sure of keeping the listener listening are going to keep the script reader reading.

What is the reader looking for as he turns over the pages of your script? SED(R), the Script Editor Drama (Radio), Richard Imison, has prepared a list of the questions a script reader should be considering when recommending a play for acceptance. This list, *Reports on Plays,* is printed here because it is good for radio playwrights to know the kind of catechism their script is going to be put through. There is no reason why they should not anticipate this

REPORTS ON PLAYS

Just for handy reference, here is a list of some important questions to be considered when recommending a script:—

1. Is it basically a good story?

2. If it is, are the characters and dialogue equally good?

3. If they are, will it make good radio?

4. If it will, to which spot is it best suited?

5. If the script is viable on all the counts listed above, is it the right length?

    If not, can it be cut or expanded without artistic loss?
    If so, where?

6. Even if the script is still viable, how might it be improved?

    Is the beginning sufficiently compelling?
    Is the cast too big?
    Does it maintain dramatic tension?
    Is everything that should be conveyed sufficiently well planted in the dialogue?

7. If it's a good story, well told in radio terms, are there any special problems?

    (e.g. controversial themes liable to misunderstanding by the audience; foreign settings calling for difficult or expensive casting; technical backgrounds likely to attract expert criticism, etc.)

8. If the play passes on all these counts, it's obviously a strong possibility for broadcast:

    How could the author make it better?

exercise and see if they cannot improve the script in certain respects before submission. By and large the points about radio plays alluded to in the questionnaire, starting with the first challenge as to whether it is 'basically a good story', are those which we have tried to emphasise in the advice given about the way to write radio drama. Not for nothing was the author of this book for many years a member of the BBC's Radio Drama Script Unit!

One of the most important facts about the Script Unit from the new, or relatively new, radio playwright's point of view is that all of the more than 15,000 scripts a year submitted to it get read. Furthermore, a great number of those playwrights whose scripts are not accepted for broadcast but nevertheless show promise in this respect or that, are written to and told why their script was not taken. This criticism may enable the writer to rework the play in such a way that it does become acceptable or, at least, helps to avoid the same mistake in subsequent plays. Not a few of those whose plays, though not accepted, show some degree of excellence in storytelling or writing dialogue will be invited in to discuss their writing with a view to achieving broadcastable quality in the future.

Seminars are run by the Script Unit for new playwrights in which they meet members of the Unit, producers and other writers and spend the day discussing the 'grammar' of the radio play, the technical facilities at the writer's disposal and practical questions of radio play production.

The reason for this helpful attitude is that the BBC Radio Drama Department needs and, therefore, encourages new writers. Broadcasting original radio plays at the rate of over 500 a year and losing established radio playwrights to other fields of writing and through natural wastage, the BBC is on the lookout for new talent in writing radio drama — and is succeeding in discovering some sixty or seventy new writers each year who have never had anything accepted for broadcasting before.

Radio drama production

The BBC Radio Drama Department is organised around its Script Unit which is responsible for finding the plays and planning the schedules for a large output not only of radio plays but of dramatic features, adaptations, serialisations and dramatic readings amounting to some 2,000 programmes in all each year. The rest of the Department is primarily concerned with the production of all this dramatic material. Both the Head of the Drama Department, Ronald Mason, and the Assistant Head, John Tydeman, are distinguished radio drama producers, and the staff producers who work with them in maintaining the standards in this field the BBC has done more to develop than any other broadcasting organisation in the world are keeping alive the great tradition of fine radio drama producers like Donald McWhinnie, Raymond Raikes, Archie Harding and so many others.

Let us say that the script of your radio play has been accepted at one of the weekly meetings when the Script Unit proposes to a departmental meeting, chaired by the Head of Radio Drama, the plays thought suitable for broadcast. In due course, perhaps six months, your play will be scheduled and offered to a producer for production.

This radio drama producer, who ought properly to be called producer-director since the post involves directorial responsibility as well as casting and costing the production, will probably want to see you beforehand, possibly to make some suggestions for improving the script but mainly to make sure of being clear about your intentions as playwright.

It is established practice for you to be invited to be present at the actual production which in the case of radio plays is feasible since even a ninety minute play usually takes only three days in the studio.

The reason for this concern with what you as playwright are saying in your play and this willingness to have you actually present in the studio is that radio play production is more script-centred than any other form of dramatic production. The imaginative world of each radio play is created entirely out of the words and sounds the playwright puts down on paper. The radio play script is the blueprint for that world and director, actors and technicians are mainly concerned with interpreting creatively what is there on the page.

There is not the opportunity in radio drama production that there is in visual dramatic production for the invention of stage business or mimed sequences or vivid expression and gesture to help the author get the dramatic message across; but then neither is there the same possibility of 'guying' or 'sending up' the play or reinterpreting it by the way it is staged. The producer has to be satisfied that the play as scripted by the writer, with whatever amendments and alterations they have agreed, is the working plan for what actors, helped by studio assistants, are going to do in the studio. There is going to be little chance of twisting or shaping the play into something else, of 'giving it the business', as it were, in the crowded time allowed for studio production.

The first thing that strikes the radio playwright on entering the control cubicle of a radio drama studio is that this is a recorded medium. It was not so in the earliest days of broadcast drama. Productions were treated as something of a theatrical event and the first real head of BBC Radio Drama, Val Gielgud, to whom the development of radio drama owes so much, used to turn up on the occasion of producing some great classic on the air, in cape and opera hat.

For a time there was some resistance to recording productions and then broadcasting the recording instead of putting performances out on the air 'live'. It was felt that the dramatic excitement of radio play production would be lost in the process of mechanical reproduction. But, of course, this argument was based on a false analogy. The 'live' radio performance is not really like a stage performance since actors have no audience reaction to help them to pace dialogue, judge effects or time laughs; there is no question of building a part or a stage relationship over a considerable run and, in any case, the parts never come off the page. Once recording techniques enabled directors and actors to broadcast as nearly perfect a production as possible in a once-only transmission, the 'live' radio performance became an artistic pseudomorph.

The basic form of radio drama production is one of rehearse and record and then tape-edit to perfect the final broadcastable recording. It is the same process with tape as the production of a moving picture with film — only radio does not go in for such a lavish expenditure of time and money with dozens of takes of every scene ending on the cutting room floor.

Whether the rehearse and record technique is used on larger or smaller sections of the play depends on the nature of the work. A technically demanding play, with a lot of complicated effects, special music and subtle acoustic changes, which does not call for any great dramatic effort on the part of the actors, is best done in small bits, setting up tape and disc machines, tying up spot effects and studio business and then, when there is synchronisation with actors' voices, freezing the whole thing in recorded form at just the right moment. If, on the other hand, the play is mainly concerned with developing human relationships which have to be brought out by actors not only mastering their own parts but also changing in sympathy with changes in the other actors, then a reasonably extensive run is necessary, something more like a live stage performance, to enable the actors to exploit their parts properly and the director to get an ensemble performance to which they have all contributed. Sometimes a whole thirty minute play will be taken in a single run.

The fact that radio drama is a recorded medium has a number of consequences for the playwright. There is the possibility of playing about with time, as when recorded snatches of dialogue or bits of a scene may be repeated at different points in a play, the way associated thoughts flash across the mind. The almost subliminal flicks in moving pictures which turn out to be a kind of precognition of something we are going to see happen later on can work for radio too. The distortion of voices by radiophonic means can achieve humorous or horrible effects. There is even a machine into which voices can be fed to come out as the speech might sound in the mouth of a lion, a monkey or a crow.

Indeed, being a recorded medium not only makes it possible to play about with time but, as in Beckett's play about a man and a tape machine *(Krapp's Last Tape)*, to play about with the idea of playing about with time.

The coming of sound to the cinema ruined many a film career of actors whose voices did not correspond with their silent image. Radio has freed many actors to star in roles they might never have been chosen for in a visual medium. It is also a boon for actors who are visibly pregnant, say, or who are disabled in various ways. The BBC Radio Drama Department maintains a 'rep' of some 35 actors who are useful as a pool of bit and character players to facilitate casting but are regularly provided with starring parts as well. Many distinguished actors have been more closely associated with radio drama than with any other dramatic medium — like Grizelda Harvey or Carleton Hobbs.

Radio playwrights sometimes write parts with a particular actor in mind and this can be mentioned to the producer, though the producer for one reason or another may not be able to act on the suggestion. And accomplished actors have often expressed their eagerness to be cast in the plays of certain radio writers they admire.

Good or slipshod productions can sometimes make a considerable difference to a radio play. A light comedy, for example, can be made or marred by the deftness of touch of those producing it. On the whole, though, new radio playwrights are well served at the BBC in terms of having their first efforts professionally handled.

Technological developments and radio drama

Radio drama came into being as the result of a technological development, and further technological developments continued to shape its history. More delicate microphones and high fidelity recording have rendered obsolete the basement drama studios in Broadcasting House, which suffer from intermittent tube train rumble, and have necessitated the building of new sound studios elsewhere.

Stereophony, with complementary signals coming out of two amplifiers, has given the radio drama listener a richer sound perspective and a more exact spatial relationship between characters, whose conversation we might follow by turning from one to the other like spectators at a ping pong match. But, of course, for every advance of this kind there is loss, too. The need for the listener to be at the right spot between two stationary amplifiers to get the best stereophonic effect means that radio drama has sacrificed its claim to be the one form of drama which can be enjoyed while doing things which keep one on the move.

Mindful of this loss and realising that many radio play listeners have not acquired stereo facilities, the BBC has ruled that the stereophonic production of radio drama should be produced in such a way as to be compatible with monaural listening. Since the quality of sound in stereo, even when heard over a single amplifier, is better and since there are advantages in standardising spoken word recordings with music recordings which are all stereophonic now, this is a happy compromise.

Quadrophony, or the arrangement of four amplifiers with the listener in the centre, is only for those who can afford a considerable amount of hi-fi equipment and a room that can be converted almost entirely into an auditorium. It completely immobilises the listener and is more suitable anyway for music or large musico-dramatic works than for straight drama.

Binaural microphones are arranged in such a way as to reproduce the stereophonic characteristics of the human ear, with the effect of placing the various sources of sound in a radio drama scene in exact geographical relationship to each other.

An interesting psychological effect of binaural listening is that many people find that all the sounds seem to come from behind them or off to one side, even when the sound source was in front of the paired microphones. This is apparently|because the brain cannot accept sounds so accurately placed at a point where there is nothing to be seen and tends to push them to either side of the cone of vision, forcing those sounds on one side or the other right around to the back. Listening with closed eyes helps to correct this effect and, in time, one gets used to experiencing exactly located sounds with no visible source.

The binaural pair of microphones can actually be worn by an

actor, with the effect of making the listener's ears almost identical with the actor's sensitive artificial ones, hearing the actor's voice as the listener's own voice would sound and hearing everything else in the same sound perspective as the actor. Since involvement is of the essence of radio play listening, a device which pulls the listener inside the skin, as it were, of one of the characters can obviously be very useful. One can imagine the chilling sensation possible in a radio horror play as some creature creeps up on us from behind and seems so close we can feel its breath on the back of our neck.

But, of course, there are, as we have seen, corresponding losses for these advantages offered us by technological advances. As playwrights we may not want to pull the listener right into the middle of the action. We may want the listener on the other side of something like a proscenium arch. Or we may not wish to surrender that geographically vague, completely subjective radio dramatic space in which things could happen with the speed of thought. Once people and things have precise geographical relationships with each other and with the listener we are going to have to exercise something of the care in moving them about and getting them on and off stage that is required in visual drama.

Developments in recording equipment make it possible now to take the radio play right out of the studio and perform and record it on location — in a park, on a farm, inside a hospital ward or a classroom. No doubt it makes an interesting change for the listener, with a suitably sensitive receiver, to hear a scene with a completely naturalistic background. And no doubt it sometimes helps the actors to get out of the claustrophobic atmosphere of the studio and act out a scene in a natural setting. But this mobility of the production team has to be paid for with the greatly reduced power of the playwright to whisk his audience anywhere at all for the briefest of scenes lit by the most ingenious of synthetic sound effects.

Since these technological developments add something to the possibilities of radio drama production while taking something else away, the answer seems fairly obvious. Use them when a particular play would be enhanced by their employment but do not try to make all production fit in with the use of any one new recording device — nor all radio drama listening fit one kind of signal reception.

In highly commercial fields the latest gadget, the latest gimmick, tends to sweep all before it. In films the development of sound or colour completely suppressed all that had gone before and a form in which some of the greatest movie masterpieces had been created, black and white mimed comedy, became a museum piece. Fortunately, radio drama is not commercial in that way and there is no reason to suppose that different forms of sound recording and propagation — stereophonic compatible with monaural, or binaural — different places of production — in studio or on various locations — and different kinds of listening — completely absorbed, the ordinary world shut out by headphones or moving about doing various chores with a transistor — should not all exist together, multiplying the variety of radio plays available to an audience able to vary the quality of the listening experience.

As radio playwrights become more experienced they may write particular scenes or, perhaps, whole plays with one or other of these new recording facilities in mind. But to begin with it is probably best to write your play simply keeping in mind that unique listener, creating out of the dialogue you write the imagined world of radio drama; and let the producer decide whether your script or a part of it might not benefit from the special treatment made possible by the latest technological developments.

A writer's medium

It should have become obvious in the course of this chapter that radio drama is, pre-eminently, a writer's medium. It is the writer's own dramatic universe which director, actors and technical staff have to realise and they have nothing to go on but the writer's script.

They cannot conceal its plot flaws with visual excitement, or cover the emptiness of lines with stage business, or make up for dull, unimaginative writing with extravagant sets or, to anything like the same extent as visual drama, with star casting. On the other hand, the writer's nicely judged dialogue and characterisation, dramatically built climaxes and marvellous resolutions are not going to be muffled or lost in some alien conception of what might make better box office.

Fewer people intervene between writer and audience in radio drama than in any other dramatic medium. There are only the director, the actors (whose number the writer has kept to the minimum), the studio manager and panel operator, grams and tape operator and someone to handle spot effects in the studio. Compare that with the endless list of credits that go up after a film or television play.

Unlike the weeks and weeks of rehearsal before a stage play can open, a radio play is rehearsed and recorded within a few days, making it possible for the writer to be present during most of the process of turning the script into a completed work ready for reproduction. This makes possible the kind of writer-director co-operation in production which took place, for example, between John Arden and Alfred Bradley in making *Pearl* one of the outstanding radio drama productions of 1978.

The radio playwright has to work hard to make sound alone fill the listener's mind with great dramatic encounters but the reward is that what the listener hears is closer to the writer's intention than can be the case in other dramatic forms.

Chapter Ten
Some Radio Plays

THE following plays have been chosen for comment and quotation because they help make some of the points we have been discussing about the way to write radio drama — and also because they just happen to be plays the author of this book likes and remembers out of the thousands that passed through his hands during his time in the BBC Radio Drama Script Unit. Every radio drama listener will have his or her own list to compare with this one, noting with approval plays common to both and extolling with justice many, many wonderful plays that have not been included here.

The first group of plays selected for mention are all by women writers. Some sixteen or seventeen years ago the BBC Radio Drama Department, in order to avoid competition with evening television viewing, established an afternoon band of radio drama. This audience is about two-thirds women and the BBC's putting out the bulk of its popular drama at that time meant that for a considerable number of women the primary dramatic experience was the radio play. Those of them who developed an interest in telling stories in dramatic form found it natural to write radio plays.

It just so happened that this new artistic platform for women writers appeared at a time when they were feeling under-represented in the arts and had a lot to say about their own plight as women in particular and about things in general from the women's point of view. While over the last century women have been holding their own as novelists, poets or diarists, relatively few have been dramatists and the theatre has remained largely a masculine preserve; but here in radio was a field of dramatic art that seemed open to them. Sometimes the author of this book on hearing one of these plays by women writers has had the interesting dramatic experience of hearing quite despicable male characters using excuses and justifications he has been known to use himself! Often their very first radio plays showed the same command over this new medium as professional writers had to learn over a considerable period of 'devisualising' scripts written as though for stage or screen. They, as it were, sprang on to the radio drama stage full grown, artistically speaking, like Athene from the head of Zeus.

Rose Tremain's play *Blossom* has already been mentioned as a good example of theatre of the mind. As a counterpoint to her daily chores in the boarding house she runs Grace carries on inner conversations, as we all do, with those who have been close to us. She cannot reconcile the brief passionate affair with young Peter Blossom, who was staying at the boarding house while on a training course, with the long years of marriage to Dennis who had died after an illness some years before. Toward the end of the play Dennis speaks to her, as the dead do in our minds and can also do, perfectly naturally, in radio plays.

Grace   It's Billy's Dad's funeral today and I promised Lil I'd be there. Lovely day for it anyway — a bright and shiny day. And I've done nothing about flowers. I must be there when the shop opens, so that they've time to make up a nice wreath. (*Hurrying on*) You remember Billy's Dad, don't you? Now there was a man who never complained. And didn't have much of a life, you know, sitting in that chair.

Dennis   Of course I remember Billy's Dad.

Grace   He was never any trouble. I often used to think, an old man like that, First World War veteran, what a burden! But he never made demands, you know? I used to marvel. Of course you could tell there was a lot going on in his head. You could *tell* that — or I could, anyway. I mean, his life hadn't always been a blank.

Dennis   That's the trouble, Grace.

Grace   Pardon, Den?

Dennis   Well, all the measuring we do in our minds; measuring one day against another, bad times against good. So unwise of us. There were days when, lying there on my own, I wished my life had been . . . well . . . more of a blank. But I couldn't remember any blanks.

Grace   Oh Den . . .

Dennis   All I could think about, you see, was how wonderful my life had been. I couldn't remember the bad bits — they didn't seem important. All I could say to myself was 'You've had the most wonderful life any man could ask for . . .'

Grace   Well, there were good times . . .

Dennis   And that was why I couldn't help crying — like you last night, Grace, crying and crying because of all the lovely things you could remember.

Grace	Den, I . . .
Dennis	Oh I know why you were crying. You were crying for Peter.
	(*Silence*)
Grace	(*Contrite*) Well, I was, Den, yes. You see, it's not that I wanted to love him. He was just a boy, young enough to be my son. But there it was.
Dennis	Of course it was.
Grace	It was long after you'd . . . well . . . gone, Den.
Dennis	I haven't gone, love. You still hear me, don't you? I'm still in your mind. Oh I know you often wish I wasn't, but I linger, don't I?
Grace	Yes.
Dennis	Well, there you are. And you see, for me you were all I ever wanted. I didn't need anyone else. And — this is odd, really — do you know what I kept thinking about? That day, oh years ago, when we had a holiday in Kent. Funny little cottage with an outside toilet. And there was some fine spring weather and we went for walks, hand in hand. We walked in the apple orchards, Grace, and — this is what's so funny, really — all the blossom was out and tumbling down around us! I'll never forget that blossom.
	(*Silence*)
	Are you there, Grace?
	(*Silence*)
Dennis	Grace?
Grace	Yes?
Dennis	I didn't want to upset you by reminding you of that.
Grace	No, it's all right, Den. I'm glad . . .
Dennis	What?
Grace	Well, I'm glad in a way we had this little talk.
Dennis	Are you?
Grace	Yes. It helps to get things straight. And Den . . .
Dennis	What, Grace?
Grace	I'd like to say, . . . I'm . . .
Dennis	No, no. There's no need for that. Now you'd better get on and order those flowers for Billy's Dad.
Grace	Yes.
Dennis	And Grace . . .
Grace	What?
Dennis	Give the old boy a good send off.
Grace	(*Tearful laughter*) Course we will, poor old bugger! Course we will, Den.

In *Moonshine* Shirley Gee deals in a poignant way with the near tragedy that results from a pleasant but feckless woman's delegation of her daughter's upbringing to a superstitious nanny. Exploration in depth of the relationship between mother and children is one of the themes of general interest the new wave of women writers is handling expertly.

> (*The Nursery*)

Ada	Close your eyes and hold your nose, one big gulp and
(Nanny)	down it goes.
Flora	Ugh. I hate it. Why do I have to have it?
Ada	Keeps you regular.
Flora	Ugh. Tell me a story, Nanny.
Ada	You'll have to pay me for it.
Flora	A kiss?
Ada	Two kisses. One on each side. Don't want one cheek to be jealous of the other.
Flora	What's jealous?
Ada	Jealousy is the green eyed god. Sometimes lives inside you. Tears you apart. *(Pause)*
Flora	Is this the story? Nan?
Ada	A monster that lives inside you, tearing at you. *(Pause)*
Flora	Come on, Nanny. You're not telling. What does he look like? Nanneee. He's got green eyes . . .
Ada	Green eyes that flash. Made of glass. Splinters of green glass that flash in the moonlight. *(Pause)*
Flora	Go on. You keep not bothering. Go on.
Ada	How much do you love your mother? Show me.
Flora	This much.
Ada	And how much do you love Nan?
Flora	The same, Nan. Exactly the same.
Ada	Good. Good. Well, when he's not living inside you he lives in a glass church. He wears a crown made of gold bones with jewels of blood, and he has a big cloak made out of poor creatures' furs and lined with the Prime Minister's skin.
Flora	Why the Prime Minister?
Ada	I've told you before, he's a wicked man. He leads people into wickedness.

Flora	How do they get his skin off? Does it hurt? Doesn't he miss it?
Ada	Don't keep interrupting, it's rude. Where was I? And the Pope's skin he uses for his cuffs and collars. His clothes are made of cobwebs, greyish yellowish cobwebs, like your mother's hair. And his throne is made of mermaids' bones.
Flora	Mummy's hair, Nan?
Ada	Like, I said, didn't I, like.
Flora	Go on. Don't stop. I won't interrupt again. Cross my heart. What does he eat?
Ada	Ah. He has a huge oven, like the Aga, only bigger, and his servants bring him all the worst things in the world, like spiders' hearts and rats' feet and old green kidneys —
Flora	— and tapioca —
Ada	— all stirred up into a deadly potion. But know what he enjoys most of all? Bad people, he gollops them up, bad people who break promises, idle people who lie about doing none of the world's work. *(Pause)*
Flora	Once upon a time it, Nan.
Ada	Well, let's see now. Once upon a time there was a queen, and this queen was beautiful beyond the dreams of man, but oh, she was a wicked one. She lay all day on a couch of leopards' fur counting her pearls . . . *(The door opens)*
Harriet	Lucky lady. Hallo, Flopkins.
Flora	*(Hissed)* Mummy, shush.
Harriet	Sorry. *(whispered)* Am I interrupting? Sorry.
Flora	Go on, Nanny.
Ada	If madam doesn't mind.
Harriet	Gracious no, of course not. So long as it's not too long.
Ada	. . . counting her pearls and drinking creme de menthe and making eyes at the poor king . . .
Harriet	Sounds like Sally Playfair.
Flora	*Sshh.*
Ada	. . . but he was bewitched by her pale beauty and held in thrall, so he never noticed how wicked she was. She had two children, a little prince and a little princess, little lambs both of them. But she was so busy . . .
Harriet	Counting her pearls.

Flora	Mummy, I *hate* you.
Ada	. . . dressing up in her furs to go to the ball and painting her dark blood nails she had no time to care for them, and slowly, slowly, gradually, gradually they shrank, from hunger and neglect. They grew thin as two washing lines, their little bones stuck through the skin, their little eyes were hollow as ghosts . . .
Harriet	Nanny! I'm sorry, I shall have to stop you there. What kind of a tale is this? She'll have nightmares.
Ada	If my Flora has bad dreams she knows where to come. Pop into Nan's bed and snuggle down and she'll be safe as houses.
Flora	It was a lovely story until you came and spoiled it.
Harriet	I'm very glad indeed I did come in. It's an appalling story.
Flora	I loved it. There was a green eyed god going to come into it and everything.
Harriet	I absolutely forbid you to say another word about it, Flora.

Fay Weldon's *The Doctor's Wife* explores the minds, as only radio drama can, of men and women caught up in the ambiguous crises of the way we live now. It firmly tracks down the satanic forces which have been such a feature of recent cinema to the subconscious mind where they lurk.

	(*In the Baileys' bedroom, the doctor and the doctor's wife dress*)
Margot	I am the doctor's wife dressing for dinner, gazing at my face in the mirror. I am so used to seeing it, I scarcely notice any changes. It was never such a pretty face that I cared much what happened to it. So long as it was clean and friendly and had no spots. So long as the mouth smiled and the eyes were kind — or so I told myself.
Dr Bailey	I am the doctor, dressing for dinner against his will. My legs are tired. I have a headache. I have had a hard day. I have put on weight. When I put on my suit I will have further evidence of that sad fact; therefore I do not want to put it on; therefore I do not want to go out to dinner. I am so very adult through the day, I am allowed to be a little childish in the evenings, surely.
Margot	I wish I hadn't said we'd go.

76

Dr Bailey	So do I. I talk to people all day. All I wanted for this evening was silence.
Margot	Yes, but we never go out.
Dr Bailey	All the more reason not to start now. Do I have to wear a suit?
Margot	I expect so. I don't know. Or perhaps they'll be wearing jeans and battle jackets.
Dr Bailey	They're not teenagers.
Margot	She's very young. And he feels he has to keep up, I daresay.
Dr Bailey	He must get very tired, that's all I can say.
Margot	Aren't you ever tempted to throw me out? Get someone less ordinary than me? I'm sure you could.
Dr Bailey	Don't be ridiculous.
Margot	It would make you feel young again.
Dr Bailey	How you do brood.
Margot	That time with your receptionist, eight years ago.
Dr Bailey	Good Lord. What a time to bring that up. A silly drunken party, when you were in Madeira sunning yourself stupid.
Margot	Sorry. It's just once I had such lovely clothes and now all I've got to wear is a purple crimplene dress, size 42.
Dr Bailey	You always look very nice to me.
Margot	Nice! That's what I mean. And she'll be wearing a crimson chiffon knickerbocker suit and black boots.
Dr Bailey	Dear God, will she?
Margot	Yes. Something like that. Why did they ask us, anyway?
Dr Bailey	Perhaps they haven't any friends. They don't sound very nice to me. I'm only going for your sake, Margot. Bread sauce, too.
	(*In the Katkin bedroom, Martin and Helen dress*)
Helen	I am Helen, the hostess, showing off in the smartest possible way. I shall write and tell mother all about it tomorrow. She never gave dinner parties. I am the second wife, showing how much better I can do it than the first one ever did. How happy I make my husband. How smart and successful we are.
Martin	I am the husband of the two wives. I drink too much. Shall I wear a suit, Helen?
Helen	A suit? No. You're not sixty yet. Wear your jeans and a jacket.
Martin	I feel awkward with doctors. Why in God's name did you ask them? And she's my secretary. It's all ridiculous.

Helen	The Blands couldn't come. I'll wear the scarlet chiffon lounger, shall I?
Martin	If you don't mind everyone staring down your bosom all evening.
Helen	Doctors are above that kind of thing.
Martin	Peter Appleby isn't.
Helen	(*calling*) Hilary! Get Jonathan into his pyjamas, will you?
Martin	She's not his nanny.
Helen	No, but she loves him and takes some trouble, which is more than you ever do. Have you seen her hair? It's really neat.
Martin	(*sarcastic*) Neat. Yeah man yeah. Wow. It doesn't suit you, honey.
Helen	What's the matter with you today? I can't do anything right.
Martin	You shouldn't have taken Hilary out of school. You've pushed Marianne right back into the lawyer's arms.
Helen	Sometimes I wonder whose side you're on.
Martin	It's not a question of sides.
Helen	I think it is. I have to account for every penny I spend of your beautiful money. She doesn't.
Martin	All twenty pounds a week of it.
	(*In the Katkin living-room the Scarlatti meanders on. Coffee is sipped and liqueurs knocked back*)
Helen	I can't bear to start worrying about cholesterol. I'm too young.
Martin	I'm not.
Martha	You should see the lunches Peter eats when I'm at home with a bowl of tinned soup. No wonder he's the size he is — all middle-aged men should be on diets, shouldn't they, Dr Bailey?
	(*The Scarlatti seems to falter; the wind blows in an open window*)
Helen	What was that? The wind? Shut the window, Martin. What did you open it for? It's cold in here. I'm shivering —
Martin	I didn't open it.
	(*and Margot moans and falls on the floor*)
Dr Bailey	Margot — what's the matter —
Margot	I can't breathe — I'm sorry —
Dr Bailey	Yes you can. Don't be silly.
	(*He slaps her*)
	Stop it, Margot. Stop it at once.

Margot	(*Breathing better*) My leg. I can't straighten it.
Dr Bailey	(*Apparently furious*) What do you mean, you can't straighten it? There!
	(*He straightens it forcibly. Margot shrieks*)
Margot	I'm sorry. I'm really sorry.
Helen	What's the matter with her?
Martin	Shall we ring the doctor?
Dr Bailey	Don't be more of a fool that you have to be — here, help me get her on to the sofa.
Margot	At moments like these — one wishes one had been on a diet — really, honestly, I'm all right now.
Helen	Listen, Jonathan's shrieking. What's Hilary thinking of — why does one ever give dinner-parties?
	(*And so Jonathan is*)
Margot	It's just suddenly I couldn't breathe. This dreadful pain in my chest. And my right leg — a pain: why should one have a pain just there? There's nothing to hurt — I'm better now.
	(*In their bedroom the doctor and Margot get ready for bed*)
Margot	What a dreadful evening. I'm glad we're home and safe. Everything looks so normal here. I'll set the alarm for seven-thirty-five. Give us an extra half-hour. I do feel foolish, Philip.
Dr Bailey	It was rather an exhibition. Never mind, it got us home early. And it should at least produce something dramatic on your disc. Perhaps that was why you did it. Of course, it might have been merely a rather vivid expression of horror at the conversation.
Margot	You mean it was hysterical? I'm not dreadfully ill after all?
Dr Bailey	Not if you get better so quickly, no. In response to a slap and a harsh word.
Margot	But it was so real. It was awful. I didn't put it on, or anything.
Dr Bailey	I'm not saying you did.
Margot	Why did I go like that?
Dr Bailey	God knows what goes on inside anyone's head.
Margot	Even mine?
Dr Bailey	Especially yours. I suppose I am a tired old man. Perhaps you'd like to be provided with a gigolo? Perhaps that's it.

Margot	I thought you were asleep, at that stage of the evening. I suppose, at my age, I'd need one. I don't like growing older, Philip, you're quite right.
Dr Bailey	Neither do I.
Margot	I am the doctor's wife, home from an evening out. An only partly welcome guest, as always; my husband's adjunct, neither smart, nor beautiful, nor successful, but useful for filling up an empty seat between two males. Mildly depressed, faintly entertained; glad to be me, not them; too full of over-rich food, and too many different kinds of drink. Creaming my face before the mirror as I have done a thousand times before, seeing the detail not the whole — as plain girls quickly learn to do, and now, I find, the ageing woman — and having, I seem to remember, behaved badly, as I have never done before.

Often plays are political without seeming to be. A home for helping prisoners who are about to be released make the transition back to normal life is set up skilfully by Gaie Houston in *Animals in the Zoo*; the dedicated staff are drawn with respect and humour and the benign effects of the treatment are shown with great compassion. We are crushed with a sense of human waste when, on grounds of economy, this venture in rehabilitation is closed down.

Dilly	What are they doing to me, then, coming down here looking me over as if I was a pound of cat's meat on the turn? They're so thick they don't even *know* what's going on in them. I know, though.
Jock	Why not try saying it as if you were a visitor?
Narrator	You can't stem a geyser, but you can dig a channel for it to flow through.
Dilly	What? One of them role-play type of things we did?
Jock	It's just a suggestion.
Narrator	Dilly, grotesque under his black eye and swollen stitched cheek, rears his small skeleton, a composition of left-over dustbin bones, to its feet. He draws breath and gazes around, as if pityingly. He points one toe and extends his undamaged arm in his version of a society pose.
Dilly	I'm the visitor then. (*Society voice*). O you poor bleeders. (*slight laughter*) What a terrible mess you are making of your lives.

	How can it be that you waste these lovely opportunities we offer you to go on the buses or peel potatoes in the filthy kitchens of our world-famous hotels! O I am sorry for you.
Narrator	Dilly mimes producing a compact and powdering his nose.
	(*mild laughter and applause*)
Derek	I always thought you were one, Dilly.
Dilly	(*Aside*). Shut up. (*In role but more intimately, forgetting accent*). Well soon I'll be back in London and drive my car back home and tell hubby I been down the zoo seen all the real criminals all walking round talking almost as if they was really free. Whipsnade they ought to call this place.
Jock	You're getting out of role, Dilly.
John	It may not be the moment . . .
Derek	Now is the only moment. You've said it enough times, John.
Narrator	A visiting probation officer who wants to work at the Centre, and who has not had a chance to shine all the morning, makes public his knowledge of the technique of role-play.
Probation Officer	I'll be you, I'll be Dilly, if that helps you.
Dilly	All right, yes.
Safari Man	I'm not entirely sure that the best interests . . .
Narrator	By now this is a meeting in which the people who say they are not entirely sure are on a losing wicket. The energy is with the role-play. Dilly's performance has already astonished the visitors, even the residents. They want more. The visiting probation officer helps them get it.
Probation Officer	Whipsnade they ought to call this place, we're trapped here, even if you can't see the fences.
Dilly	(*His own voice*). Well that's your fault, ain't it? You ought to get a job down the factory and stop living off my taxes.
Narrator	He has picked up a response which most visitors have tried their best to suppress. They lean forward, awed, like children watching two conjurers. The visiting probation officer is getting into it now. He is standing with folded arms, sneering at Dilly. He speaks again.

Probation Officer	I hate — I hate standing eight hours a day in front of a machine in such a racket I can't even hear myself speak.
Dilly	That's what's wrong with these criminals, they're lazy. Why don't they do something for society for once, get a job as hospital porter, twenty quid a week for washing down sluices and wheeling the stiffs down to the morgue.
Jock	Your role's slipping again, Dilly.
Narrator	Dilly turns on Jock with the masterly ease of a good comedian riding the heckling in a Northern club.
Dilly	You watch it, Jock. You may be able to talk to your criminals like that, but don't you come that with me. I'm the middle classes and I've got friends on committees and things and I can get you put out of your job soon as look at you. You might think you're something, but to a judge or a real lady a probation officer ain't half just a speck of muck to pick off the end of your nose and drop on the floor. *(loud applause and laughter)*
Probation Officer	*(as himself)* You seem to have got there, Dilly. Do you need to go on?
Dilly	I had a talk with this judge. Where are you? Yes, him. He's the one who sent me down last time; but he's all right. You're all right.
Judge	Thank you.
Dilly	Except you was too soft with me. I should've got the maximum.
Nelson	There's always a next time, Dilly.
Dilly	Shut up. Only that made me think what I'd do if I was a judge. I'd sit up there in my wig and all the clobber, and I'd have them put my dad in the dock. And my old woman. And most other people's too, from what I've heard. And next to them I'd cram in the school-teacher who used to knuckle my head when I tried to ask to go to the toilet when I was a little kid of five . . .
Nelson	This woman in the home where I was used to take away my models when I'd spent the whole weekend painting them, and just break them up, stamp on them in front of me . . .
Dilly	Yes. And all the screws and the Old Bill . . .
Tom	That bus inspector this morning . . .
Derek	Some of the clerks from the Social Security . . .

82

Dilly	P.O.'s. Judges. I'd ram them into the dock like sardines and I'd give them a look — I'd talk to them so they'd curl up, so they'd wish they'd never been born. Then I'd march them out to dig their own grave and shoot the lot of them. Not you. None of you here. And then I'd turn round and sign a paper so we took over all the big hotels, and any boy who'd ever been in care or been in trouble could help hisself to a nice room and good food and a four-figure giro every week, without showing no photograph or signing nothing not giving a number not having to prove nothing to no-one. (*Immensely pleased*). Wah. I think that'll do for now. Thanks.
Mrs A.	As this lady was saying, I feel that we visitors here this morning have been privileged to glimpse a — very vivid . . . (*laughter*) community life here.
Judge	I should like to support Mrs Amberley.
Dilly	(*Aside*) Need to do a bit of weight-training first, mate.
Nelson	Be quiet, man. It's your friend the judge.
Dilly	He's all right.
Judge	And I should like to thank John and the rest of the staff for inviting me here. An alternative to prison. And one that I can feel a certain degree of respect for. You see, one of the most difficult parts of my job is deciding what to do with people when they've been found guilty. I daresay that many of you would agree with me, that in an imperfect society, there is a place for prisons . . .
Nelson	(*Aside*) I'll tell you the place if you like.
Dilly	Shut up.
Judge	Society must be protected. And some offenders seem themselves to need the degree of protection that prison gives. But that is certainly not true of the men I have met here today. On this farm you are making use, so far as I can see, of a chance to let a little more order, a little more peacefulness, into your lives, as well as learning particular trades or skills as some of you are doing. This place does not function on fear, and my guess is that for some of you that is quite a new experience in your lives.
Dilly	(*Aside*) I'll still end up inside.
Jock	I wish you'd not mutter, Dilly.

Dilly	(*Aloud*) I said I'll still die in the nick, like my old man kept telling me I would.
Jock	That's your choice, Dilly. You don't have to.
John	(*To Judge*) Sir. I'd like to thank you for what you've said. It's nice to be recognised.
Judge	My job would certainly be a little easier if there were more places of this kind to which men — and women — might be referred. (*Some chuckles and foot-stamping*)
John	Yes. Well, with your support, sir . . .
Mrs A.	And the support of many of us here today, I feel sure. Such influence as we have . . . (*Fade*)
Official Voice	Dear John, just an unofficial word before next Tuesday's meeting, to thank you most sincerely for all the dedicated work you and your staff have put in at the Day Centre, and to tell you of the immense regret I share with my committee in having to face the economic realities of the time and bring this in many ways successful experiment to a close. I would ask you to accept no more referrals, from the date of this letter, as the present financial climate makes it impossible to leave even the present community there for more than a few weeks . . .

The radio play can be an excellent vehicle for horror. In the visual media when the monster or ghost or evil thing finally materialises it is apt to be a bit of an anticlimax — not so terrible as we expected; but in the radio play the most frightening thing each listener can imagine is exactly the shape that haunts this particular example of the genre. *Boo!* by David Campton is a very imaginative horror play. It is about Bill Halliday, a man who does not understand or like children very much and who, having taunted the children of the neighbourhood, allows himself one night to be lured into a game of hide and seek.

Tony	We'll count to a hundred.
Sylvie	One.
Tony	Two.
Girl	Three.
Children	Four.
Sylvie and Children	Five. Six. Seven . . . (*Fade out*) (*Fade in*)

Bill	(*in panting whisper*) Damn fool place to hide — behind spare room curtains. Bound to show. Panic, of course. Should have cheated. Slip out through back door, and come back when they give up. Too late now, though. On their way. Mustn't breathe so hard. They can hear a heart beating. All over the house, now, scrabbling and scuffling. Like rats. Sniffing into cracks and corners. Just like rats. What happens when they find . . .? Here. Alone. He set this up. Dead cunning. No way out . . . It's a game. Just a game. Laugh, and switch on the lights. The stairs creaked. They're closer. Trying bedroom doors. Are they scattered, or in a pack? Perhaps they won't think to draw back the curtains. Perhaps they'll give up and go away. Persistent little devils, though. It's a game. Only a game. Hush now. Hold your breath. They're here.
	(*Door opens. Scuffling of tiny feet. A whisper which is shushed. Heavy breathing*)
Child	(*In loud whisper*) The curtains.
	(*The whisper is taken up by the others. 'The curtain, curtain, curtain . . .'*)
Tony	Sssh.
	(*The curtains are drawn*)
	(*Bill gasps, then laughs uneasily*)
Bill	I give up.
	(*There is no sound from the children*)
Bill	All of you here? Well, well, well. All together. What's the routine now? Give three hearty cheers?
	(*He pauses. There is no sound from the children*)
Bill	You won, didn't you? Why don't you say 'We won'? One of you. Any of you. Say something. Anything.
	(*Pause*)
Bill	If it's all over, switch on the light. No future in standing around in the dark. Even if there is a full moon shining. You at the back there, switch on the lights. The switch is in the usual place by the door.
	(*Pause*)
Bill	What the hell are you waiting for? The grand transformation scene? I can't do it. Not even standing in the full moonlight. I can't change myself into a wolf or a bat. I can't even eat a little boy for you. I'm not built that way. Forget what I told you. Just sounding off. Sorry if I put you to any inconvenience, ladies and gentlemen. I'd be obliged if you would accept my apologies.
	(*Pause*)

85

Bill	You're still there, I know. I can see your teeth. Sharp, white, bone-picking teeth, shining in the moonlight. Did I ever tell you that you have too many teeth? And eyes. You have too many eyes. They stare. If you won't switch on the light, then let me. Break ranks and let me through.
	(*Pause*)
Bill	I could force my way to the door. It's only you against me.
	(*Pause*)
Bill	I know the way to beat you. By not having you. You know it, too, don't you? You'll look sick if you're never born. That's the way we monsters work. Backwards. I'm not giving way. Stop crawling forwards. Rows of pale faces like marigold tops. Back. Did you hear me? Back. This is the window. There's no way out through the window. I remember what I said, but I can't. Not fly. The way through the window would be fatal to a man of my opinions. Don't crush me. I won't have it. I won't have you. I have my own life to lead. You were not included. Get back. Back to where you came from. You are not wanted. Status symbol. Accidents. You weren't planned. Don't press in so. Smothering. Sticky fingers. Can't breathe. Messy. Smelly. Back. You're pushing me through the . . .
Tony	Do you know how to catch bears?
Bill	(*Screams*)
Sylvie	(*Distant, calling*) What was that? What are you doing? Put the lights on at once.
Tony	I think you ought to come up, Mrs Halliday. I think Mr Halliday may be ill.
	(*Footsteps on stairs*)
Sylvie	What happened? What's wrong?
Tony	Mr Halliday talked and talked. Then he suddenly stopped talking. He made a funny noise and fell down. He isn't asleep because his eyes are open.
Sylvie	Bill? What's the matter? Bill! . . . Get some water, Tony. From the bathroom. Quickly.
Tony	Yes, Mrs Halliday.
Sylvie	Bill. It's me, darling. Oh, Bill!
Bill	I — I . . .
Sylvie	Thank heavens you're coming round. You frightened us.

86

Bill	Where's . . . ? I — I want . . .
Sylvie	You'll be all right. You fainted.
Bill	I want . . . where is she?
Sylvie	Here, darling. I'm here.
Bill	My Mummy. I want my Mummy.
Sylvie	(*Horrified whisper*) Bill!
Bill	Where's my Mummy? I want my Mummy.
Sylvie	(*Almost a scream*) Bill!
Bill	Mummy. Mummy. Mummy. Mummy. Mummy. (*Fade out*)

Something the radio play can do particularly well is fantasy. In Ken Whitmore's *Jump*, the moles explain to a sympathetic human being about the work seventy million and seven of them have to do to prop up the Earth's crust when man's wickedness keeps mining and tunnelling and sending off underground explosions. But there's a way the moles might still save the situation.

Frederick	Aye, but . . .
Mole	Wait a bit. Listen. What if there's somebody else under the bedcover, besides the sleeper, to make sure it keeps still whatever happens? To prop it up? To maintain the equilibrium, the status quo? Frederick, lad, there is somebody down there to prop it up. Somebody down there under the earth's crust. Leastwise, some bodies. Seventy million and seven, if you want to be fussy. Moles.
Frederick	Nay!
Mole	The sleeper turns and by all the laws of God and gravity the bedcover sinks and tosses. (*Pause*) But we don't let it. At the smallest stirring of the sleeper we spring to our posts — digging and delving, shoring and shelving.
Frederick	You what?
Mole	Dragging and hauling and pushing and heaving. Deep down in the true dark. A masterpiece of engineering by seventy million and seven moles of one mind. And up above a blade of grass wouldn't wave to tell you what was happening under its roots.
Frederick	I still don't see where jumping comes into it.
Mole	Too many people up on top. Think of that great load of people pressing down from above! Four thousand million people on this planet — pressing down, pressing

down. So any gap between the bedcover and the sleeper's filled in a flash and packed down tight like snow stamped down by a foot on a flagstone. A weight like that's too much even for the moles. We're flattened and fossilised between the rocky layers. Turned to mole coal in the blink of an eye. Now. If that pressure could be relieved . . . just for as long as it takes to blink . . . we could get the job done. We're that fast. And relieving the pressure for that long's as easy as blinking. All it needs is for the people above to . . .

Frederick   Jump?

Mole   With one accord. And while they're in mid-air we'd finish the stabilising. (*Pause*) But nobody's ever jumped. Nobody jumped in Shen-Si. Nobody jumped in the Sunken Land of Bus, or the Lost Continent of Mu. That's why they are Sunken and why they are Lost.

Frederick   Nay, but you couldn't expect folk to jump if nobody told 'em.

Mole   But somebody did. We always do. In Shen-Si it was a girl named Weng Lak Sang. She ran to tell the Mandarins and princes but they preferred to die with their precious incredulity intact. Man's strongest faith is in his own capacity for disbelief, Frederick. It'll be the downfall of London on Friday and the end of civilisation the Friday after. June the tenth.

Frederick   Aye, but why?

Mole   The sleeper's waking up. For century heaped on century he slept in peace. Oh, he gave a twitch and capsized a Mu or an Atlantis every few thousand year, but mostly he slept like a bairn. But now he's rousing himself. Who sleeps easy when his bloodstream's filled wi' poison? Who lies gentle when jumping jacks and thunderbolts are going off around his lugs? It's all man's wickedness with his underground fireworks and his dyeing of the rivers sky blue pink. Is it a wonder old Magma's running a fever? We've been keeping him under observation and there's no doubt. He's going to throw up his left arm on Friday. And his left arm lies directly under London.

Frederick   (*whispering*) Get off! (*Pause*) And what about the Friday after that?

Mole   On that day — at ten past three in the afternoon — Magma will jump up with a terrible cry and fling off his bedcover — just as if a cockroach had run up his pyjamas. And the earth's crust'll go whizzing through the universe as it might be the skin off a rice pudding.

Beach Games by Derek Coltman pits against each other in a vast comic clash two different views of the universe — a woman librarian, Dewey, who represents the pigeonhole classificatory logic of the West and an ex-sailor who represents the Eastern idea of the fundamental identity of all things, both offering the most absurd illustrations as proof of their respective attitudes. The scene on a deserted Venetian sandbank entirely surrounded by the sea where Dewey and her friend Estelle are joined by the man who has just swum in from the shipping lanes is sketched in surrealistically with a few brushstrokes of words.

> (*A fine summer morning on a sandbank facing the open sea. A boat scrunches on to it. Dewey and Estelle disembark. Estelle, large herself, is carrying a large lunch basket, another basket containing a large book, a card-index, towels, and a two-piece swimming costume. Dewey carries a folding stool*)

Dewey   Excellent. Not another boat in sight. We shall have the sandbank to ourselves today. There is nothing that clears the mind quite so well as being surrounded entirely by the sea.

Estelle   Of course I'd been very impressed by him at first. Not just because he was a count, or because of those dark, burning eyes. He was so kind too, so courteous, lending me those gold sunglasses of his when I dropped mine off the . . . off the . . . Dewey, what do you call one of those little steamboats in Venice?

Dewey   Estelle, you may continue with your fantasy when we have unpacked. For the moment I have to get to work.

Estelle   Oh all right.

Dewey   My stool, please. Thank you. My book. And my card-index. Good. Now you may put that repulsive oil all over yourself if you wish. And the word you are looking for is vaporetto.

Estelle   Oh, yes! But of course I sensed the change the moment we set foot inside his palazzo. Or did I? I probably didn't. I was so dazzled by all those treasures he had there, you see. Yes, there were Picassos, Rembrandts . . . um, chandeliers, um . . . Einsteins? Anyway, there it all was, spread before me. A banquet of culture. So how could I possibly know he'd be so crude, so unimaginative. But he was. All that artistic heritage, that lovely silk suit, that terribly expensive gold watch, those slender sensitive hands . . . But oh, what a beast. No delicacy at all. The very moment we got inside the lounge he simply made a lunge at me.

Dewey (*Without looking up*) Palazzi don't have lounges.

Estelle (*With a sigh of mingled exasperation and resignation*) Well, the moment he got me near a sofa, then, he just went for me. I was appalled. If you hadn't taught me judo I don't know where I'd have been.

Dewey Estelle.

Estelle (*Sullen*) What?

Dewey You know what. I have no wish to appear in your fantasies at all, but I absolutely insist that you do not misrepresent me. It is totally untrue that I ever taught you judo, or any other form of unarmed combat. You know perfectly well that I don't know judo. Only karate.

Estelle Oh all right. If my mother hadn't taught me judo. Will that do?

Dewey Why can't you make someone up? You could hardly have learned judo before the age of five, and by that time your mother had already developed arthritis in both knees. Fiction is fiction. Reality is reality. Are we going to have that fight again?

Estelle (*Cowed by this terrible threat*) No, Dewey. Well, if I hadn't been taught judo by Lars Svenson, my Swedish skiing instructor. Yes, he had beautiful golden, golden hair and . . . and coal black eyes. Yes, I like that. You're always complaining I'm so unoriginal . . .

(*A man who has been on the landward side of the sandbank appears*)

He I'm sorry to interrupt, but I thought I'd better let you know I'm here. I can hear every word you're saying, you see. Not that I was listening, but it is a very small sandbank. And there's not much wind, is there?

Dewey We would hardly have come if it had been windy. How did you get here? I didn't see another boat.

He I swam from a ship. Out there. Then I went to sleep with my head on the sand. I think I must have heard the crunch when you beached your boat.

Dewey You swam in from the shipping lanes? How long did it take?

He	About twenty-four hours, I think. Do you happen to have anything to eat or drink?
Dewey	We have our lunch with us. You may share it.
He	That's very kind of you.
Estelle	Oh not at all. Really.
Dewey	And you may come and sit with us in the meantime.
He	The meantime?
Dewey	There are still fifty-six minutes before lunchtime yet, you know.
He	Couldn't I have just *something* now? Swimming is really very hard work. And it's *over* twenty-four hours since I last ate.
Estelle	Yes, but not really.
He	What do you mean? Not really.
Estelle	Well *I* agree it's really. But Dewey won't.
Dewey	She means I would refuse to accept that you could be hungry in reality simply because you had swum for twenty-four hours in fantasy.

In the field of comedy the radio play has made a considerable contribution to the nation's rich storehouse of humour. The thought-quick transformations and juxtapositions of radio drama encourage witty and humorous writing and radio comedy shows like *The Goons* or *Take It From Here* pioneered a comic grammar of sound which could be exploited by the playwright as, for example, *Made in Heaven* by Andrew Sachs.

Mrs Avon	Yes, well as I say . . .
	(*Avon eats*)
	. . . and then there's the children. One of them cut his head open today. That meant a plaster. And it all has to come out of the housekeeping.
Avon	Which one?
Mrs Avon	Which one what?
Avon	Which one of the children?
Mrs A	Which one of the children?
Avon	Yes.
Mrs A	Well — how do I know?
Avon	Oh.
Mrs A	My concern was with the wound. You don't ask for names in an emergency like that.
Avon	But didn't you recognise him?
Mrs A	You're so tiresome, Avon. Of course I recognised him. How else would I know it was one of ours? I can't

	afford to go sticking plaster all over other people's children you know.
Avon	Are they all in bed?
Mrs A	Yes. Washed, dried —
Avon	(*To himself*) — And polished.
Mrs A	Clean clothes ready for school as usual and I changed the sheets this morning. That's besides everything else.
Avon	You're working too hard, my little darling.
Mrs A	Hm!
Avon	Perhaps we can get a daily — next year say.
Mrs A	That means somebody else to clean up after.
Avon	No, no, a daily is supposed to clean up after you.
Mrs A	Me? *Me*, Avon? *I* need cleaning up after? You're not home five minutes before the insults start.
Avon	I didn't mean . . . I mean clean up before you . . . that is — I wouldn't dream of . . . everything's so tidy and lovely because of you —
Mrs A	Oh, get on with your fish.
	(*He eats quietly*)
	Besides, you don't earn enough for a daily.
Avon	I could ask for a rise.
Mrs A	Ten pence? Fifty? . . . Don't be ridiculous. Perhaps if you'd had a bit of ambition and drive in the past, changed your job, I wouldn't need to slave like this now.
Avon	Oh, I couldn't change my job. It's a good steady job. It suits me very well. I meet a lot of forms in my work.
	(*Mrs Avon's voice begins to distort and recede*)
Mrs A	Yes of course, that's all that matters. I have to sacrifice, but you — no. I had the chance of a career once, but it was taken away like everything else.
	(*A groaning sigh from Avon close to mike*)
	You and your forms. I wish everything could be so easy for me. Some people enjoy looking after a house and children — they'd be unhappy away from the routine and chores.
Avon	(*Singing to himself*) Here we go again, Happy as can be —
Mrs A	They actually like washing and ironing. It gives them a thrill because they haven't been brought up to anything else.
Avon	What a bore you are, my little loveheart.
Mrs A	I suppose you think I'm like that too. If you only understood what I go through every single day, you'd

	have some idea what a pain and torture it is to be sensitive.
Avon	If your whining hasn't stopped in five seconds, my love, something will go snap! inside me and I shall become an uncontrollable monster with a deep delightful urge to push your ugly face in. (*He begins to count five*)
Mrs A	And my pains don't make it any easier. When did I last have an operation? I mean a *really satisfying* operation I can talk about; and then a lovely holiday afterwards to recuperate away from the house and those children. Just lying in the sun all day . . .
Avon	. . . Five. I'm sorry, my little hunnybunny, this is going to hurt you more than it does me. (*A vicious thumping sound, and heavy breathing from Avon*)
Mrs A	(*Hardly affected*) . . . with no worry about the laundry or we've run out of this and that. See how you'd cope looking after everyone . . .
Avon	No good? Let's have that bread-knife, then. (*He picks it up*)
Mrs A	And it always comes down to money. I have to ask for every single penny. You've robbed me of all independence.
Avon	I want to see blo-o-o-d . . . (*He stabs her with the breadknife*)
Mrs A	(*Recovering quickly*) And then you tease me by asking which one of the children cut his head. It's the one with the plaster on if you must know. It's funny how it's always me that has to go dragging them off to the doctor or stick plaster all over them.
Avon	Very well. I'm going to strangle you with my own clawed, hairy hands, while I sink my vampire fangs into your scrawny flesh. (*He does so with a satisfying crunch of bones*)
Mrs A	But there's nobody for me to run to when there's trouble (*As though being shaken and choked*), or when I want a bit of company except those boring neighbours. All they know is small talk and Majorca.
Avon	The window! Out of the window and on to the spiked railings below! Yes! (*He opens the window and drags her over as she continues*) Come on. Over here.

Mrs A	What good is small talk to me? I was meant for better things than this. A housewife! That's no life for someone like me. I wish I didn't have a house.
Avon	Out you go, you oafish, lumpy great millstone!
Mrs A	All I want is myself and my care-e-e-e-e-r!
	(*Her voice recedes quickly on echo into the distance as she falls. There is a sickening squelch as the body impales itself below. Avon giggles gleefully. Sound back to normal. Mrs Avon is quite unperturbed*)
	(*On*) You're not listening, Avon.

In radio comedy it is possible to put humour on the stage in a way that would not be so easy in visual drama — as is shown in Gerry Jones' delightful send-up of a God-tormented Welshman, his down-to-earth wife and their son, whose birth was such a disaster: *Taybridge*.

	(*A gentle wind is moaning as we hear a small group of carollers sing*):
	'In the bleak midwinter
	Frosty winds made moan
	Earth stood hard as iron,
	Water like a stone.'
	(*The carol singers move away slowly, their voices fading*)
	'Snow had fallen, snow on snow,
	Snow on snow.
	In the bleak midwinter,
	Long, long ago.'
	(*They have gone. We are left with the moaning wind*)
	(*Exterior*)
Harold	In the name of mercy, why can't I see the Lord? This telescope cost me thirty pounds — *thirty pounds* . . . you'd think that a thirty pound telescope would give me a peep at God, even a blurry peep. Thirty pounds to sit frozen in a garden staring at the Man in the Moon. What do I have to do? What magic piece of living creates an earthly calling card that opens a crack in the Golden Gates and sends the cherubs buttling for the Master? What? What?
Pearl	(*Quietly*) Harold!
Harold	(*Wild with excitement*) Yes, Lord? Yes, I'm listening. Speak my name again, pour your words like golden rain

	that I may soak them up in the sponge of my body. Speak . . . speak again . . . show yourself and warm my soul, grown cold in a vacuum. Punch a hole in heaven, tear away the clouds, turn up the stars and show yourself. Stand at the gate of my year, O Lord and tip a humble sinner a wink.
Pearl	Harold . . . it's me . . . Pearl. (*Pause*) I'm sorry.
Harold	For a moment I thought . . .
Pearl	I'm sorry.
	(*There is silence apart from the moaning wind*)
	Come inside Harold, it's too cold to be out here.
Harold	Not yet . . . not yet.
Pearl	Every night it's the same, every night . . . sitting on your stool like a cow-less milkmaid peeping through a keyhole at heaven. Every night, looking for God in your telescope.
Harold	And I'll find Him, too . . . one night I'll find Him . . . one night . . . in focus. Think of it, Pearl, think of it, what a wonderful night.
Pearl	Wonderful.
Harold	I'll point my instrument at the distant dark and there He'll be, smiling the smile of love from His many mansions and saying 'Well done, Harold, I've reserved you a place.' There'll be a fire in my soul that night, Pearl, and a singing in my heart fit to crack a glass.
Pearl	It's just that . . .
Harold	What?
Pearl	Nothing.
Harold	What?
Pearl	It's just that I can't help wondering sometimes why you haven't managed to get him in focus yet.
Harold	The Good and Gracious Lord, my dear Pearl, doesn't hang about the heavens waiting to be spotted like the promise of good weather.
Pearl	Well, He should . . . He should.
Harold	He has His reasons.
Pearl	I know, love, I know, but He ought to give a *glimpse* . . . people get tired.
Harold	He'll come . . . one night . . . in the telescope . . . He'll come. The world has *got* to be a two-way mirror, Pearl, it doesn't make sense to suffer in a box.
Pearl	Come inside, now, let's have something to eat.
Harold	Belly, belly, that's all you think of.

Pearl	I'm only suggesting a bowl of soup.
Harold	As God is my judge, Pearl, you may well reach the Golden Gates, but it's doubtful if you'll ever squeeze through. Food, food, the weapon of the Devil.
Pearl	You know what you're like when your insides get cold.
Harold	Fats instead of faith . . . soup instead of the spirit . . . look at the world . . . look at it.
Pearl	Stop shouting.
Harold	Look at it . . . filling its belly, emptying its mind, trudging the path of depravity . . . a weary line of constipated agnostics.
Pearl	Language!
Harold	Constipation is a *condition,* not a swear word.
Pearl	Condition or not, it's sixpence in the swear box.
Harold	(*Suddenly*) Listen!
	(*Away in the distance we hear the sound of the carol singers*)
	Carols . . . can you hear them, Pearl? Tomorrow is Christmas Eve . . . then the birthday of our Lord. (*Shouting*) He'll come, Pearl . . . I know it.
Pearl	Well you must remember he's very old.
Harold	What are you talking about?
Pearl	I mean God . . . God is very old.
Harold	So?
Pearl	Well, perhaps that's why He can't hear you . . . perhaps He's hard of hearing.
Harold	(*Yelling*) Hard of hearing!!!
Pearl	Shhhh!
Harold	(*Louder*) *Hard of hearing*?!! How many times do I have to tell you that God doesn't suffer from faculties.
Pearl	Quiet now, love, shouting's not Christian and you'll waken the cat.
Harold	Cats are supposed to be awake at night.
Pearl	It makes him poorly to move about and well you know it.
Harold	He never moves . . . sleeps, that's what he does, sleeps, sleeps, sleeps.
Pearl	Only since you had it doctored.
Harold	I wasn't having the evil thing stalking around, stalking around with filthy thoughts.
Pearl	It wasn't its filthy thoughts it lost.
Harold	Wash the dirt from your mouth, woman, I'm surprised at you. Sometimes I think the devil is in permanent residence just behind your teeth.

Pearl	Oh, Harold . . . it's sometimes hard to cope, with it all.
Harold	Of course it is . . . that's the point! Make salvation easy and *everyone* would get it. Suffer, Pearl, suffer and struggle and squirm.
	(*Seconds pass*)
Pearl	Can you see anything?
Harold	Quiet, woman.
	(*Seconds pass*)
Pearl	Anything?
Harold	Nothing . . . nothing.
Pearl	There's sad.
Harold	It's not God's fault I can't see Him . . . it's the telescope. I should have known better than to expect a vision on a mail order instrument. Let's go inside.
Pearl	Give me a kiss, love.
Harold	I've told you before . . . not in the *open*.
Pearl	Just a little kiss now, a Christmas time kiss.
Harold	Kissing in the open is for the English . . . the Welsh do it inside and in the dark.
Pearl	Well kiss me in English . . . nobody's watching.
	(*There is a second's pause then the sound of a quick smacking kiss*)
Harold	Again?
Pearl	Yes, please.
Harold	All right, but this is the . . .
Pearl	What is it?
Harold	We're being watched.
Pearl	By God?
Harold	By Taybridge . . . our awful son, Taybridge . . . he's looking at us from the attic window.
Pearl	Did he see us kiss?
Harold	He must have done (*suddenly shouting*) Peeping Tom . . . Peeping Tom . . . in the attic . . . son of the Devil. What a way to spend Christmas Eve . . . looking for God and only kissing you . . . and our son Taybridge watching our disgrace then no doubt plunging his head into the water tank.
Pearl	What for?
Harold	It's what he does when he gets excited.
Pearl	He'll catch his death.

A comedy might result from something unexpected happening to break a fixed pattern of behaviour as when Albert Chipchase, in Alan Plater's *The What on the Landing*, goes to relieve himself, on the night he spends alone watching television while Edna Chipchase is at her evening class in Elementary Archaeology, and finds the loo on the landing occupied. Someone else is in the house!

Narrator	The police.
Albert	It's all gone far enough.
Narrator	The police?
Albert	I pay rates, I pay taxes, I have my rights as a citizen, I am not acting in a rash or irresponsible manner.
Narrator	The police.
Albert	(*Doubt growing*) I'm simply putting my trust in those who've been democratically elected . . .
Narrator	The police?
Albert	Oh that's a point. (*Suddenly pedantic*) Course, they're not elected . . . where do they come from? Well, they're just produced from a special source of supply. A source of supply of policemen. Funny. Policemen just seem to happen.
Narrator	All he knows is that they do happen.
Albert	Excuse me sir would you mind stepping this way? I'm sorry constable I can't, you're standing on my hand and there's a chair wedged against my living room door.
Narrator	Albert Chipchase is frightened of policemen.
Albert	It's just that they tend to be dark blue.
Narrator	But he is also frightened of the man in the lavatory.
Albert	They tend to be red . . . and yellow.
Narrator	Which is he most frightened of?
	Pause
Albert	Nine nine nine then, here goes . . .
F/X	*Dialling*
	(*Rehearsing*) Hello, sorry to bother you but I need help, without fear or favour and it's getting near the end of the day.
Operator	Hello, which service do you require?
Albert	Service?
Operator	Fire, police, ambulance . . .
Albert	I've got a nice fire thanks . . . I'd like a policeman please.
Operator	One moment please.
F/X	*Assortment of buzzing and clicks*
Spilsby	Hello.
Albert	Hello, is that the police?
Spilsby	That would appear to be a correct assumption.

Albert	Good.
Spilsby	What would be the nature of your inquiry?
Albert	I've got a bit of a problem . . .
Spilsby	You're not alone, my friend. The whole world's got a bit of a problem. Name.
Albert	Chipchase . . . Albert Chipchase.
Spilsby	Address?
Albert	23, Windermere Close.
Spilsby	A good address to have, Mr Chipchase . . .
Albert	Well, we like it here . . .
Spilsby	Oh yes, very desirable. What we term a violence and rape-free zone, in technical language. I often say to my chief super, give me Windermere Close and I'll give you a haven of tranquillity . . .
Albert	Actually, it's about my toilet.
Spilsby	Your what?
Albert	Toilet. Lavatory.
Spilsby	Somebody pinched it, have they?
Albert	No.
Spilsby	That gives us a head start.
Albert	There's somebody in there.
Spilsby	When you've got to go, you've got to go, Mr Chipchase . . .
Albert	What I mean is . . . I'm alone in the house, but there's somebody in the toilet.
	Pause
Spilsby	There's a contradiciton there, you realise that . . .
Albert	I'm sorry . . .
Spilsby	If you're alone there can't be anybody in the toilet. If, on the other hand, there's somebody in the toilet, you can't be alone . . . you see what I'm driving at?
Albert	I see what you mean.
Spilsby	Defending Counsel would drive a horse and cart through it . . .
Albert	Yes, I understand . . .
Spilsby	Let's try again. Resolve the contradiction.
Albert	I *thought* I was alone in the house . . .
Spilsby	Better . . .
Albert	Till I discovered the toilet door locked, the light on inside, and heard the chain being pulled.
Spilsby	Excellent. Simple thoughts, clearly expressed.
Albert	Can you do something?
Spilsby	Well now . . .
	Pause

	I can't pretend there's a lot of this going on because frankly there isn't . . . so we can't apply the modus operandi. A fairly unique case.
Albert	I don't care how unique it is . . .
Spilsby	That would appear to be a rather off-hand attitude . . .
Albert	I don't mean . . .
Spilsby	Not unlike saying . . . I don't care how many murders there are as long as nobody murders me. How long's it been going on?
Albert	It came after the News, I think. This . . . er, Red Chinaman.
Spilsby	How did you know it was Chinese communists? (*Heavily*) Oh. I see, I understand, yes.
Albert	Is there something going on, something afoot, something the public doesn't know about?
Spilsby	There's always a few things the public doesn't know about.
Albert	And you get special information, don't you?
Spilsby	It can happen, from time to time, we have our sources . . .

In the field of comedy, women writers have contributed delightfully fresh and funny plays. *Trouble on the Line* was the first of half a dozen little plays written by Jennifer Phillips for the wonderful comedy team Beryl Reid and Patricia Hayes.

> (*The sound of coins inserted into phone box.*
> *Announcer's voice above continuing effects*)

Announcer	Trouble on the line . . .
	(*Madge and Lillian are sitting in Madge's living room having their tea. There is the sound of a telephone ringing in the room*)
Madge	Don't answer it. It'll be a wrong number.
Lillian	Why?
Madge	It'll be a wrong number.
	(*The ringing stops*)
Lillian	It stopped sudden anyway. Didn't it stop sudden?
Madge	That's just what I mean, there wasn't anybody there.
Lillian	Not a genuine caller?
Madge	No, they'd have held on longer.
Lillian	It was sudden.

100

Madge	As I was saying Lillian . . .
Lillian	Before we were interrupted.
Madge	Mrs Gramson. She was eating sardines in a bath bun.
Lillian	Madge . . . no!
Madge	She was.
Lillian	She showed you?
Madge	She made no attempt to hide it.
Lillian	Madge, how did you know it was a wrong number just then as soon as the phone started ringing?
Madge	I get so many. I know what to expect.
Lillian	You could ring the operator.
Madge	She wouldn't know anything about it.
Lillian	You dial a hundred.
Madge	I know you dial a hundred. I did the other night when the phone rang at half past twelve — that was last week.
Lillian	I heard it ring late. What did she say?
Madge	Who?
Lillian	The operator when you rang her.
Madge	It was a he, a very nice young man, very polite, he apologised.
Lillian	I suppose he had to. It's this new system they've installed.
Madge	That's what he said.
Lillian	Automatic . . . I knew it.
Madge	It tinkled all this morning.
Lillian	I didn't hear it.
Madge	On and off . . . on and off all the time.
Lillian	Did you pick the receiver up?
Madge	Yes.
Lillian	Who was it?
Madge	No one.
Lillian	Did you say anything?
Madge	I said 'Hello . . . hello.' There was no one there.
Lillian	Leastways you didn't think so.
Madge	No . . . I listened for breathing.
Lillian	They might have held their breath so . . .
Madge	And then I rang him.
Lillian	Who?
Madge	The operator.
Lillian	He doesn't mind you ringing often?
Madge	No, it was a she this time. She's very polite too . . . well educated. She said it was probably workmen.
Lillian	Tampering . . .

Madge	On the line, so she said . . .
Lillian	Is the tea still warm?
Madge	Yes.
Lillian	I'll have another cup if you don't mind.
Madge	Pour me one too while you're at it.
	(*Sound of tea being poured*)
	(*Sound of the telephone ringing*)
Lillian	It's ringing longer this time . . . you'd better answer it.
Madge	All right I will . . . (*She picks up the receiver and speaks abruptly*) Yes?
Voice	Is that the vet's surgery?
Madge	(*Gasps and slams down the receiver*) There, what did I tell you?
Lillian	You all right, Madge?
Madge	I will be.
Lillian	Have a sip of your tea. (*Madge sips her tea, the cup rattles on to the saucer as she puts it down*) You're trembling — look, what did they say?
Madge	I've had that one before . . . I know that one of old.
Lillian	What?
Madge	'Is that the vet's surgery?'
Lillian	Who do they think they're taking in? Who do they think they're deceiving?
Madge	Not us, Lillian, that's for sure. (*Pause*) They're checking up again.
Lillian	Checking up?
Madge	Checking to see if we're in.
Lillian	Oh, no, Madge.
Madge	Better go and see if the back door is locked.
Lillian	You locked it after me when I came in from putting the cat's fish to cool on the kitchen window sill.
Madge	Are you sure I did?
Lillian	Yes, and you put the key on top of the stove.
Madge	Did I put it under the jug?
Lillian	Yes.
Madge	The back of the house is secure then. What about the French windows from your room into the garden? What about them?
Lillian	It's too cold to have had them open.
Madge	Where's the key for them?
Lillian	Under the carpet, under the sideboard.
Madge	How long is it since you looked to see if it was still there?
Lillian	Anyway Madge, you've stuck over that keyhole with sticky tape.

Madge	Oh, yes.
Lillian	Madge, who d'you think it is . . . checking up?
Madge	Someone who wants to make sure we're out. It's a very old trick you know to make sure that the house is empty first.
Lillian	First, yes . . . Maybe it's always best to answer the phone when it rings. It must be if they want to catch us out, then if you answer it they know you're in.
Madge	(*Pause*) I wouldn't be too sure, Lillian.
Lillian	What? Why not?
Madge	Because on the other hand they might want to find us in.
Lillian	Oh no, you don't really think . . . I mean burglars, burglars would want to find us out . . . to have the place to themselves.
Madge	They're not fussy.
Lillian	Who?
Madge	Men.
Lillian	Oh, Madge, you don't surely think . . .
Madge	I told you a teenager stood on my foot, didn't I?
Lillian	(*Shocked*) No. Where?
Madge	In the bus queue. And he must have seen that I was wearing elastic stockings.
Lillian	They don't pay heed to anything.
Madge	He must have seen because we'd been stood there for ages.
Lillian	That your legs were bad. It doesn't matter to them.
Madge	That's what I mean.
Lillian	It doesn't bear thinking about.

The radio play is particularly suited to zany, innocent comedy. Its surrealistic quality of existing in a landscape which can change as quickly as the mind and imagination of writer and listener want it to is susceptible to the most ridiculous comic effects.

The very limitations of a medium restricted to sound, making it necessary to appeal to the audience's imagination, help to establish a rapport of provocative stimulus and receptive response which can be ideal for laughter — rather like the old silent two-reelers of Keaton or Chaplin, similarly limited and relying on the same kind of audience participation to supply the missing sense.

The innocence which is partly enforced in the interest of a daytime audience made up of people of all ages turns out, anyway, to be one of the characteristics of the best humour, the nasty, the vicious or the pretentious having no part in it.

David Marshall has written a number of such comedies. *When the Music Stops* is about a change of image of the corporate man.

	(*J.B.'s office. Door bursts open*)
King	(*App*) (*Hums pop tune and snaps fingers*) Afternoon, J.B. Going to be a lovely evening.
J.B.	Afternoon, King. No — don't sit down. What I have to say won't take long.
King	(*Laughs uncertainly*) J.B. baby, you and I have —
J.B.	Cut it out, King . . . You're a senior executive grade two, I believe?
King	Right. I —
J.B.	I see you're wearing a pink shirt and orange side whiskers.
King	Oh, do you think the colours clash?
J.B.	Don't be flippant with me, King.
King	Sorry.
J.B.	The fact is that a man who wears a pink shirt to the office is making a statement about himself — a statement which we in management would prefer not to hear. Your pink-shirted man is saying: 'I'm still young enough to go to discos. I can still make the scene.' Or something of that sort.
King	Not quite with you, J.B.
J.B.	Don't be so obtuse, man. Do I have to spell it out for you? Look, the Board of Directors have decided — rightly in my opinion — that the sixties are over. The permissive society has been closed down . . . I am drafting the appropriate Resolution at this minute.
King	Not sure I can go along with you on this one, J.B. Where I live — just off the King's Road — the permissive society is alive and —
J.B.	Then I'll put it another way, King. Your membership of it has been cancelled with immediate effect. There will be no more of that nonsense between you and your secretary — what's her name? Ann? Do you hear music, King?
King	No, sir, I was lis-
J.B.	That's because there isn't any. It's stopped and when the music stops you make sure you're in the right seat with the right woman on your knees. With me? Senior executives — senior executives who want to get on, that is — have wives. Haven't you got a wife, King?
King	Well . . . yes and no. I mean — sort of.
J.B.	(*Blows up*) Well, have you or haven't you?

King	Yessir.
J.B.	Get her over here tomorrow morning. One o'clock sharp. Directors' luncheon room. Best bib and tucker, mind. One o'clock luncheon. You've got till then to get your private life in order . . . You *do* want to be a grade one executive?
King	Naturally, sir. Thank you very much, sir.
J.B.	Pass the message down. Homes, wives, hobbies, eh? No more swinging. Clear?
King	Yes, sir. I'm glad the sixties are over. I —
J.B.	Good. That's all. (*Pause*) Oh and, King.
King	(*Off*) Sir?
J.B.	Do you really live off the King's Road?
King	I'm afraid so.
J.B.	Then move. Get right out.
King	Hampstead sir?
J.B.	No! Try Surrey. I'll circulate a list of suitable districts. Off you go then.

In *Vienna ABC*, David Marshall describes how one of the greatest documentary programmes of our time came to be written.

	(*Two-finger typing. Paper is pulled from typewriter*)
Len	(*Calls*) Kay, I've made a start on my outline.
Kay	(*Off*) Read it to me.
Len	Right. Ready? June the fourteenth, 1914. Lenin, an up-and-coming revolutionary who only three short years later was to catch the plague and be transported to Russia in a sealed railway carriage, was on the train from Berlin to Vienna. With him was his wife. Her name? Madame Lenin . . . Well, what do you think of it?
Kay	Marvellous, Len. Punchy.
Len	It's for a new documentary series on telly — 'Major Mischief-Makers of Our Time'. I'm also doing Dr Schweitzer and Einstein . . . What are you up to?
Kay	Still on that novel about the life of Kafka. Want to hear the start of chapter six?
Len	Love to.
Kay	It was a warm musky evening in early summer when the young shock-haired man with fine sensitive features boarded the train at the Berlin Bahnhof. The heavy air was scented with the smell of the lime trees and charged

	with a sense of expectancy. The young man's heart sang. For Franz Kafka — or K as he now preferred to be called — was in love . . .
Len	Go on. It's not bad.
Kay	That's all, I'm afraid. I'm blocked.
Len	How early in the summer was it?
Kay	I'm not sure.
Len	You're working from the Diaries, aren't you?
Kay	I dip into them occasionally.
Len	Listen, Kay, could it have been as early as June the fourteenth, 1914? I mean, that's early summer.
Kay	Well —
Len	So it *was* June the fourteenth. You know what, don't you? Kafka was only on the same train as the Lenins, that's all. We've got ourselves a scoop.
Kay	Hang on. According to the Diaries he spent the whole of that summer in Prague —
Len	Codswallop. That was just a cover while he was having it off with Lenin's wife . . . Hot sultry summer, war in the air, restless young author, Mrs Lenin bored stiff with hubbie's plots — it all adds up to the eternal triangle, the good old ABC. Ah, ah, ah. I know what you're going to say. I've been in the documentary game too long to pass up a chance like this . . . Listen . . . The train was crowded with Viennese intellectuals arguing about politics. There was standing room only as the train steamed heavily out of the station. The Lenins, astride their suitcases in the corridor, knew they were in for a night of it. Lenin —
Kay	A tough but incredibly —
Len	A small but wiry man —
Kay	Incredibly wiry man.
Len	Right. Lenin, a small but unbelievably wiry man, fought his way to the lavatory, shut himself in and began to re-think the revolution. Instead of being bloodless, as his wife had urged, it was to be a massacre . . . Cut to Lenin on the lav —
Kay	Fully buttoned.
Len	Fully buttoned, as you say. This is a serious programme for adults who want to learn something. Cut to Lenin, sitting there, seething at not having got a seat. Cut to wildly spinning railway wheels to indicate the speed and ferocity of his thoughts.
Kay	Their ruthlessness and utter implacability.

106

Len	Exactly. Then . . . Come on, Kay, feed me an idea.
Kay	Meantime, Madame Lenin had struck up a conversation with a young shock-haired man whose fine sensitive features revealed him to be an intellectual . . . No . . . fine sensitive features revealed a capacity for suffering —
Len	Well . . . OK. . . . yes.
Kay	Close up of Kafka.
Len	Looking unbelievably sensitive. After all, he hadn't got a seat either. Now what?
Kay	Play your recording of steam trains.
Len	You're a genius, Kay. (*Interior sound of steam train in motion*) There you go. Kafka is chatting up Madame Lenin in the corridor. (*Train noises reach a peak of noisiness then fade out*)
Kafka	My God, we're in for a night of it, Fraulein.
Mme L	Frau, if you please. I am a married woman. (*Giggles*)
Kafka	But you are so unbelievably young. How careless of your husband to desert you on a train crowded with Viennese intellectuals.
Mme L	Not at all, Herr —?
Kafka	Kafka. But please call me Franz.
Mme L	My husband, Herr Lenin, is just excusing himself.
Kafka	Now I come to think of it, I saw you on the platform with a short bald man, unbelievably wiry.
Mme L	That was he — the dreamer who will one day change the world.
Kafka	(*Low, close*) I too am a dreamer.
Mme L	You have the eyes of a poet.
Kafka	I work for an insurance company.
Mme L	Ah, a salesman. A man of action.
Kafka	No. I sit at my desk in a dream — in a nightmare — my desk crawling with paper clips.
Mme L	You have a drink problem?
Kafka	Sometimes, on a Saturday night . . . with the boys. You understand?
Mme L	Perfectly. You are lonely, oppressed by your endless capacity for suffering. You are seeking love.
Kafka	(*Sighing*) I thought I had found it in Berlin. I believed myself to be on to a good thing. Unfortunately . . .

Another author who has supplied the same sort of delightfully wacky comedy is Tony Allen. *Cloth Caps, Mufflers and Ill-Fitting Suits* is set in an employment office.

107

Monty	(*Whispering*) I hope they've got something for me today, I've been coming here for ages.
Bert	(*Whispering also*) No vacancies in the market gardening then?
Monty	Isn't there?
Bert	I don't know, you're the market gardener.
Monty	No, I'm not a market gardener.
Bert	You distinctly told me you were a market gardener, not five minutes ago.
Monty	I only said market gardener as an example, I could have said anything, I could have said nuclear scientist, but you would probably have thought that a bit ostentatious.
Bert	I beg your pardon?
Monty	(*Explaining*) I've been doing a lot of crosswords lately.
Bert	Oh . . . If you're not a market gardener, what do you do?
Monty	I don't do nothing.
Bert	You must do something for a living.
Monty	No I don't, that's why I come down here, see if they can fix me up.
Bert	Well what did you do before you came down here?
Monty	I had a cup of tea and a bacon sandwich in the cafe over the road.
Bert	No, no, no, you fail to understand. What I meant was, what was your previous occupation, job. What did you do for a living?
Monty	Oh, I see. I was with the RSPCA for a bit.
Bert	(*Lightly*) Oh, nothing serious I hope.
Monty	No, it's not for people, it's the Royal Society for the pre —
Bert	(*Interrupts*) Yes, yes, I know that, it was just a joke.
Monty	Oh. (*half laughs*) Oh. Subtle.
Bert	What did you do there anyway?
Monty	Caretaker I was, nice little number, fourteen pound a week, uniform and luncheon vouchers, provided.
Bert	Provided what?
Monty	I don't know. I wasn't there long enough to find out.
Bert	How come you left then?
Monty	I was invalided out.
Bert	Invalided out of the RSPCA?
Monty	Yes, savaged by a hamster one Saturday morning. I was. Lost the use of my little finger, kept dropping me squeegee and upsetting me bucket.
Bert	How is it now?

108

Monty	It gnawed through the bottom of its cage and escaped. The finger still plays up too.
Bert	And you haven't worked since?
Monty	No but I've been for a few things though . . . Porter stroke Janitor at the Hanger Lane primary . . . Caretaker with a little bit of driving, at the St Cecilia in The Fields Convent, Harlesden. I even tried Caretaker stroke Handyman at the Wormald Street Art Gallery, but he said he wanted someone with a bit of experience with works of art.
Bert	(*Authoritatively*) Yes, well he would, wouldn't he? It's valuable some of that stuff. You can't have inexperienced hands dusting old masters. One foul flick of your feather duster and you could set the national assets back half a million.
Monty	What, at the Wormald Street Gallery?
Bert	Yes, oh yes, all that old gear's worth a few bob. Why only the other day, I was reading about a Stradivarius going for ten thousand pounds.
Monty	(*Impressed*) Oooo.
Bert	Yes. That's a lot for one painting, isn't it?
Monty	Er, wasn't Stradivarius to do with violins?
Bert	No, oh no, he was a painter, little bloke, short legs, cut his ear off.
Monty	Are you sure?
Bert	Course I'm sure. (*Authoritatively*) I see the film, didn't I? Marlon Brando . . . brilliant acting, three and half hours with his legs strapped up his back. (*Afterthought*) I wonder how they got his shoes to stay on his knees?
Monty	I'm sure I read something about a Stradivarius violin.
Bert	No, no, you're wrong there. I think you'll find he painted horses.

The Day Willy Put His Ear to the Wall by David Fitzsimmons starts out with two young men sharing digs who start kidding each other about their physical deficiencies and end up saying more about themselves than they intended.

Jim	She is not. You're only jealous.
Willy	Jealous of you and a knock-kneed schoolgirl?
Jim	She is not knock-kneed.

Willy	You look at her knees. You just look at them. Have you really looked at her knees?
Jim	Her knees are OK.
Willy	Six foot tall, knock-kneed and with a squint.
Jim	What squint?
Willy	Hasn't she? That's something anyway. (*Pause*) (*friendly*) Now look here, Jim. Could you live with yourself if you . . . A schoolgirl, I ask you. She's only just out of ankle socks and Enid Blyton. And she's not . . . I know I joke about her knees and that, and I know she's a nice girl, but is she much cop? Really, is she? Is she what you've been saving yourself for?
Jim	I've not been saving myself. It's just happened that way.
Willy	Well the first time should be . . . should be something special, something like . . . So I suggest you wait until . . . What are you doing?
	(*Jim is reading paper*)
Jim	I'm reading the paper.
Willy	I can see you're reading the paper.
Jim	That's OK then.
	(*Pause*)
Willy	I'm not putting you off Jean only because . . . That's not the news section, it's the classified ads.
Jim	So I'm reading the classified ads.
Willy	Are you looking for anything in particular?
Jim	If you must know, I'm looking for a flat.
Willy	A what?
Jim	A flat of my own.
Willy	Why?
Jim	Where I can do as I like. Where I can lose my virginity to whom I like.
Willy	(*mocking*) To whom!
	(*Jim searches frantically*)
	You couldn't live on your own. You'd have nobody to talk to. You'd talk to yourself and go off your head.
	(*Jim searches*)
	I know you. You'd be off your head within a week. They'd take you away and put you in a padded cell.
Jim	I'd get along fine on my own. I've had you and Buddy Holly up to here.
	(*Jim throws paper down*)
	Blast.
Willy	Aren't there any in?

Jim	I'm going to look in the newsagent's window.
Willy	There won't be any in there. They only advertise old prams and French lessons.
	(*Jim picks up the paper again and searches*)
Willy	What are you looking for now? What's that? Cars? What are you looking at cars for?
Jim	I want a car.
Willy	One second you want a flat, next second you want a car. What's got into you?
	(*Pause*)
Willy	What do you want a car for?
Jim	What you can't do in a flat you can do in the back of a car.
Willy	I see.
	(*Jim searches*)
	There is a snag.
	(*Jim searches*)
	You can't drive. Unless of course you intend to park it permanently behind the Essoldo.
Jim	I can learn.
Willy	Impossible. Your feet wouldn't reach the pedals.
Jim	Charlie's got a car. That's why he's such a big success with the women.
Willy	Charlie's car's never working. It's always round the back with its wheels off, supported on bricks. And it's nasty and flashy. With holiday resort stickers and a nodding dog in the back and leopard skin upholstery and . . .
Jim	What's that got to do with anything?
Willy	You want a car like Charlie's?
Jim	It doesn't have to be like Charlie's. I don't have to have a nodding dog.
Willy	What are you going to buy it with?
Jim	I could borrow the money.
Willy	Who from?
Jim	You.
Willy	I don't have any money.
Jim	You must have money. You're as mean as hell.
Willy	There's your answer then. I'm not lending you any money because I'm as mean as hell.
Jim	Please.
Willy	Please?
Jim	I'd take you trips in it.
Willy	I don't want to go anywhere.

Jim	We could be joint owners.
Willy	(*as if pleased with the idea*) Could we?
Jim	So you'll put up the money.
Willy	I might.
Jim	Great!
Willy	But you do realise that as joint owner I wouldn't allow any funny business in it. (*Laughs*)
Jim	I can't win.
Willy	Seems that way. (*Pause*) I know, why don't you get your friend Charlie to let you use his car. Although you wouldn't have to move about much or it'd fall off its bricks. (*Pause*) (*as though praying*) Please, Lord, make me grow a little more like Charlie every day. (*Pause*) It wouldn't be right anyway. Owning a car. Think of all that pollution you'd be adding to the atmosphere.
Jim	What pollution?
Willy	Carbon monoxide. Do you realize that car fumes are so bad in Tokyo that policemen on point duty carry oxygen cylinders and masks.
Jim	This isn't Tokyo.
Willy	Tokyo today, us tomorrow. And everyone in Tokyo wears a smog mask. I've seen pictures. Little Japs, carrying transistor radios and wearing smog masks. So what is needed is for individuals to make firm moral stands. To say, 'I'm not adding to the pollution. I'm not running a car.'
Jim	Like you?
Willy	Like me.
Jim	That's really big of you, Willy, making a sacrifice for humanity.
Willy	I've been thinking of wearing a smog mask myself when I go out.
Jim	If you go out tonight, I'll buy you a smog mask. I'll buy you a whole box of smog masks.
Willy	I don't think Jean will anyhow.
Jim	Will what?
Willy	You'd have more of a chance with Big Alice I reckon.
Jim	No.
Willy	Because I reckon she fancies you. (*Jim groans*) You could do worse, you know. A lot worse. (*Jim groans again*) You'd probably have to marry her before she would though. And then she might not.

Jim	Shut up.
	(*Willy laughs*)
	You're the one.
Willy	I'm the one what?
Jim	You're the one that ought to team up with her.
Willy	Me?
Jim	She's more your size.
Willy	No.
Jim	You wouldn't be able to go anywhere though. (*Pause*) Aren't you going to ask why?
Willy	No.
Jim	Because you wouldn't both fit on the bike. (*Laughs*)
Willy	I don't think that's funny.
Jim	(*Laughing*) She'd have to buy a sidecar. (*Pause*) There's one thing about Charlie, you know.
Willy	Only one thing.
Jim	There's one thing you can't take away from him. He's a snappy dresser.
Willy	Snappy?
Jim	He always has the cuff links, the tie pin.
Willy	What sort of a word's 'snappy'?
Jim	Button-down collars, matching shirt and tie.
Willy	Eau de Cologne.
Jim	He's a snappy dresser all right.
Willy	Does he still work at that men's boutique?
Jim	Yes.
Willy	I wouldn't buy any clothes there.
Jim	You couldn't. They don't cater for outsize men.
Willy	Does that puff work there?
Jim	Who do you mean?
Willy	That puff.
Jim	Do you mean Joseph?
Willy	That's him. Joseph. Does he?
Jim	He's not a puff.
Willy	Course he's a puff. Why does he call himself Joseph if he's not a puff?
Jim	What?
Willy	Whoever heard of anybody christened Joseph who didn't call himself Joe?
Jim	Joseph's all right.
Willy	You like Joseph, do you?
Jim	I said, he's all right.
	(*PAUSE*)

Willy	Jim. . . . Jim, have you ever thought. . . . have you ever thought of. . . . of becoming one yourself?
Jim	What?
Willy	A puff.
Jim	Are you serious?
Willy	Well look at it this way . . . .
Jim	You are serious.
Willy	You don't have much success with girls. Right?
Jim	What about Jean?
Willy	No, let me finish. You don't have much success with . . . in fact you don't have any success.
Jim	Jean . . .
Willy	You, you'd go down a bomb as a puff.
Jim	Take a running jump.
Willy	Don't be hasty. Think about it. Consider it. And you said yourself, Joseph's all right.
Jim	I don't want to be a puff.
Willy	Are you worried about the psychological conflict?
Jim	What?
Willy	It's a myth. Most puffs are well adjusted individuals.
Jim	You're sick.
Willy	It could be the making of you.
Jim	I don't want to hear any more.
Willy	And you don't really like girls.
Jim	I do.
Willy	With their false eye-lashes and their false everything else. And what have they ever done for you?
Jim	Willy?
Willy	Nothing. They've done nothing for you.
Jim	Willy, are you trying to tell me something?
Willy	They pass you over for pock-faced Charlie.
Jim	Willy, are you . . .? Have you become . . .? Are you a puff?
Willy	What?
Jim	You aren't one yourself, Willy?
Willy	Me?
Jim	You keep on about . . .
Willy	Now listen here . . .
Jim	Why are you selling it so strong?
Willy	You know I'm not a . . .
Jim	I've always thought of you as sort of not bothered.
Willy	I'm not a puff.
Jim	I've never questioned why you don't bother with girls.

114

Willy	Believe me.
Jim	Why, Willy? Why don't you?
Willy	You know why.
Jim	Because you're a puff.
Willy	No.
Jim	Why?
Willy	Because . . .
Jim	Why, Willy?
Willy	Because I'm big and fat and ugly.
Jim	I'm sorry.
Willy	I'm not a puff.
Jim	I'm sorry, Willy.
Willy	You know damn well I'm not.
Jim	I know.
Willy	I've never . . .
Jim	I know you haven't. I'm sorry.
Willy	Do you think I'm not bothered?
Jim	No.
Willy	I am bothered.

There are so many delightful radio comedies one could quote from if there were space. In *Just the Job* Liane Aukin plays about deliciously with the idea that what most women really need is a wife, a woman who can take care of household chores, children and husbands so that they will have more freedom to, among other things, earn enough money working for some other woman to pay the one 'doing' for them.

J. C. W. Brook's alien from outer space in *Blop* arrives by spaceship in a Herefordshire village to take over Earth for colonisation and gets fatally involved in a local feud about who grows the best roses.

It had been thought that farce was too visual to work on sound; but John Graham triumphantly disproved this with *A Slip of the Disc*. By using a blind piano tuner to introduce us to the scene of the farcical proceedings and cramming to bursting point the Hills' London flat, John Graham can find sound gag equivalents of sight gags, like the similarity to some ears of modern music and instrumental tuning. The very difficulty in radio drama of identifying voices is turned here to hilarious advantage and generates the kind of misunderstandings that come from all that scurrying between adjacent bedrooms in visual farce. Underlying all the fun and giving it an added satirical spice is our awareness that the rather farcical world of popular television entertainment is being amiably sent up from the point of view of the piano tuner who belongs to our blind world of radio drama.

The best political radio drama has not proclaimed itself as such by shouting the slogans or waving the banners of this or that particular persuasion but has dealt with those fundamental feelings of compassion and loyalty out of which specific political commitment springs. A really horrifying picture of what Britain could be like a few years from now, if those urging us 'back to Victorian values' got their way, is shown in Gilly Fraser's *Somewhere Else*. A jingoistic call for a return to a glorious past can be a summons to a fascistic future.

In *The Quarter Million Boys* Bloke Modisani shows what a powerful weapon ridicule can be against racist tyranny. The larger-than-life characters of the shebeen are able to carry out their grand caper of snatching a security van-load of money simply by, at each point in their plan, knowing how the ingrained racism of Afrikaaner clerks, guards and police will make them act in certain situations.

The importance of a good strong storyline for radio drama has often been referred to and many good storytellers have written many good radio plays like Philip Levene or, more recently, Rodney Wingfield. A good example of Rodney Wingfield's work is *A Test to Destruction* in which a man being tested for his toughness to see if he qualifies for security work blows the men setting the test to smithereens.

It is only possible to mention the tiniest fraction of the thousands of excellent Afternoon Theatre plays which have been broadcast. Just as Jill Hyem's *Equal Terms,* already mentioned, has been used in training social workers, her Afternoon Theatre play *Thank You,* about a woman who tries to make an acquaintance witness her suicide as a punishment for being so uncaring, has been used to help people volunteering for the Samaritans.

Many Afternoon Theatre plays deal with serious contemporary themes. Fay Weldon's *Polaris* deals, very obliquely, in terms of the infidelity of the wife of a member of a nuclear submarine crew, with the way a country's possession of such diabolic things as nuclear weapons seeps into and poisons the lives of its people.

John Graham's *We Hardly Ever Lose a Boffin* deals in a charmingly comic way with the same subject.

In *Korsakoff's Psychosis,* Geoffrey Parkinson wittily satirises contemporary mores by observing that there is not really much wrong with the world but love. If it were not for love we could get on with grabbing all we can for ourselves, satisfying our lusts and destroying ourselves and others as we were intended to. It is love that is filling the psychiatrists' waiting rooms.

Benefit of Clergy is one of a half-dozen period comedies set in the time of the Duke of Wellington written by Geoffrey Hubbard. In this one there is the mystery of some twenty or thirty clergymen apparently stealing mailbags.

More Cherry Cake by Jehane Markham uses a family tea party in a garden on a hot summer's day, like a spread of iron filings when tapped, to show the magnetic pattern of criss-crossing relationships beneath the surface.

In *Mary, Mary,* Rachel Billington makes the shock of the possibility that the fantasisings of a becalmed husband and wife may be true fill their sails and get them underway again.

Around the question of whether their ten-year-old son should remain in a private school or not, Rose Tremain draws the complete dissolution of a relationship and a marriage in *Don't Be Cruel.*

Heather Stevens in *The Gardener* shows how the perspective in a radio play can be kept shifting from one character to another, with dramatic and humorous results, and how something imagined, like the garden in this play, can remain ambiguous, changing from lovesome to noxious as the perspective changes.

In *My Name Is Bird McKai* Anne Leaton exploits the radio play's marvellous capacity for imaginative settings in the desert scenes when her heroine, among the Indians, does indeed, as every woman is meant to do at least once and must prepare her daughter to, fly.

And so one could go on and on recalling plays one has enjoyed from this Afternoon Theatre grab-bag, from a very funny play about parents' day at a public school, written by a fourteen year-old boy, to the first play written by an 85-year-old man just to prove to his doubting family that he was still capable of the concentration it took.

Long may the BBC continue to put out such a quantity of radio drama that there is no chance of its being monopolised by current fads in theme or treatment and new writers will go on having the best opportunity in Britain today for getting a public for their first dramatic work.

Chapter Eleven

Other Forms of Radio Dramatic Writing

SOMETIMES writers new to radio drama think that the easiest way to get started is to adapt for radio an existing work in another medium, a novel or a short story. This can be a mistake. It may take a more intimate knowledge of radio drama to adapt for it successfully, translating a work from one medium into an entirely different one, than to write for it originally. However, there are writers who have made distinguished careers for themselves in the field of adaptations — just as literary careers have been made by translators from one language to another.

Adaptation

We have described the way the radio play has emerged from narrative storytelling through the narrator's becoming split up into the characters of the story and then acting out in the present what had formerly been recounted as happening to them in the past. When we adapt a narrative piece for radio, that is the process we are applying to some particular work.

The first question we have to ask about a book or story we are thinking of adapting is: can the characters be got to act out their story for us without the help of a narrator to describe them and to explain what is happening to them? The ease with which this can be done depends on the perspective from which the work to be adapted is written. If the perspective is the usual one of the Victorian novelist, with the author standing outside the characters and presenting them to us objectively, then the transition to radio drama is relatively simple, as the fine adaptations of Dickens, George Eliot or Trollope show. If a more contemporary stream-of-consciousness perspective is used, characters bobbing along the flow of the writer's peculiar reflective process, adaptation is more difficult. Indeed, it may be quite impossible to transform such a work into radio drama without such damage to its spirit that it would be better to have it read on the air by an actor who assumes the author's voice.

Sometimes the theme of a novel or short story is so much a matter of the writer's subjective state that externalising it dramatically and acting it out results inevitably in too great a loss of subtle shades of meaning. Henry James' fine ghost story, *The Jolly Corner,* is a case in point.

Of course, there is a range of choice for the adaptor from eliminating the narrator altogether to making use of the narrator's voice to a lesser or greater extent. By and large if the work in question is a good yarn told by a writer with no particular distinction of style, like Edgar Wallace, one wants to get rid of the narrator entirely and let no one come between characters and listeners. But if the work being adapted is by a great novelist and if there is narrative work to be done, let it by all means be done in the voice and style of the writer.

Scene-setting or scene-changing paragraphs, in the words of the author, not only perform a narrative function but also help to set the mood and period of the original. What has to be remembered is that the greater the use of a narrator, the more the characters are distanced from us. There is a loss in immediacy to exactly the extent that the storyteller materialises as a middleman between us and his characters.

The reason why the works of the great Victorian novelists serialise so well is that many of them were written to begin with as instalments published in periodicals. Shorter contemporary novels written in a more tightly constructed way for publication as a complete work usually lend themselves to adaptations as a single ninety minute radio play and sometimes they can be done in sixty minutes.

One of the things to be considered when it comes to deciding what to adapt is the amount of dialogue provided in the original work. If it is a novel whose scenes are conceived dramatically, there will be a good deal of dialogue which the adaptor can make use of; but if the book is largely descriptive, like a novel by W. H. Hudson, it may mean that a great deal of dialogue is going to have to be invented and made to sound appropriate for, perhaps, a South American jungle.

Some novels or short stories have so much dialogue that there is not much point in adapting them. A story like Hemingway's *The Killers* can practically be cast and broadcast as it is.

The BBC takes account of the difficulties of adapting a work in fixing the fees, allowing as much as 80% of the fee for an original work for a very complicated adaptation.

Literary dialogue presents a problem for the adaptor. We have noted that naturalistic dialogue does not work well in the radio dramatic medium; but then neither does dialogue as artificially

119

contrived as late Henry James. The adaptor has to follow a middle course of keeping the Jamesian flavour while making the lines sufficiently colloquial to be spoken credibly by actors. This is possible because masters of prose style, however tortuous their language may look on the page, are always testing it by reciting it to an inner ear as they compose. Such dialogue lends itself more easily to the heightened language of drama than the flat, literal speech of many contemporary novels or short stories.

The main problem about adaptations for the writer new to radio is that over many years of broadcasting the classics in radio dramatic form, most of the great novels have been done; and even if a new production is wanted the BBC may use the same old scripts. Of course, if a writer claims to have a new slant on one of the classics which would involve a different treatment, there might be some interest.

Although the better-known American, French, Italian, German and Russian novels have also been broadcast there are many novels now from South and South East Asia, from Africa and from Latin America which have not been done and are well worth adapting.

Contemporary novels may present difficulties over copyright, some film company having acquired an exclusive option. In any case the writer, before embarking on the task of a major adaptation, should find out from the BBC Drama Script Unit if the book has been done and if any other writer has a prior claim on it, if the book is available for broadcast and if the BBC is interested, in principle, in an adaptation. The BBC will pursue questions of copyright, though the writer can usually assume that any book whose author has been dead for over fifty years is out of copyright.

Dramatic features

Dramatic features come under the control of the Radio Drama Department, like radio plays. They can be distinguished from documentary features, which come under another department, by having parts in them which are played by actors. They can be distinguished from the radio play, not so much on the ground that the play is fiction while the dramatic feature is fact, as that the radio play has both theme and plot while the dramatic feature usually develops as the creative exploration of a theme only.

A radio play may deal with a factual event or a historical personage; but insofar as it tells a dramatic story about its characters which is distinct from news accounts or from history, it is a play. Shirley Gee's *Typhoid Mary* is a radio play about a historical character. Geoffrey Bridson's *March of the Forty Five* is a poetic reconstruction of a historical event but it does not tell a story about its characters distinct from history. It is a dramatic feature.

Lyrical evocations of a real or imagined place, like Henry Reed's *Streets of Pompeii,* and even that radiophonic masterpiece, Dylan Thomas' *Under Milk Wood,* are best described as dramatic features. Naturally any attempt at classification is going to encounter works which will not fit neatly into our pigeonholes.

Charles Parker's radio ballads, like *Singing the Fishing,* use documentary material collected from a particular section of workers, creatively assembled and edited, combined with traditional and original work songs, to give a portrait in sound of a whole working community. Like other imaginative feature productions they have pioneered a grammar of expressiveness in sound which was going to be at the disposal of the radio playwright proper. An interesting radio play written by a media arts student in the Central London Poly uses the idea of a documentary producer collecting material for a programme on the political situation in a Central American country. He allows himself to be persuaded by compradore businessmen, the American ambassador and certain tough undercover agents to make good safe recordings of 'reliable' people, but what is heard on the tapes when he is putting the programme together back in London is a people's agony and their determination to liberate themselves — the very material he ought to have collected and did not!

Series

Sometimes a radio playwright will create a character so interesting that additional plays can be written to exploit this same character — like Andrew Davies' Steph. Each play is self-contained and they may be separated by considerable gaps of time; but eventually there are enough of them to be repeated in a series of perhaps half a dozen.

Geoffrey Hubbard produced six period detective plays centring around the character of the Duke of Wellington, and Rodney Wingfield wrote several series of plays called *The Secret Life of Kenneth Williams* that were in every way very close to light entertainment.

121

Serials

The daily radio serial, which in the United States was so closely associated with soap advertisements that it gave a name to a whole genre, was launched by the BBC with a more public service mission. *Mrs Dale's Diary,* about the family and professional concerns of a general practitioner, was a useful way of providing information to the public about the National Health Service and *The Archers* was a bucolic version of soap opera for spreading ideas in rural areas about good farming methods.

When it was felt after many, many years that *Mrs Dale's Diary* had largely served its purpose, Keith Williams replaced it with *Waggoners Walk,* a new series having a more contemporary feel to it and coming to grips with some of the new social and moral problems of the Sixties and Seventies. Unfortunately, during retrenchment in radio drama, this daily serial was dropped.

That meant that only *The Archers* was left to provide four resident writers on its panel with the one guaranteed living wage radio can offer to writers. Changes in the panel offer opportunities for new or relatively new writers to serve their apprenticeship in radio writing as members of a team which has included such experienced writers as the distinguished novelist and radio playwright, Susan Hill.

Chapter 12

The Future of Radio Drama

THE FUTURE of radio drama in Britain is largely tied up with the continuation of public service broadcasting.

The Writers' Guild of Great Britain and the Society of Authors, representing writers in general and radio playwrights in particular, together with Actors Equity and the Musicians Union, regularly campaign for the government of the day to fix the annual fee at a high enough rate to enable the BBC to provide an excellent public service in broadcasting. Support for public service broadcasting is an important part of the writers' collective struggle for jobs, for the right to work at their chosen profession.

The BBC, for its part, is expected to give certain assurances to those who work creatively in broadcasting on such issues as the maintenance of the quantity and quality of radio drama and the acceptance of limits on the importation of relatively cheap television dramatic material from the US which deprives of jobs writers, actors and directors here.

The BBC sometimes makes the mistake of thinking that it can better secure its existence by courting cheap popularity by offering the kinds of programmes the public at its most undiscriminating is assumed to want than by fulfilling its proper public service responsibility of gaining through excellence the widest possible audience for the kinds of programme it ought to provide.

It was this kind of mistake which inspired the move to rigid generic radio at the beginning of the Seventies, with nothing on Radio 1 but disc-jockeyed pop music; little on Radio 2 but light music; all news, talks and spoken word generally, including drama, on Radio 4; and Radio 3, when it was not a channel for classical music, a much-restricted cultural ghetto into which a highbrow hodge podge was crowded.

Generic radio means dividing the public up into those who only like pop music and those who only like classical music instead of regarding the majority of people as possibly preferring lighter music but being susceptible to an appreciation of classical music as well; or of dividing the audience for radio drama into those who like plays which simply tell a good story and those who like plays which are more demanding, instead of thinking of listeners to radio plays as sometimes wanting dramatic entertainment while they are doing other things and sometimes being prepared to drop everything else and give their full attention to a radio play which may challenge or change their attitudes and sentiments.

During the period when BBC radio was shared by Home, Light and Third Programmes, some of the most imaginative programming, like 'Music in Miniature' which was made up of the most tuneful items from classical compositions, persuaded people who normally listened to the Light Programme that there was much attractive music to be heard on Third. By introducing a challenging new play by Pinter, say, on the Third and then repeating it on Home, the BBC was broadening horizons of appreciation and entertainment instead of dividing people up permanently into categories of age, class or brow levels. Just as the most exciting academic discoveries are made in the borderland between different disciplines, so some of the most exciting programming is that which moves listeners from channel to channel selectively.

Fortunately, the BBC has modified its adherence to strictly generic radio but the move away from lazy, unimaginative programming needs to go further. We do not need a public service radio organisation, supported by licence fees, to put out a programme of endless recorded pop music as Radio 1 has tended to do. It might as well be selling soap!

What is very serious from our point of view as writers of radio drama is that the BBC is not recruiting from the Radio 1 captive audience of British youth any listeners for the radio drama of the future. Unless radio plays can be devised which engage the interest of young people, radio playwrights will find themselves writing for a dwindling audience of older and older people who are not being replaced by younger devotees of radio drama.

Short plays or serials with short episodes are ideal for introducing people to radio drama and for giving writers practice in a new medium. While the arrangement of fees for actors is such that short plays are one of the most expensive ways of filling air time, the disappearance of the 'Just before Midnight' fifteen minute plays on Friday, Saturday and Sunday at 11.45 p.m. and the daily serial *Waggoners Walk* must be deplored.

Radio writers and BBC programmers should put their heads together and think of ways of presenting an element of drama on Radio 1 in such a way as to encourage young people, in this country so renowned for its drama and its dramatists, to begin to appreciate radio drama and the literature of ours and other cultures which can be enjoyed in radio dramatic form. Just as putting out radio plays in an afternoon band heard by a predominantly women's audience resulted in a wonderful crop of radio plays by women writers, so making radio drama available to young people, perhaps in playlets that can be seeded through a pop music format or a suitably devised mini-serial, will yield a rich harvest of young voices speaking in terms of radio drama and giving it fresh life.

Radio drama fees

At the first Radio Literature Conference held at the University of Durham in April, 1977, R. D. Smith, the well-known radio play producer, said that creative writers had two things against working for radio — 'the money is abysmal and, more seriously, the work is fleeting, impermanent, forgotten as soon as done.'

The fees for writing radio drama may seem low compared with writing television drama, the going rate for radio plays being about one-third that for television plays. This discrepancy has nothing to do with the relative difficulty of writing for the two media. The BBC in negotiations with the Writers' Guild of Great Britain and the Society of Authors frankly admits that fees for television drama cannot be allowed to fall too far behind what commercial television can offer writers while no such competitive pressure is pushing up fees for radio drama.

At the same time writers' organisations are aware of what a boon it is to have so much radio dramatic writing being bought, far greater than the amount of dramatic writing bought by television, and they would not wish to raise radio fees drastically at the cost of a considerable reduction in the number of radio plays being broadcast. The high cost of television plays, including the much higher fees for writers, has meant a reduction in the number of television plays and a tendency to play safe with those that are done by discriminating against new writers or innovative themes and treatment.

In any case, radio drama fees do not compare all that unfavourably with other forms of writing. A newly established radio playwright, one, that is, who has had only two or three plays accepted, can expect to receive a fee of around £23 per minute at present (1984). This means that the fee for a Monday Night or Saturday Night Theatre play of ninety minutes, with a built-in repeat, comes to at least £3105. There must be many writers who have made less than that on a novel which took far longer to write.

There is also the possibility that the radio play may be taken by the Transcription Service for distribution abroad in recorded form or may be broadcast by the BBC's External Service or, as a result of the BBC's circulation to broadcasting organisations all over the world of its quarterly output of radio drama, some foreign radio service may buy the script of a radio play written here for translation and use in another country. This further use attracts additional fees because the copyright of radio plays remains with the playwright, the BBC only buying the right to broadcast them. Indeed, there is nothing to keep the playwright from turning a radio play which has been broadcast on the BBC into a television play or a stage play. From time to time broadcast radio plays have even been bought for films.

It would not be sound advice to suggest to someone taking up radio dramatic writing that there was much chance of making a reasonably good living out of writing radio plays alone. But then that must be true of other fields of writing these days and more and more professional writers try their hand at a variety of writing jobs — radio and television drama, stage plays, books, whatever seems to provide an opening. That is one of the reasons why the writers' trade union, the Writers' Guild of Great Britain, has evolved from being mainly concerned with screen and television writers into covering radio, books and, most recently, stage playwrights, with the intention of becoming the single union representing all professional writers in Britain whatever fields they work in.

Certainly the fact that the Writers' Guild now negotiates with the BBC on behalf of television, radio and book writers means that those in a comparatively weak bargaining position, like radio writers, are strengthened by linking their BBC negotiations with television writers. There are other issues than fees that have to be dealt with, like the Code of Practice governing relations between BBC and radio playwrights which has been adopted as paragraphs 12 through 19 of the Radio Drama Agreement between the BBC and the Writers' Guild of Great Britain.

Radio plays in published form

The other point made at that Durham conference about the unattractiveness of radio drama as a field for the efforts of the creative writer was the ephemeral character of the radio play.

Of course so much writing these days is ephemeral. Who can remember last year's best sellers? Who would want to! The disposability of razors, watches and tableware now extends to culture and so much that is produced is only meant to while away a few hours and be thrown away and forgotten.

CODE OF PRACTICE PROVISIONS FOR ADDITION TO THE RADIO DRAMA AGREEMENT

12. Consultation on Director and Casting

It is agreed to be good practice for the choice of director and cast to be discussed between Drama Department and the writer so far as may be practicable given the constraints of time, the writer's availability and his experience. Nevertheless the final choice of director, cast and other participants in the production of work shall be in the BBC's discretion.

13. Access to Rehearsals and Recording

It is agreed to be good practice for reasonable access to rehearsals and recordings of their work to be afforded to writers and to this end they will be notified in advance of the dates and times of such rehearsals and recordings. It is acknowledged that the producer has responsibility for the conduct of rehearsals and recordings and that there may be exceptional occasions when in proper exercise of this responsibility he may exclude a writer from a rehearsal or recording. The writer will be entitled to travel expenses and subsistence allowance in accordance with the BBC's standing instructions when attending rehearsals and recordings at the request of the producer.

14. Promotional Hearings and Audience Reaction

a. Writers shall be informed of and should consider themselves welcome at any formal promotional pre-hearings of their works.

b. It is agreed to be good practice for a writer to ask to be informed of professional reaction within Drama Department to the broadcast of his work, and also of any response from the press or public (including any response reported by the BBC's Audience Research Department) known to Drama Department. Any such information supplied to a writer shall be treated by him as having been supplied in confidence and shall not be divulged by him to a third party.

15. Notification of Proposed Dates of Broadcasts and Repeats

Writers will be notified as far in advance as possible of the scheduled dates of first broadcast and repeat broadcast and of any changes thereto.

16. Final Script

It is agreed to be good practice for the writer to be supplied with 6 copies of the final script (2 copies in the case of External Services) as soon as they are available and the BBC shall endeavour to send one to the writer to reach him at least 48 hours before the scheduled recording whenever practicable.

17. Cancelled Productions or Broadcasts

If at any time after a date has been set for the first rehearsal of a work the BBC decides that the work or the production thereof is not suitable for broadcasting, the BBC shall take all reasonable steps to inform the writer forthwith of its intention not to proceed with production or transmission and a period of 48 hours shall be allowed to elapse before the intention is implemented. During the 48 hour period, the BBC shall at the request of the writer or, if he is a member of the Guild or of the Society at the request of the Guild or Society, convene a meeting under the conciliation procedure set out in Clause 18 hereof.

18. Conciliation

If a dispute relating to material covered by this Agreement arises between a Society or a Guild member and the BBC which cannot be settled by informal contact between the Society or the Guild and the BBC, then either side will have the right to convene a meeting between the Society or the Guild and the BBC to investigate the dispute and if possible to resolve it. This clause shall not however be invoked in a manner to override any other clause in the Agreement, or to call in question the BBC's reasonable and proper discretion to accept or reject a script or a programme.

19. Arbitration

Any dispute regarding the interpretation of this Agreement or regarding the interpretation of the individual Agreement between the BBC and the writer which cannot be resolved by discussion between the parties shall be referred to an Arbitration Committee consisting of representatives of the BBC and the Society or the Guild as the case may be or, if the writer is not a Society or a Guild member, consisting of representatives of the BBC and of the writer. Failing settlement it shall then be referred to a single Arbitrator mutually acceptable to both sides who shall determine the issue and whose decision shall be binding on both parties.

This clause shall not apply to disputes arising under Clauses 12 and 18 hereof.

128

But probably what was being referred to was the impermanence of a work which is broadcast at a particular time and then vanishes into the ether to be heard no more. But the radio play is no different in this respect from the television play and in both cases, being media which are based on recording, the originals can be preserved and reproduced whenever they are wanted.

As far as another form of cheating evanescence is concerned, the endurance of publication, the radio play has an advantage over all other forms of drama. Because all the descriptions of settings and characters, all the stage directions and notes for actors are in the dialogue, the radio play goes more readily and readably into print than any other kind of play. The script of a radio play does not contain all those arcane instructions like C.U. or L.S. or whip-pan or tracking often going on for several pages before we get to any dialogue at all. It does not start with a diagram of a set and two or three pages of descriptions of props and, when they appear, characters. The climax of a radio play is never some bit of visual business which may look fine on a stage but reads like nothing at all. The whole drama of a radio play and nothing else is right there on the page.

Several collections of radio plays like New Radio Drama (1966) and plays by a particular writer like Don Haworth were brought out by BBC Publications, and Eyre Methuen brought out a collection of radio plays by Harold Pinter and the individual plays, *Pearl* by John Arden and *The Ruffian on the Stairs* by Joe Orton. But these publications were too infrequent to create a market for radio plays in print.

A co-operative venture between BBC Publications and the Radio Drama Script Unit took the form of printing very economically a number of copies of the script of a radio play likely to be popular before transmission. Then in a microphone announcement at the end of the broadcast the audience was told that scripts of the play were available at a very reasonable price.

The first three scripts dealt with in this way were *Don't Be Cruel* by Rose Tremain, *Giving Up* by J. C. W. Brook and *The Clerks* by Rhys Adrian. But the scheme seems to have been allowed to lapse.

In 1977 the author of this book, then acting BBC Radio Drama Script Editor, approached Nicholas Hern of Eyre Methuen with the idea of a joint BBC-Eyre Methuen annual publication of an anthology of the best radio plays. This proposal was agreed and those whose plays were selected for inclusion in each successive volume were called Giles Cooper Award Winners. The first volume was published in 1978 and the winners were:

Episode on a Thursday-Evening — Don Haworth
Halt! Who Goes There — Tom Mallin
Daughters of Men — Jennifer Phillips
Remember Me — Jill Hyem
Polaris — Fay Weldon
Is It Something I Said — Richard Harris

Each year since, another volume has been produced. Before the war, when short stories were the most popular form of literature and appeared in a great number of periodicals, there was an anthology of the Best Short Stories for each year. With the folding up of so many of those periodicals no such anthology appears anymore. We may be moving into a time when the radio play takes the place of the short story as one of the most popular forms of current literary culture.

Radio drama on cassettes

The most important way in which the ephemeral character of radio drama will be mitigated is in making radio plays available on cassettes.

We have explained why the BBC puts out the bulk of its popular radio drama in the afternoon; but this means that a great number of people who may like radio drama are unable to listen at the time when so much of it is transmitted. Making radio plays available on cassettes frees this dramatic form from having to be heard at a particular time on one fixed date and gives it a currency extending far beyond the original broadcast.

No matter how much circulation there should be of radio plays in recorded form, freed from the temporal tyranny of a single broadcast, distribution of cassettes should always be grounded in an actual broadcast play. It is in terms of radio broadcasting with its peculiar limitations and freedoms that the radio play developed and it is in remaining broadcastable that the radio play will be true to its own nature.

There are several features about the experience of having one's radio play broadcast which contribute to the feeling that radio drama is very ephemeral. The very bulk of radio drama which is a boon to the writer trying to sell a play means that when the play goes out it seems to be lost among all the other plays broadcast even in the same week. After the excitement of participating in the production of the play and feeling that it has worked out very well, the writer may have to wait some time before the broadcast. Then the great day arrives announced by a tiny billing in Radio Times; friends and relatives are alerted; the play goes out; and then — nothing! In all probability no critical notice anywhere, nothing from the BBC; and the writer may indeed feel that the play on which such care was lavished might never have existed for all the stir its broadcast seems to have created.

Mass media newspapers devote space for criticism and review of the arts on the basis of the kind of mass following those arts command. Radio drama does not get all that much notice paid to it. All the more credit then to those, like David Wade and Gillian Reynolds, who have made radio drama a field for serious critical attention and have put their time and pens at the disposal of the cause of maintaining the highest standards in broadcast radio plays.

The BBC Radio Drama Department might do more to remedy the fact that the radio playwright has no equivalent of first night applause, film festival acclaim or columns of comment on television. The gist of any letters written in about a play, any comments in the Department or at radio review boards, and the relevant Listener Research figures, should be made available to the writer. If, on the whole, this response is favourable, the writer will be encouraged by it; if unfavourable, the writer will learn from it.

The BBC maintains a Listener Research Department to keep tabs on audience response to various programmes and most radio plays are reported on. Listener Research figures cannot be taken literally and have to be interpreted in various ways. Audience sizes, for example, can vary with the weather, with Wimbledon or a cup final; but over a period of time the figures will show whether the audience for plays at a particular time is growing, diminishing or staying about the same. Radio plays are not subject to sudden increases in audience because the writer is so well known or because a popular star has been cast, as tends more to be the case with television. Radio's drama audiences are built on the basis of maintaining a high standard of excellence of a wide variety of plays in a regular spot over a considerable period of time.

The programme appreciation figure also has to be taken with certain reservations. Foibles and prejudices of those who volunteer as panel members can result in such influences on judgement as intellectual snobbery which makes panel members give higher marks to plays they think they ought to like even if they do not, as resistance to what is new in theme or treatment, as downgrading of all comedy for not being serious enough to deserve high marks even if they enjoyed it.

Some of these prejudices and preferences are characteristic of a whole radio audience like, for example, the Afternoon Theatre audience. It is worthwhile for the playwright to know something of the likes and dislikes of an audience, if only the better to circumvent them. Certainly no writer will ever write well for an audience held in contempt.

But if the play was chosen because it was thought to be good popular entertainment and it gets an unusually low appreciation figure then some Script Editor has to be concerned and, of course, any charges by the panel that a play was hard to follow always have to be taken seriously.

Sometimes a low appreciation figure is taken, particularly by those working in Radio 3, as a sign of merit on the mistaken assumption that there is some necessary connection between excellence and inaccessibility, so that an audience too small to be measured at all is the ultimate accolade. At the other extreme those working in Radios 1, 2 and 4 can play the game of their commercial rivals and sacrifice all other considerations to achieving high appreciation figures as the way to big audiences. Public service broadcasting is always about winning through excellence the widest possible audience for the whole range of enlightening, inspiring and entertaining programmes that ought to be made available to the public. It is to a BBC doing that job and acting as honest broker between artist and public that the playwright sends the script of a radio play.

Radio drama's place in the cultural scene

The enormous popularity of television made it seem that radio was a stop-gap form of dramatic entertainment until technological progress could restore the sense radio was missing. After all, was not sight the most important sense of all, as we acknowledge in such expressions as 'seeing is believing', or 'out of sight, out of mind'?

Television and film, dramatically speaking, seemed to be the legitimate children of a very old and firmly established theatrical tradition. Blind radio was a kind of unfortunate stepchild. This attitude is encouraged by the fact that, on the plea that it would be too hard to collect a licence fee based on possession of a radio, only those with television sets pay for BBC public service broadcasting. Radio programmes are given away like free prizes to make us buy something else. Members of BBC staff who work on the radio side of the house are often made to feel like second-class citizens in the world of broadcasting.

But radio drama, as our analysis and history of the form has shown, should not be considered as a deprived or disabled heir of the theatre. It is a different kind of theatre — a theatre of the mind — and its progenitors go right back to storytellers around a campfire, to reciters of the great epics. It is cognate with other forms of theatre in deriving directly from the oral tradition which is the origin of all literature.

The pervasiveness of literacy and the cultural dominance of the printed word can make us forget that writing began as a kind of computer for storing information and recording the creative achievements of the spoken word. Much of the rhythm, rhyme and rhetoric of literature have their origin as aids to the memory of a narrator in an extemporised oral performance of some great theme. Even the elaborate prose of a writer like Sir Thomas Browne must have been put down with a recitation ringing in the author's mind. As writing has got farther and farther away from the sound of a human voice, has it not suffered an increasing impoverishment of style, has not some poetry become more recognisable as such from its appearance on a page than from the way it sounds?

Certainly to hear on the air a recitation of *The Faerie Queene* or a dramatisation of *Paradise Lost* is to realise that what looks forbidding on the printed page listens very well indeed and is much more accessible to ear than eye.

People are most accustomed to receiving instruction or pursuing entertainment by way of the eye, and the attentive ear attuned to the voice of mentor or storyteller has ceased to be the basic learning or enjoying faculty it once was. Radio can help restore sharpness and discernment to that faculty. The radio playwright is one of the recruits in the war that has to be fought against all the pointless, mindless din of modern life which dulls and atrophies our hearing.

Dramatic language in the theatre or on the radio is spoken language. The text, the script is never anything but the means to the end of a vocal performance. Radio drama is one of the ways in which passion and humour, hope and despair, the whole gamut of human emotions and aspirations fall directly on our ears. But more than that, radio drama, in which the spoken word is the whole essence of the artistic form, cannot but have a revivifying effect on language, inspiring radio playwrights with a lively appreciation of what language can so vigorously do and of how resonantly beautiful, haunting and moving it can sound.

The radio play is thus a link for us with the rich oral tradition on which literate culture floats like a barque on a sea. It puts us in touch with cultures less printed-word-dominated than our own and, indeed, plays its part in keeping open for continuous creative exploration the question of the division of labour between oral and literate traditions in meeting all the demands of human expression.

That is the context in which you are writing radio drama. The best of luck in your efforts!

Index

135

was born in 1940. She published her first novel, *Shadow Dance*, in 1965. Her second novel, *The Magic Toyshop*, won the John Llewellyn Rhys Prize in 1967 (Virago, 1981), and her third, *Several Perceptions*, won the Somerset Maugham Award in 1968. *Heroes and Villains* was published in 1969, *Love* in 1971, *The Infernal Desire Machines of Dr Hoffman* in 1972 and *The Passion of New Eve* in 1977 (Virago, 1982). *Nights at the Circus* was joint winner of the James Tait Black Memorial Prize for 1985. Angela Carter also published three collections of short stories, *Fireworks* (1974, published by Virago in 1988), *The Bloody Chamber*, which was received with great acclaim in 1979 and won the Cheltenham Festival of Literature Award, and *Black Venus* (1985). *The Sadeian Woman* (Virago, 1979) was her first work of non-fiction. Virago also publishes *Nothing Sacred* (1982), a collection of her journalism from *New Society* and elsewhere. *Expletives Deleted*, a second collection of her articles, was published in 1992. She also edited the highly successful short story anthologies: *Wayward Girls and Wicked Women* (1986), *The Virago Book of Fairy Tales* (1990), and *The Second Virago Book of Fairy Tales* (to be published in autumn 1992). Her final novel was the much-lauded *Wise Children*, published in 1991.

Angela Carter died in London, aged 51, in February 1992. In the *Independent*'s obituary Robert Coover wrote she was 'a true witness of her times, an artist in the here and now of both life and art, Bloody Chamber though it may be.'

ANGELA CARTER

The

Sadeian Woman

AN EXERCISE IN CULTURAL HISTORY

Published by VIRAGO PRESS Limited 1979
20–23 Mandela Street, Camden Town, London NW1 0HQ

Reprinted 1982, 1983, 1984, 1987, 1990, 1992 (twice)

A CIP catalogue record for this book is available from the British Library

Typeset by Malvern Typesetting Ltd
and printed and bound in Great Britain
by Cox & Wyman Ltd, Reading, Berks

CONTENTS

INTRODUCTORY NOTE

Sade was born in 1740, a great nobleman; and died in 1814, in a lunatic asylum, a poor man. His life spans the entire period of the French Revolution and he died in the same year that Napoleon abdicated and the monarchy was restored to France. He stands on the threshold of the modern period, looking both backward and forwards, at a time when the nature of human nature and of social institutions was debated as freely as it is in our own.

Sade's work concerns the nature of sexual freedom and is of particular significance to women because of his refusal to see female sexuality in relation to its reproductive function, a refusal as unusual in the late eighteenth century as it is now, even if today the function of women as primarily reproductive beings is under question. *The Sadeian Woman* is neither a critical study nor a historical analysis of Sade; it is, rather, a late-twentieth-century interpretation of some of the problems he raises about the culturally determined nature of women and of the relations between men and women that result from it – an opposition which is both cruelly divisive in our common struggle to understand the world, and also, in itself, a profound illumination of the nature of that struggle.

one

POLEMICAL PREFACE:
PORNOGRAPHY
IN THE SERVICE OF WOMEN

> Sadism is not a name finally given to a practice as old
> as Eros; it is a massive cultural fact which appeared
> precisely at the end of the eighteenth century, and
> which constitutes one of the greatest conversions of
> Western imagination: unreason transformed into
> delirium of the heart, madness of desire, the insane
> dialogue of love and death in the limitless presumption
> of appetite.
>
> > *Madness and Civilisation,*
> > Michel Foucault

> I am not the slave of the Slavery that dehumanised my
> ancestors.
>
> > *Black Skin White Masks,*
> > Frantz Fanon

Pornographers are the enemies of women only because our
contemporary ideology of pornography does not encompass
the possibility of change, as if we were the slaves of history
and not its makers, as if sexual relations were not
necessarily an expression of social relations, as if sex itself
were an external fact, one as immutable as the weather,

creating human practice but never a part of it.

Pornography involves an abstraction of human intercourse in which the self is reduced to its formal elements. In its most basic form, these elements are represented by the probe and the fringed hole, the twin signs of male and female in graffiti, the biological symbols scrawled on the subway poster and the urinal wall, the simplest expression of stark and ineradicable sexual differentiation, a universal pictorial language of lust – or, rather, a language we accept as universal because, since it has always been so, we conclude that it must always remain so.

In the stylisation of graffiti, the prick is always presented erect, in an alert attitude of enquiry or curiosity or affirmation; it points upwards, it asserts. The hole is open, an inert space, like a mouth waiting to be filled. From this elementary iconography may be derived the whole metaphysic of sexual differences – man aspires; woman has no other function but to exist, waiting. The male is positive, an exclamation mark. Woman is negative. Between her legs lies nothing but zero, the sign for nothing, that only becomes something when the male principle fills it with meaning.

Anatomy is destiny, said Freud, which is true enough as far as it goes, but ambiguous. My anatomy is only part of an infinitely complex organisation, my self. The anatomical reductionalism of graffiti, the *reductio ad absurdum* of the bodily differences between men and women, extracts all the evidence of me from myself and leaves behind only a single aspect of my life as a mammal. It enlarges this aspect, simplifies it and then presents it as the most significant aspect of my entire humanity. This is true of all mythologising of sexuality; but graffiti lets it be *seen* to be true. It is the most explicit version of the idea of different sexual essences of men and women, because it is the crudest. In the face of this symbolism, my pretensions to any kind of social existence go for nothing; graffiti directs me back to my mythic generation as a woman and, as a woman, my symbolic value is primarily that of a myth of patience and receptivity, a dumb mouth from which the teeth have been pulled.

Sometimes, especially under the influence of Jung, a more archaic mouth is allowed to exert an atavistic dominance. Then, if I am lucky enough to be taken with such poetic pseudo-seriousness, my nether mouth may be acknowledged as one capable of speech– were there not, of old, divinatory priestesses, female oracles and so forth? Was there not Cassandra, who always spoke the truth, although admittedly in such a way that nobody ever believed her? And that, in mythic terms, is the hell of it. Since that female, oracular mouth is located so near the beastly backside, my vagina might indeed be patronisingly regarded as a speaking mouth, but never one that issues the voice of reason. In this most insulting mythic redefinition of myself, that of occult priestess, I am indeed allowed to speak but only of things that male society does not take seriously. I can hint at dreams, I can even personify the imagination; but that is only because I am not rational enough to cope with reality.

If women allow themselves to be consoled for their culturally determined lack of access to the modes of intellectual debate by the invocation of hypothetical great goddesses, they are simply flattering themselves into submission (a technique often used on them by men). All the mythic versions of women, from the myth of the redeeming purity of the virgin to that of the healing, reconciling mother, are consolatory nonsenses; and consolatory nonsense seems to me a fair definition of myth, anyway. Mother goddesses are just as silly a notion as father gods. If a revival of the myths of these cults gives women emotional satisfaction, it does so at the price of obscuring the real conditions of life. This is why they were invented in the first place.

Myth deals in false universals, to dull the pain of particular circumstances. In no area is this more true than in that of relations between the sexes. Graffiti, the most public form of sexual iconography, one which requires no training or artistic skill in its execution and yet is always assured of an audience, obtains all its effects from these false universals of myth. Its savage denial of the complexity of human relations is also a consolatory nonsense.

In its schema, as in the mythic schema of all relations between men and women, man proposes and woman is disposed of, just as she is disposed of in a rape, which is a kind of physical graffiti, the most extreme reduction of love, in which all humanity departs from the sexed beings. So that, somewhere in the fear of rape, is a more than merely physical terror of hurt and humiliation – a fear of psychic disintegration, of an essential dismemberment, a fear of a loss or disruption of the self which is not confined to the victim alone. Since all pornography derives directly from myth, it follows that its heroes and heroines, from the most gross to the most sophisticated, are mythic abstractions, heroes and heroines of dimension and capacity. Any glimpse of a real man or a real woman is absent from these representations of the archetypal male and female.

The nature of the individual is not resolved into but is ignored by these archetypes, since the function of the archetype is to diminish the unique 'I' in favour of a collective, sexed being which cannot, by reason of its very nature, exist as such because an archetype is only an image that has got too big for its boots and bears, at best, a fantasy relation to reality.

All archetypes are spurious but some are more spurious than others. There is the unarguable fact of sexual differentiation; but, separate from it and only partially derived from it, are the behavioural modes of masculine and feminine, which are culturally defined variables translated in the language of common usage to the status of universals. And these archetypes serve only to confuse the main issue, that relationships between the sexes are determined by history and by the historical fact of the economic depen-

dence of women upon men. This fact is now very largely a
fact of the past and, even in the past, was only true for
certain social groups and then only at certain periods.
Today, most women work before, during and after marriage.
Nevertheless, the economic dependence of women remains a
believed fiction and is assumed to imply an emotional
dependence that is taken for granted as a condition inherent
in the natural order of things and so used to console working
women for their low wages. They work; see little profit from
it; and therefore conclude they cannot really have been
working at all.

This confusion as to the experience of reality – that what I
know from my experience is true is, in fact, not so – is most
apparent, however, in the fantasy love-play of the archetypes, which generations of artists have contrived to
make seem so attractive that, lulled by dreams, many
women willingly ignore the palpable evidence of their own
responses.

In these beautiful encounters, any man may encounter
any woman and their personalities are far less important to
their copulation than the mere fact of their genders. At the
first touch or sigh he, she, is subsumed immediately into a
universal. (She, of course, rarely approaches him; that is not
part of the fantasy of fulfillment.) She is most immediately
and dramatically a woman when she lies beneath a man, and
her submission is the apex of his malehood. To show his
humility before his own erection, a man must approach a
woman on his knees, just as he approaches god. This is the
kind of beautiful thought that has bedevilled the history of
sex in Judaeo-Christian culture, causing almost as much
confusion as the idea that sex is a sin. Some of the scorn
heaped on homosexuals may derive from the fact that they
do not customarily adopt the mythically correct, sacerdotal
position. The same beautiful thought has elevated a
Western European convention to the position of the only
sanctified sexual position; it fortifies the missionary
position with a bizarre degree of mystification. God is in-

voked as a kind of sexual referee, to assure us, as modern churchmen like to claim in the teeth of two thousand years of Christian sexual repression, that sex is really sacred.

The missionary position has another great asset, from the mythic point of view; it implies a system of relations between the partners that equates the woman to the passive receptivity of the soil, to the richness and fecundity of the earth. A whole range of images poeticises, kitschifies, departicularises intercourse, such as wind beating down corn, rain driving against bending trees, towers falling, all tributes to the freedom and strength of the roving, fecundating, irresistible male principle and the heavy, downward, equally irresistible gravity of the receptive soil. The soil that is, good heavens, myself. It is a most self-enhancing notion; I have almost seduced myself with it. Any woman may manage, in luxurious self-deceit, to feel herself for a little while one with great, creating nature, fertile, open, pulsing, anonymous and so forth. In doing so, she loses herself completely and loses her partner also.

The moment they succumb to this anonymity, they cease to be themselves, with their separate lives and desires; they cease to be the lovers who have met to assuage desire in a reciprocal pact of tenderness, and they engage at once in a spurious charade of maleness and femaleness.

The anonymity of the lovers, whom the act transforms from me and you into they, precludes the expression of ourselves.

So the act is taken away from us even as we perform it.

We become voyeurs upon our own caresses. The act does not acknowledge the participation of the individual, bringing to it a whole life of which the act is only a part. The man and woman, in their particularity, their being, are absent from these representations of themselves as male and female. These tableaux of falsification remove our sexual life from the world, from tactile experience itself. The lovers are lost to themselves in a privacy that does not transcend but deny reality. So the act can never satisfy them, because it does not affect their lives. It occurs in the mythic dream-time of religious ritual.

But our flesh arrives to us out of history, like everything else does. We may believe we fuck stripped of social artifice; in bed, we even feel we touch the bedrock of human nature itself. But we are deceived. Flesh is not an irreducible human universal. Although the erotic relationship may seem to exist freely, on its own terms, among the distorted social relationships of a bourgeois society, it is, in fact, the most self-conscious of all human relationships, a direct confrontation of two beings whose actions in the bed are wholly determined by their acts when they are out of it. If one sexual partner is economically dependent on the other, then the question of sexual coercion, of contractual obligation, raises its ugly head in the very abode of love and inevitably colours the nature of the sexual expression of affection. The marriage bed is a particularly delusive refuge from the world because all wives of necessity fuck by contract. Prostitutes are at least decently paid on the nail and boast fewer illusions about a hireling status that has no veneer of social acceptability, but their services are suffering a decline in demand now that other women have invaded their territory in their own search for a newly acknowledged sexual pleasure. In this period, promiscuous abandon may seem the only type of free exchange.

But no bed, however unexpected, no matter how apparently gratuitous, is free from the de-universalising facts of real life. We do not go to bed in simple pairs; even if we choose not to refer to them, we still drag there with us the cultural impedimenta of our social class, our parents' lives, our bank balances, our sexual and emotional expectations, our whole biographies – all the bits and pieces of our unique existences. These considerations have limited our choice of partners before we have even got them into the bedroom. It was impossible for the Countess in Beaumarchais' *The Marriage of Figaro* to contemplate sleeping with her husband's valet, even though he was clearly the best man available; considerations of social class censored the possibility of sexual attraction between the Countess and Figaro before it could have begun to exist, and if this convention restricted the Countess's activities, it did not affect those of her husband; he happily plotted to seduce his valet's wife. If middle-class Catherine Earnshaw, in Emily Brontë's *Wuthering Heights*, wants to sleep with Heathcliff, who has the dubious class origins of the foundling, she must not only repress this desire but pay the socially sanctioned price of brain-fever and early death for even contemplating it. Our literature is full, as are our lives, of men and women, but especially women, who deny the reality of sexual attraction and of love because of considerations of class, religion, race and of gender itself.

Class dictates our choice of partners and our choice of positions. When fear, shame and prudery condemn the poor and the ignorant to copulate in the dark, it must be obvious that sexual sophistication is a by-product of education. The primal nakedness of lovers is a phenomenon of the middle-class in cold climates; in northern winters, naked lovers must be able to afford to heat their bedrooms. The taboos regulating the sight of bare flesh are further determined by wider cultural considerations. The Japanese bathed together in the nude for centuries, yet generations of Japanese lovers fucked in kimono, even in the humidity of summer, and did not even remove the combs from their chignons while they did so. And another complication – they did not appreciate the eroticism of the nude; yet they looked at one another's exposed genitalia with a tender readiness that still perturbs the West.

Control of fertility is a by-product of sexual education and of official legislation concerning the availability of cheap or free contraception. Even so, a poor woman may find herself sterilised when all she wanted was an abortion, her fertility taken out of her own control for good by social administrators who have decided that poverty is synonymous with stupidity and a poor woman cannot know her own mind.

The very magical privacy of the bed, the pentacle, may itself only be bought with money, and lack of privacy limits sexual sophistication, which may not be pursued in a room full of children.

Add to these socio-economic considerations the Judaeo-Christian heritage of shame, disgust and morality that stand between the initial urge and the first attainment of this most elementary assertion of the self and it is a wonder anyone in this culture ever learns to fuck at all.

Flesh comes to us out of history; so does the repression and taboo that governs our experience of flesh.

The nature of actual modes of sexual intercourse is determined by historical changes in less intimate human relations, just as the actual nature of men and women is capable of infinite modulations as social structures change. Our knowledge is determined by the social boundaries upon it; for example, Sade, the eighteenth-century lecher, knew that manipulation of the clitoris was the unique key to the female orgasm, but a hundred years later, Sigmund Freud, a Viennese intellectual, did not wish to believe that this grand simplicity was all there was to the business. It was socially permissible for an eighteenth-century aristocrat to sleep with more women than it was for a member of the nineteenth-century bourgeoisie, for one thing, and to retain a genuine curiosity about female sexuality whilst doing so, for another. Yet Freud, the psychoanalyst, can conceive of a far richer notion of human nature as a whole than Sade, the illiberal philosopher, is capable of; the social boundaries of knowledge expand in some areas and contract in others due to historical forces.

Sexuality, in short, is never expressed in a vacuum. Though the archaic sequence of human life – we are born, we fuck, we reproduce, we die – might seem to be universal experience, its universality is not its greatest significance. Since human beings have invented history, we have also invented those aspects of our lives that seem most im-mutable, or, rather, have invented the circumstances that determine their nature. Birth and death, the only absolute inescapables, are both absolutely determined by the social context in which they occur. There is no longer an inevitable relationship between fucking and reproducing and, indeed, neither fucking nor reproducing have been activities practiced by all men and women at all times, anyway; there has always been the option to abstain, whether it is exercised or not. Women experience sexuality and reproduction quite differently than men do; rich women are more in control of the sequence than poor women and so may actually enjoy fucking and childbirth, when poor women might find them both atrocious simply because they are poor and cannot afford comfort, privacy and paid help.

The notion of a universality of human experience is a confidence trick and the notion of a universality of female experience is a clever confidence trick.

Pornography, like marriage and the fictions of romantic love, assists the process of false universalising. Its excesses belong to that timeless, locationless area outside history, outside geography, where fascist art is born.

Nevertheless, there is no question of an aesthetics of pornography. It can never be art for art's sake. Honourably enough, it is always art with work to do.

Pornographic literature, the specific area of pornography with which we are going to deal, has several functions. On one level, and a level which should not be despised, it might serve as an instruction manual for the inexperienced. But our culture, with its metaphysics of sexuality, relegates the descriptions of the mechanics of sex to crude functionalism; in the sex textbook, intercourse also takes place in a void. So pornography's principal and most humanly significant function is that of arousing sexual excitement. It does this by ignoring the first function; it usually describes the sexual act not in explicit terms – for that might make it seem frightening – but in purely inviting terms.

The function of plot in a pornographic narrative is always the same. It exists purely to provide as many opportunities as possible for the sexual act to take place. There is no room here for tension or the unexpected. We know what is going to happen; that is why we are reading the book. Characterisation is necessarily limited by the formal necessity for the actors to fuck as frequently and as ingeniously as possible. But they do not do so because they are continually consumed by desire; the free expression of desire is as alien to pornography as it is to marriage. In pornography, both men and women fuck because to fuck is their raison d'etre. It is their life work.

It follows that prostitutes are favourite heroines of the pornographic writer, though the economic aspects of a prostitute's activity, which is her own main concern in the real world, will be dealt with only lightly. Her labour is her own private business. Work, in this context, is *really* dirty work; it is unmentionable. Even unspeakable. And we may not talk about it because it reintroduces the question of the world. In this privatised universe pleasure is the only work; work itself is unmentionable. To concentrate on the prostitute's trade *as* trade would introduce too much reality into a scheme that is first and foremost one of libidinous fantasy, and pornographic writers, in general, are not concerned with extending the genre in which they work to include a wider view of the world. This is because pornography is the orphan little sister of the arts; its functionalism renders it suspect, more applied art than fine art, and so its very creators rarely take it seriously.

Fine art, that exists for itself alone, is art in a final state of impotence. If nobody, including the artist, acknowledges art as a means of *knowing* the world, then art is relegated to a kind of rumpus room of the mind and the irresponsibility of the artist and the irrelevance of art to actual living becomes part and parcel of the practice of art. Nevertheless, pornographic writing retains this in common with all literature – that it turns the flesh into word. This is the real transformation the text performs upon libidinous fantasy.

The verbal structure is in itself reassuring. We know we

are not dealing with real flesh or anything like it, but with a cunningly articulated verbal simulacrum which has the power to arouse, but not, in itself, to assuage desire. At this point, the reader, the consumer, enters the picture; reflecting the social dominance which affords him the opportunity to purchase the flesh of other people as if it were meat, the reader or consumer of pornography is usually a man who subscribes to a particular social fiction of manliness. His belief in this fiction prevents him from realising that, when he picks up a dirty book, he engages in a game with his own desire and with his own solitude, both of which he endlessly titillates but never openly confronts.

Therefore a cerebral insatiability, unacknowledged yet implicit, is a characteristic of pornography, which always throws the reader back on his own resources, since it convinces him of the impotence of his desire that the book cannot in itself assuage, at the same time as he solaces that loneliness through the medium of the fantasy extracted from the fiction.

The one-to-one relation of the reader with the book is never more apparent than in the reading of a pornographic novel, since it is virtually impossible to forget oneself in relation to the text. In pornographic literature, the text has a gap left in it on purpose so that the reader may, in imagination, step inside it. But the activity the text describes, into which the reader enters, is not a whole world into which the reader is absorbed and, as they say, 'taken out of himself'. It is one basic activity extracted from the world in its totality in such a way that the text constantly reminds the reader of his own troubling self, his own reality – and the limitations of that reality since, however much he wants to fuck the willing women or men in his story, he cannot do so but must be content with some form of substitute activity. (The fictional maleness of the pornography consumer encompasses the butch hero of homosexual pornography; it is a *notion* of masculinity unrelated to practice.)

The privacy of the reader is invaded by his own desires, which reach out towards the world beyond the book he is reading. Yet they are short-circuited by the fantastic nature of the gratification promised by the text, which denies to flesh all its intransigence, indeed its sexed quality, since sexuality is a quality made manifest in being, and pornography can only allow its phantoms to exist in the moment of sexual excitation; they cannot engage in the wide range of activity in the real world in which sexual performance is not the supreme business of all people at all times.

Yet the gripping nature of pornography, its directly frontal assault upon the senses of the reader, its straightforward engagement of him at a non-intellectual level, its *sensationalism*, suggest the methodology of propaganda. Indeed, pornography is basically propaganda for fucking, an activity, one would have thought, that did not need much advertising in itself, because most people want to do it as soon as they know how.

The denial of the social fact of sexuality in pornography is made explicit in its audience. Produced in the main by men for an all-male clientele, suggesting certain analogies with a male brothel, access to pornography is usually denied to women at any level, often on the specious grounds that women do not find descriptions of the sexual act erotically stimulating. Yet if pornography is produced by men for a male audience, it is exclusively concerned with relations between the sexes and even the specialised area of homosexual pornography divides its actors into sexual types who might roughly be defined as 'masculine' and 'feminine'. So all pornography suffers the methodological defects of a manual of navigation written by and for landlubbers.

Many pornographic novels are written in the first person as if by a woman, or use a woman as the focus of the narrative; but this device only reinforces the male orientation of the fiction. John Cleland's *Fanny Hill* and the anonymous *The Story of O*, both classics of the genre, appear in this way to describe a woman's mind through the fiction of her sexuality. This technique ensures that the gap left in the text is of just the right size for the reader to insert his prick into, the exact dimensions, in fact, of Fanny's vagina or of O's anus. Pornography engages the reader in a most intimate fashion before it leaves him to his own resources. This gap in the text may also be just the size of the anus or mouth of a young man, subsuming him, too, to this class that is most present in its absence, the invisible recipients of the pornographic tribute, the mental masturbatory objects.

So pornography reinforces the false universals of sexual archetypes because it denies, or doesn't have time for, or can't find room for, or, because of its underlying ideology, ignores, the social context in which sexual activity takes place, that modifies the very nature of that activity. Therefore pornography must always have the false simplicity of fable; the abstraction of the flesh involves the mystification of the flesh. As it reduces the actors in the sexual drama to instruments of pure function, so the pursuit of pleasure becomes in itself a metaphysical quest. The pornographer, in spite of himself, becomes a metaphysician when he states that the friction of penis in orifice is the supreme matter of the world, for which the world is well lost; as he says so, the world vanishes.

Pornography, like satire, has an inbuilt reactionary mechanism. Its effect depends on the notion that the nature of man is invariable and cannot be modified by changes in his social institutions. The primordial itch in the groin existed before multinational business corporations and the nuclear family and will outlast them just as it illicitly dominates them. The disruptiveness of sexuality, its inability to be contained, the overflowing of the cauldron of id – these are basic invariables of sexuality, opines the pornographer, and in itself pornography is a satire on human pretensions. The judge conceals his erection beneath his robes of office as he passes judgement on the whore. The cabinet minister slips away from his office early to visit the call girl. The public executioner ejaculates as the neck of his victim snaps. And we laugh wryly at the omnipotence of Old Adam, how he will always, somehow or other, get his way; and we do ourselves and Old Adam the grossest injustice when we grant him so much power, when we reduce sexuality to the status of lowest common denominator without asking ourselves what preconceptions make us think it should be so.

Since sexuality is as much a social fact as it is a human one, it will therefore change its nature according to changes in social conditions. If we could restore the context of the world to the embraces of these shadows then, perhaps, we could utilise their activities to obtain a fresh perception of the world and, in some sense, transform it. The sexual act in pornography exists as a metaphor for what people do to one another, often in the cruellest sense; but the present business of the pornographer is to suppress the metaphor as much as he can and leave us with a handful of empty words.

Pornographic pictures, movies and narrative fiction are the pure forms of sexual fiction, of the fiction *of* sex, where this operation of alienation takes place most visibly. But all art which contains elements of eroticism (eroticism, the pornography of the elite) contains the possibility of the same methodology – that is, writing that can 'pull' a reader just as a woman 'pulls' a man or a man 'pulls' a woman.

And all such literature has the potential to force the reader to reassess his relation to his own sexuality, which is to say to his own primary being, through the mediation of the image or the text. This is true for women also, perhaps especially so, as soon as we realise the way pornography reinforces the archetypes of her negativity and that it does so simply because most pornography remains in the service of the status quo. And that is because its elementary metaphysic gets in the way of real life and prevents us seeing real life. If the world has been lost, the world may not be reassessed. Libidinous fantasy in a vacuum is the purest, but most affectless, form of day-dreaming. So pornography in general serves to defuse the explosive potential of all sexuality and that is the main reason why it is made by and addressed to the politically dominant minority in the world, as an instrument of repression, not only of women, but of men too. Pornography keeps sex in its place. that is, under the carpet. That is, outside everyday human intercourse.

The sexuality of the blue movie queen, contained by her social subservience, exhibits no menace. Linda Lovelace does not believe in the Women's Liberation Movement; how could she? Fanny Hill gladly gives up the dominant role of mistress for the subservient role of wife and hands to her Charles all her hard-earned money too, which is an infinitely more far-reaching gesture of submission than that of accepting his sexual mastery and opting for domestic monogamy and motherhood under his exclusive economic sanction. Fanny knows in her heart that her Charles is really her last, most efficient, pimp. O, less complex because her economic means of support are not explored as closely as Cleland explores Fanny's, is more content simply to rejoice in her chains, a model for all women.

It is fair to say that, when pornography serves – as with very rare exceptions it always does – to reinforce the prevailing system of values and ideas in a given society, it is tolerated; and when it does not, it is banned. (This already suggests there are more reasons than those of public decency for the banning of the work of Sade for almost two hundred years; only at the time of the French Revolution and at the present day have his books been available to the general public.) Therefore an increase of pornography on the market, within the purchasing capacity of the common man, and especially the beginning of a type of pornography modelled on that provided for the male consumer but directed at women, does not mean an increase in sexual licence, with the reappraisal of social mores such licence, if it is real, necessitates. It might only indicate a more liberal attitude to masturbation, rather than to fucking, and reinforce a sollipsistic concentration on the relationship with the self, which is a fantasy one at the best of times.

When pornography abandons its quality of existential solitude and moves out of the kitsch area of timeless, placeless fantasy and into the real world, then it loses its function of safety valve. It begins to comment on real relations in the real world. Therefore, the more pornographic writing aquires the techniques of real literature, of real art, the more deeply subversive it is likely to be in that the more likely it is to affect the reader's perceptions of the world. The text that had heretofore opened up creamily to him, in a dream, will gather itself together and harshly expel him into the anguish of actuality.

There is a liberal theory that art disinfects eroticism of its latent subversiveness, and pornography that is also art loses its shock and its magnetism, becomes 'safe'. The truth of this is that once pornography is labelled 'art' or 'literature' it is stamped with the approval of an elitist culture and many ordinary people will avoid it on principle, out of a fear of being bored. But the more the literary arts of plotting and characterisation are used to shape the material of pornography, the more the pornographer himself is faced with the moral contradictions inherent in real sexual encounters. He will find himself in a dilemma; to opt for the world or to opt for the wet dream?

Out of this dilemma, the moral pornographer might be born.

The moral pornographer would be an artist who uses pornographic material as part of the acceptance of the logic of a world of absolute sexual licence for all the genders, and projects a model of the way such a world might work. A moral pornographer might use pornography as a critique of current relations between the sexes. His business would be the total demystification of the flesh and the subsequent revelation, through the infinite modulations of the sexual act, of the real relations of man and his kind. Such a pornographer would not be the enemy of women, perhaps because he might begin to penetrate to the heart of the contempt for women that distorts our culture even as he entered the realms of true obscenity as he describes it.

But the pornographer's more usual business is to assert that the function of flesh is pure pleasure, which is itself a mystification of a function a great deal more complex, apart from raising the question of the nature of pleasure itself. However, the nature of pleasure is not one with which the pornographer often concerns himself; for him, sexual pleasure is a given fact, a necessary concomitant of the juxtaposition of bodies.

It is at this point that he converts the sexed woman, living, breathing, troubling, into a desexed hole and the breathing, living, troubling man into nothing but a probe; pornography becomes a form of pastoral, sex an engaging and decorative activity that may be performed without pain, soil, sweat or effect, and its iconography a very suitable subject for informal murals in public places. If, that is, the simplest descriptions of sex did not also rouse such complex reactions.

And that is because sexual relations between men and women always render explicit the nature of social relations in the society in which they take place and, if described explicitly, will form a critique of those relations, even if that is not and never has been the intention of the pornographer.

So, whatever the surface falsity of pornography, it is impossible for it to fail to reveal sexual reality at an unconscious level, and this reality may be very unpleasant indeed, a world away from official reality.

A male-dominated society produces a pornography of universal female aquiescence. Or, most delicious titillation, of compensatory but spurious female dominance. Miss Stern with her rods and whips, Our Lady of Pain in her leather visor and her boots with sharp, castratory heels, is a true fantasy, a distorted version of the old saying 'The hand that rocks the cradle rules the world.' This whip hand rocks

the cradle in which her customer dreams but it does nothing
else. Miss Stern's dominance exists only in the bedroom.
She may utilise apparatus that invokes heaven, hell and
purgatory for her client, she may utterly ravage his body,
martyrise him, shit on him, piss on him, but her cruelty is
only the manifestation of the victim or patient's guilt before
the fact of his own sexuality, of which he is ashamed. She is
not cruel for her own sake, or for her own gratification. She
is most truly subservient when most apparently dominant;
Miss Stern and her pretended victim have established a
mutually degrading pact between them and she in her weird
garb is mutilated more savagely by the erotic violence she
perpetrates than he by the pain he undergoes, since his pain
is in the nature of a holiday from his life, and her cruelty an
economic fact of her real life, so much hard work. You can
describe their complicity in a pornographic novel but to
relate it to her mortgage, her maid's salary and her laundry
bills is to use the propaganda technique of pornography to
express a view of the world, which deviates from the notion
that all this takes place in a kindergarten of soiled innocence. A kindergarten? Only small children, in our
society, do not need to work.

The pornographer who consciously utilises the propaganda, the 'grabbing' effect of pornography to express
a view of the world that transcends this kind of innocence
will very soon find himself in deep political water for he will
begin to find himself describing the real conditions of the
world in terms of sexual encounters, or even find that the
real nature of these encounters illuminates the world itself;
the world turns into a gigantic brothel, the area of our lives
where we believed we possessed most freedom is seen as the
most ritually circumscribed.

Nothing exercises such power over the imagination as the
nature of sexual relationships, and the pornographer has it
in his power to become a terrorist of the imagination, a
sexual guerilla whose purpose is to overturn our most basic
notions of these relations, to reinstitute sexuality as a

primary mode of being rather than a specialised area of vacation from being and to show that the everyday meetings in the marriage bed are parodies of their own pretensions, that the freest unions may contain the seeds of the worst exploitation. Sade became a terrorist of the imagination in this way, turning the unacknowledged truths of the encounters of sexuality into a cruel festival at which women are the prime sacrificial victims when they are not the ritual murderesses themselves, the ewe lamb and Miss Stern together, alike only in that they always remain under the constant surveillance of the other half of mankind.

The pornographer as terrorist may not think of himself as a friend of women; that may be the last thing on his mind. But he will always be our unconscious ally because he begins to approach some kind of emblematic truth, whereas the lackey pornographer, like the devious fellows who write love stories for women's magazines, that softest of all forms of pornography, can only do harm. But soon, however permissive censorship may be, he will invade the area in which censorship operates most defensibly, that of erotic violence.

This area of taboo remains theoretically inviolate even though violence, for its own sake, between men, escapes censorship altogether. The machine-gun of the gangster can rake as many innocent victims as the writer or film-maker pleases, the policeman can blast as many wrongdoers to extinction as serves to demonstrate the superiority of his institutions. Novels and movies about warfare use violent death, woundings and mutilations as a form of decoration, butch embroidery upon a male surface. Violence, the convulsive form of the active, male principle, is a matter for men, whose sex gives them the right to inflict pain as a sign of mastery and the masters have the right to wound one another because that only makes us fear them more, that they can give and receive pain like the lords of creation. But to show, in art, erotic violence committed by men upon women cuts too near the bone, and will be condemned out of hand.

Perhaps it reveals too clearly that violence has always been the method by which institutions demonstrate their superiority. It can become too vicious a reminder of the mutilations our society inflicts upon women and the guilt that exacerbates this savagery. It suggests, furthermore, that male political dominance might be less a matter of moral superiority than of crude brute force and this would remove a degree of glamour from the dominance itself.

There is more to it than that, though. The whippings, the beatings, the gougings, the stabbings of erotic violence reawaken the memory of the social fiction of the female wound, the bleeding scar left by her castration, which is a psychic fiction as deeply at the heart of Western culture as the myth of Oedipus, to which it is related in the complex dialectic of imagination and reality that produces culture. Female castration is an imaginary fact that pervades the whole of men's attitude towards women and our attitude to ourselves, that transforms women from human beings into wounded creatures who were born to bleed.

It is a great shame we can forbid these bleedings in art but not in life, for the beatings, the rapes and the woundings take place in a privacy beyond the reach of official censorship. It is also in private that the unacknowledged psychological mutilations performed in the name of love take place.

Sade is the connoisseur of these mutilations. He is an extreme writer and he describes a society and a system of social relations *in extremis*, those of the last years of the ancien régime in France. The stories of Justine and Juliette are set at a time immediately preceding the French Revolution. *The Hundred and Twenty Days at Sodom* is set in the seventeenth century. Its heroes have financed their murderous holiday by vast profits made from the Thirty Years War. *Philosophy in the Boudoir* takes place sometime between 1789 and 1793; outside the room in which the action of this dramatic interlude takes place, they are selling revolutionary pamphlets on the steps of the Palace of

Equality but the actors in the boudoir are aristocrats, members of a privileged class. In all this fiction, Sade is working primarily in the mode of pornography; he utilised this mode to make a particularly wounding satire on mankind, and the historical time in which the novels are set is essential to the satire.

But Sade is unusual amongst both satirists and pornographers, not only because he goes further than most satirists and pornographers, but because he is capable of believing, even if only intermittently, that it is possible to radically transform society and, with it, human nature, so that the Old Adam, exemplified in God, the King and the Law, the trifold masculine symbolism of authority, will take his final departure from amongst us. Only then will freedom be possible; until then, the freedom of one class, or sex, or individual necessitates the unfreedom of others.

But his work as a pornographer is more descriptive and diagnostic than proscriptive and prophetic. He creates, not an artificial paradise of gratified sexuality but a model of hell, in which the gratification of sexuality involves the infliction and the tolerance of extreme pain. He describes sexual relations in the context of an unfree society as the expression of pure tyranny, usually by men upon women, sometimes by men upon men, sometimes by women upon men and other women; the one constant to all Sade's monstrous orgies is that the whip hand is always the hand with the real political power and the victim is a person who has little or no power at all, or has had it stripped from him. In this schema, male means tyrannous and female means martyrised, no matter what the official genders of the male and female beings are.

He is uncommon amongst pornographers in that he rarely, if ever, makes sexual activity seem immediately attractive as such. Sade has a curious ability to render every aspect of sexuality suspect, so that we see how the chaste kiss of the sentimental lover differs only in degree from the vampirish love-bite that draws blood, we understand that a disinterested caress is only quantitatively different from a disinterested flogging. For Sade, all tenderness is false, a deceit, a trap; all pleasure contains within itself the seeds of atrocities; all beds are minefields. So the virtuous Justine is condemned to spend a life in which there is not one single moment of enjoyment; only in this way can she retain her virtue. Whereas the wicked Juliette, her sister and antithesis, dehumanises herself completely in the pursuit of pleasure.

The simple perversions, available in any brothel, documented in the first book of *The Hundred and Twenty Days at Sodom*, will insatiably elaborate, will never suffice in themselves, will culminate in the complex and deathly rites of the last book, which concludes in a perfectly material hell. The final passion recounted by the sexual lexicographer, Madame Desgranges, is called the Hell-game; its inventor, assisted by torturers disguised as demons, himself pretends to be the devil.

In the perpetual solitude of their continually refined perversions, in an absolute egotism, Sade's libertines regulate and maintain a society external to them, where the institutions of which they are the embodiment are also perversions.

These libertines are great aristocrats, landowners, bankers, judges, archbishops, popes and certain women who have become very rich through prostitution, speculation, murder and usury. They have the tragic style and the infernal loquacity of the damned; and they have no inner life, no introspection. Their actions sum them up completely. They are in exile from the world in their abominable privilege, at the same time as they control the world.

Sade's heroines, those who become libertines, accept damnation, by which I mean this exile from human life, as a necessary fact of life. This is the nature of the libertine. They model themselves upon libertine men, though libertinage is a condition that all the sexes may aspire to. So Sade creates a museum of woman-monsters. He cuts up the bodies of women and reassembles them in the shapes of his own delirium. He renews all the ancient wounds, every one, and makes them bleed again as if they will never stop bleeding.

From time to time, he leaves off satire long enough to posit a world in which nobody need bleed. But only a violent transformation of this world and a fresh start in an absolutely egalitarian society would make this possible. Nevertheless, such a transformation might be possible; at this point, Sade becomes a Utopian. His Utopianism, however, takes the form of Kafka's: 'There *is* hope – but not for us.' The title of the pamphlet describing the Sadeian Utopia inserted in *Philosophy in the Boudoir* is: *Yet Another Effort, Frenchmen, If You Would Become Republicans*. It is possible, but improbable, that effort will be made; perhaps those who make it will have hope.

Sade describes the condition of women in the genre of the pornography of sexual violence but believed it would only be through the medium of sexual violence that women might heal themselves of their socially inflicted scars, in a praxis of destruction and sacrilege. He cites the flesh as existential verification in itself, in a rewriting of the Cartesian cogito: '*I fuck therefore I am*'. From this axiom, he constructs a diabolical lyricism of fuckery, since the acting-out of a total sexuality in a repressive society turns all eroticism into violence, makes of sexuality itself a permanent negation. Fucking, says Sade, is the basis of all human relationships but the activity parodies all human relations because of the nature of the society that creates and maintains those relationships.

He enlarges the relation between activity and passivity in the sexual act to include tyranny and the acceptance of physical and political oppression. The great men in his novels, the statesmen, the princes, the popes, are the cruellest by far and their sexual voracity is a kind of pure destructiveness; they would like to fuck the world and fucking, for them, is the enforcement of annihilation. Their embraces strangle, their orgasms appear to detonate their partners. But his great women, Juliette, Clairwil, the Princess Borghese, Catherine the Great of Russia, Charlotte of Naples, are even more cruel still since, once they have tasted power, once they know how to use their sexuality as an instrument of aggression, they use it to extract vengeance for the humiliations they were forced to endure as the passive objects of the sexual energy of others.

A free woman in an unfree society will be a monster. Her freedom will be a condition of personal privilege that deprives those on which she exercises it of her own freedom. The most extreme kind of this deprivation is murder. These women murder.

The sexual behaviour of these women, like that of their men, is a mirror of their inhumanity, a magnified relation of the ambivalence of the word 'to fuck', in its twinned meanings of sexual intercourse and despoliation: 'a fuck-up', 'to fuck something up', 'he's fucked'.

Women do not normally fuck in the active sense. They are fucked in the passive tense and hence automatically fucked-up, done over, undone. Whatever else he says or does not say, Sade declares himself unequivocally for the right of women to fuck – as if the period in which women fuck agressively, tyrannously and cruelly will be a necessary stage in the development of a general human consciousness of the nature of fucking; that if it is not egalitarian, it is unjust. Sade does not suggest this process as such; but he urges women to fuck as actively as they are able, so that powered by their enormous and hitherto untapped sexual energy they will then be able to fuck their way into history and, in doing so, change it.

One of Sade's singularities is that he offers an absolutely sexualised view of the world, a sexualisation that permeates everything, much as his atheism does and, since he is not a religious man but a political man, he treats the facts of female sexuality not as a moral dilemma but as a political reality.

In fact, he treats all sexuality as a political reality and

that is inevitable, because his own sexuality brought him directly against the law. He spent the greater part of his adult life in confinement because his own sexual tastes overrode his socialisation; his perversion has entered the dictionary under his own name.

Although he documented his sexual fantasies with an unequalled diligence, and these fantasies delight in the grisliest tortures (even if, in the context of his fictions, he creates an inverted ethical superstructure to legitimise these cruelties) his own sexual practice in life remains relatively obscure. From the evidence of the two court cases in which he was involved, the affair of Rose Keller in 1768 and the charges made against him by a group of Marseilles prostitutes in 1772, he seems to have enjoyed both giving and receiving whippings; voyeurism; anal intercourse, both active and passive; and the presence of an audience at these activities. These are not particularly unusual sexual preferences, though they are more common as fantasies, and are always very expensive if purchased. When they take place in private, the law usually ignores them even when they are against the law, just as it turns a blind eye to wife beating and recreational bondage. Sade, however, seems to have been incapable of keeping his vices private, as if he was aware of their exemplary nature and, perhaps, since the notion of sin, of transgression, was essential to his idea of pleasure, which is always intellectual, never sensual, he may have needed to invoke the punishment of which he consciously denied the validity before he could feel the act itself had been accomplished.

The Rose Keller affair in particular has a curious quality of theatre, of the acting-out of a parable of sex and money. This woman, the thirty-six-year-old widow of a pastry cook, was begging in Paris on Easter Sunday, a day of special significance to the anti-clerical Sade; a day that cried out to be desecrated. According to the deposition she later gave the police, a gentleman, well-dressed, even handsome, approached her in a public square and suggested she might

like to earn herself a crown. When she concurred, he took her
to a room in a private house; whipped her; gave her food and
offered her money, both of which she refused. Then he
locked her in the room but she soon escaped through the
window and went to tell her tale. Sade admitted freely that
he had indeed hired her and whipped her but he said that
Rose Keller had known perfectly well he did not intend her
to sweep his house, as she claimed, and they had agreed
beforehand she would go off with him for a session of
debauchery. The matter was settled out of court. Rose
Keller was persuaded to withdraw her charge on a payment
of an enormous indemnity of two thousand four hundred
francs and expenses of seven louis d'or for dressings and
ointments for her wounds.

The affair enchants me. It has the completeness and the
lucidity of a script by Brecht. A woman of the third estate, a
beggar, the poorest of the poor, turns the very vices of the
rich into weapons to wound them with. In the fictions he is
going to write, Sade will make La Dubois, the brigand chief,
say that the callousness of the rich justifies the crimes of
the poor; Rose Keller, who expected, perhaps, to have sex
with the Marquis but for whom the whip came as a
gratuitous, unexpected and unwelcome surprise, turns her
hand to blackmail and who can blame her? An ironic
triumph for the beggar woman; the victim turned victor.

Sade himself, at this point, is by no means the plain
Citizen Sade he became after the French Revolution. He is
Donatien-Alphonse-Francois, Marquis de Sade, Seigneur of
Saumane and of La Coste, with other lands in Bresse,
Bugey, Valromey and Gex – he owns most of Provence, with
sizeable chunks of other parts of France and, if the rents from
his tenants are not always forthcoming, he remains good for
credit in spite of his extravagances for, besides, he has a rich
wife. His title of nobility dates from the twelfth century; he
is related to the royal family; there is nothing in his life that
does not convince him the world owes him a living and that
he can do as he pleases, except the protests of a beggar

woman who objected to being whipped even though he gave her bread and beef and offered her money. Sade is not yet Sade; he is the Marquis. He is the very type of aristocrat who provoked the vengeance of the revolutionaries.

Four years later, he took a box of aniseed balls flavoured with cantharides with him to a brothel in Marseilles and fed the girls with them, to make them fart, which he enjoyed. There was a good deal of whipping and his valet, who accompanied him, buggered him but the girls, cannily, refused to be buggered because they knew they could get into trouble for it. Later that day, the girls who had eaten the sweets began to vomit. One girl, Marguerite Coste, thought she had been poisoned and went to the magistrate.

The public prosecutor issued warrants for the arrest of the Marquis and his valet, Latour, but they had fled from the Sade ancestral mansion, La Coste, some miles from Avignon. They were tried in absentia and found guilty of 'poisoning and sodomy', although the girls were all quite well by now. In absentia, both men were burned in effigy at Aix-en-Provence. Sodomy was at that time a capital crime in France.

If a brothel is a fine place in which to learn misogyny, it is inevitable that Sade, the frequenter of brothels, treated his wife, the unfortunate Renée Pélagie de Montreuil, abominably, teasing her, ignoring her, impregnating her, forcing her to pimp for him and to take part in his orgies, persuading her to pay off the outraged fathers whose daughters he had seduced, scandalously running off with her own sister and, when his adventures ended in prison, further tormenting her with ingenious jealousies. But their married life began badly; without their own consent. Renée Pélagie was a rich bourgeois and Sade an aristocrat with a perennial problem of funding his extravagances. Their two families arranged the match as a business contract, Renée Pélagie's expectations in exchange for Sade's title, although it seems both knew quite well that Sade had already engaged himself to another woman at the time of the betrothal. Nevertheless, they were married and Renée Pélagie did not leave him until 1790, after twenty-seven years of a marriage the rigours of which must have been eased by Sade's lengthy imprisonment.

The same year that Renée Pélagie finally abandoned him, Sade met a young actress, Constance Quesnet, whose husband, a draper, had recently deserted her and her young son. To complicate the question of his misogyny, Sade remained devoted to this young woman from their meeting until his death some twenty years later, although they were very poor and often separated by force of circumstance and the need to earn a living. He nicknamed this young woman 'Sensitivity' and dedicated *Justine* to her, perhaps an ambivalent gesture. Yet it is not so much sexual abnormality and ambivalence towards women that are the keys to Sade's bleak imaginary universe; it is the combination of sexual obsession – for he was undoubtedly obsessed with sex to a most unusual degree – and imprisonment.

He first went to prison in 1772, at the age of thirty two, for five months. He had fled the Marseilles affair to Chambery, in Savoy, then under the control of the King of Sardinia. As if to extract the final ounce of scandal and retribution from the notorious business, he had chosen to elope with his sister-in-law, Anne de Launay – thus, according to the Catholic church, committing incest. Her outraged mother, his mother-in-law, personally requested the King of Sardinia for his arrest and he was sent to the Fortress of Miolans, to escape shortly afterwards. This period of freedom lasted for five years. In June 1778, he returned to Aix-en-Provence for a retrial of the Marseilles poisoning charges. Since the poisoned women had long ago recovered and were now all alive and well, the charge of poisoning was dropped; the accusation of sodomy was withdrawn by the girls. The charge was altered to one of 'debauchery and excessive licentiousness', for which Sade received a public admonition; was fined; and ordered to keep away from Marseilles for three years. In fact, he spent all those years and many more in prison, under a *lettre de cachet* obtained by Madame de Montreil which meant he could be kept in preventive detention, without trial, for an indefinite time. In Sade's case, this was thirteen years.

Except for a charge of moderatism brought against him under the Terror because of his opposition to the death penalty, he was never again publicly charged with any further offence. Rather than his misdeeds, it seems it was the ferocity of his imagination that led to his confinement. His was a peculiarly modern fate, to be imprisoned without trial for crimes that existed primarily in the mind. It is not surprising that *Justine*, with its dominant images of the trial and the castle, recalls Kafka, nor that it arrives to us out of the confinement of its creator at the beginning of the modern period of which it is one of the seminal, if forbidden, books. Sadism, suggests Michel Foucault, is not a sexual perversion but a cultural fact; the consciousness of the 'limitless presumption of the appetite'. Sade's work, with its compulsive attraction for the delinquent imagination of the romantics, has been instrumental in shaping aspects of the modern sensibility; its paranoia, its despair, its sexual terrors, its omnivorous egocentricity, its tolerance of massacre, holocaust, annihilation.

It was prison, the experience of oppression, that transformed the rake into the philosopher, the man of the Age of Reason into the prophet of the age of dissolution, of our own time, the time of the assassins. Deprived of the fact of flesh, he concentrated his notable sexual energy on a curious task of sublimation, a project that involved simultaneously creating and destroying that which he could no longer possess, the flesh, the world, love, in a desolate charnel house of the imagination. It is as well to remember that, when given the opportunity of carrying out this project in practice during the Reign of Terror, he rejected it, at the price of further confinement.

Although Sade's sexual practices would hardly be

punished so severely today (and it was punishment that inflamed his sexual imagination to the grossest extent) his sexual imagination would always be of a nature to violate any law that governed any society that retained the notions of crime and punishment. This would be especially true of those societies that most rigorously practice punitive justice, that habitually utilise legislative murder, that is, capital punishment, flogging, mutilation and torture as methods of punishment and intimidation towards their members. For these legal crimes to be described by an honest pervert, or a moral pornographer, as 'pleasure' is to let the cat out of the bag; if Sade is to be castigated for tastes he exercised only in the privacy of his mind or with a few well-paid auxiliaries, then the hanging judge, the birching magistrate, the military torturer with his hoods and his electrodes, the flogging schoolmaster, the brutal husband must also be acknowledged as perverts to whom, in our own criminal folly, we have given a licence to practice upon the general public. Since Sade had no such licence, and, indeed, deplored the fact that licences were granted, his imagination took sexual violence to an extreme that may, in a human being, only be accompanied by an extreme of misanthropy, self-disgust and despair.

His solitude is the perpetual companion and daily horror of the prisoner, whose final place of confinement is the self. 'When I have inspired universal disgust and horror, then I will have conquered solitude', said Baudelaire, who read Sade again and again. Sade projects this diabolic solitude as an absolute egoism; that is the result of thirteen years solitary meditation on the world. The desires of his imaginary libertines may no longer be satisfied by flesh; flesh becomes an elaborate metaphor for sexual abuse. World, flesh and the devil fuse; when an atheist casts a cool eye on the world, he must always find Satan a more likely hypothesis as ruling principle than a Saviour. Criminality may present itself as a kind of saintly self-mastery, an absolute rejection of hypocrisy. Sade directly influenced

Baudelaire; he is also the spiritual ancestor of Genet. Swift
saw mankind rolling in a welter of shit, as Sade does, but
Sade's satire upon man is far blacker and more infernal than
Swift's – for Sade, mankind doesn't roll in shit because
mankind is disgusting, but because mankind has over-
weening aspirations to the superhuman. Of his own contemporaries, he has most in common with the painter Goya;
of our contemporaries, the polymorphous perversity and the
intense isolation of his characters recall William Burroughs.
If Sade is the last, bleak, disillusioned voice of the
Enlightenment, he is the avatar of the nihilism of the late
twentieth century. His overt misogyny is a single strand in
a total revulsion against a mankind of whom, unlike Swift,
he cannot delude himself he is not a member.

During the thirteen years in prison, he compiled that
immense taxonomy of all the inhumane functions of the
sexuality of what the sexual radical, Norman O. Brown,
calls 'the immortal child within us', to which Sade gave the
title *The Hundred and Twenty Days at Sodom*. He rolled up
the manuscript and hid it in a hole in the wall of his cell in
the Bastille, where he was now lodged, shortly before July 2
1789. On this day, he was observed shouting through his
window that the prisoners in the Bastille were having their
throats cut and he should be released; he judged, accurately,
that one at least of the cities of the plain was shortly about
to suffer a mortal shock. Sade was immediately transferred
from the Bastille to the Asylum of Charenton, a hospital for
madmen and epileptics, a place to which he would return, to
prevent him from further inciting the crowd to storm the
prison. They stormed it of their own accord on July 14, the
day on which modern history begins.

He was released from Charenton nine months later, as
poor as he had once been rich, and signed away his titles to
become Citizen Sade. He took up a modest bureaucratic role
in the revolutionary government of Paris. Briefly, during
the Terror, he acted as a judge and went to prison again for
lenience but they soon let him out. It was Napoleon who

sent him to prison for the last time, after they found the manuscript copy of *Justine* in Sade's own hand at his publishers. Sade had said he would gladly be a martyr for atheism, if any were needed; to be a martyr for pornography may have struck him as a less glorious fate. Anyway, he always strenuously denied he had written *Justine* and, indeed, all the works by which he has acquired such lasting if scabrous fame.

Sade was transferred speedily from his last prison to the Asylum of Charenton, again, in 1803. His condition was diagnosed as 'sexual dementia', a diagnosis as therapeutically dubious then as now. Nobody considered him mad in everyday terms; nevertheless, he must be put away for the protection of society and there he stayed, in relative comfort, surrounded by books, accompanied by Madame Quesnet, his mistress, posing as his daughter, until he died in 1814. The biographical facts of Sade's life are fully recounted in Gilbert Lely's monumental biography; I don't propose to deal with them any more fully. It was a curious life and its intellectual terms of reference may be found among the books included in the inventory of his effects at Charenton; they include the complete works of Jean-Jacques Rousseau, *The Princess of Cleves*, *Don Quixote* and the 1785 edition of Voltaire in eighty-nine volumes. It is of this world of reason that Sade produces a critique in the guise of a pornographic vision; his heroine, the terrible Juliette, can say, as a hero of Voltaire might: 'I have no light to guide me but my reason.' Yet rationality without humanism founders on itself. On the title page of *Les Liaisons Dangereuses*, Laclos put a quotation from Rousseau's *La Nouvelle Heloise:* 'I have seen the manners of my time and I have published these letters.' Sade might have said that, of the novel *La Nouvelle Justine*, whose title teasingly echoes that of Rousseau's. His fiction blends the picaresque narrative of the late sixteenth and early seventeenth century with the fictions of moral critique of his own youth, and adds to them the sharp outlines of the nightmare.

Sade. An unusual man: aristocrat; atheist; sodomite; novelist; old lag; dramatist; flagellant; glutton; master, as André Breton was the first to point out in his *Anthologie de L'Humeur Noir*, of black humour. This man who was capable of inventing the most atrocious massacres felt sick when he smelt the blood from the guillotine. This curious and self-contradictory person placed pornography at the service of the French Revolution in the shape of the lengthy, picaresque double novel: *The Adventures of Justine and of Juliette, Her Sister*, and the three different versions of *Justine*. The manuscript of *The Hundred and Twenty Days at Sodom* was lost, to Sade's great regret, and not discovered again until the twentieth century. *Philosophy in the Boudoir* was written in 1795. The rest of his pornographic writing has been lost or destroyed. His voluminous other writings, plays, moral tales, treatises, political pamphlets, have been largely ignored by commentators; it is on the above books that Sade's reputation as a pornographer rests.

He was unusual in his period for claiming rights of free sexuality for women, and in installing women as beings of power in his imaginary worlds. This sets him apart from all other pornographers at all times and most other writers of his period.

In the looking-glass of Sade's misanthropy, women may see themselves as they have been and it is an uncomfortable sight. He offers an extraordinary variety of male fantasies about women and, because of the equivocal nature of his own sexual response, a number of startling insights. His misanthropy bred a hatred of the mothering function that led him to demystify the most sanctified aspects of women and if he invented women who suffered, he also invented women who caused suffering. The hole the pornographer Sade leaves in his text is just sufficient for a flaying; for a castration. It is a hole large enough for women to see themselves as if the fringed hole of graffiti were a spyhole into territory that had been forbidden them.

This book, which takes as its starting point of cultural exploration the wealth of philosophically pornographic material about women that Sade provides, is an exercise of the lateral imagination. Sade remains a monstrous and daunting cultural edifice; yet I would like to think that he put pornography in the service of women, or, perhaps, allowed it to be invaded by an ideology not inimical to women. And give the old monster his due; let us introduce him with an exhilarating burst of rhetoric:

> Charming sex, you will be free: just as men do, you shall enjoy all the pleasures that Nature makes your duty, do not withold yourselves from one. Must the more divine half of mankind be kept in chains by the others? Ah, break those bonds: nature wills it.

two

THE DESECRATION OF THE TEMPLE:
THE LIFE OF JUSTINE

All the idealisations of the female from the earliest days
of courtly love have been in fact devices to deprive her
of freedom and self-determination.

Love and Death in the American Novel,
Leslie Fiedler

*Dans le sacrifice, la victime était choisie de telle manière
que sa perfection achevat de render sensible la brutalité
de la mort.*

L'Erotisme, Georges Bataille

. . . it's so different a life from what all girls expect.

Letter quoted from a woman seeking
birth control in *Motherhood in Bondage*,
Margaret Sanger

I ANGEL-FACE ON THE RUN

Justine is a good woman in a man's world. She is a good
woman according to the rules for women laid down by men
and her reward is rape, humiliation and incessant beatings.
Her life is that of a woman martyrised by the circumstances
of her life as a woman.

The Justine of *Justine, or The Misfortunes of Virtue,* edition of 1791, is a beautiful and penniless orphan, the living image of a fairy-tale princess in disguise but a Cinderella for whom the ashes with which she is covered have become part of the skin. She rejects the approaches of a fairy godmother because the woman is a criminal; she falls in love, not with a handsome prince, but with a murderous homosexual who sets his dogs upon her and frames her for a murder he has himself committed. So she is the heroine of a black, inverted fairy-tale and its subject is the misfortunes of unfreedom; Justine embarks on a dolorous pilgrimage in which each preferred sanctuary turns out to be a new prison and all the human relations offered her are a form of servitude.

The recurring images of the novel are the road, the place of flight and hence of momentary safety; the forest, the place of rape; and the fortress, the place of confinement and pain. She is always free only in the act of escape for the road down which she perpetually flees is, in spite of its perils, always a safer place than the refuges she spies with such relief, that offer her only pain, humiliation and a gross genital acting-out of the hatred of men for the women whose manners they have invented, and related to this, of the pure and impersonal hatred of the strong for the weak.

Always the object of punishment, she has committed only one crime and that was an involuntary one; she was born a woman, and, for that, she is ceaselessly punished. The innocent girl pays a high price for the original if imaginary crime of Eve, just as Saint Paul said she should, and her protracted and exemplary Calvary makes her a female Christ whom a stern and patriarchal god has by no means forsaken but takes an especial delight in tormenting. Our revulsion at this spectacle is not unrelated to the uncomfortable truths it contains.

But there is no mysterious virtue in Justine's suffering. The martyrdom of this Christ-figure is absolutely useless; she is a gratuitous victim. And if there is no virtue in her suffering, then there is none, it turns out, in her virtue itself; it does nobody any good, least of all herself.

Justine is first introduced to the reader almost at the end of her unfortunate career, swathed to the eyes in a black cloak, bound securely hand and foot, a parcel of bereft humanity on its way to the gallows. This pathetic bundle is handed down unceremoniously from the roof of a carriage by a detachment of policemen at a coach stop and she narrates her life from its beginnings to a pair of sympathetic listeners, the first sympathy she has encountered for years.

Left penniless when her parents died of grief on becoming bankrupt, Justine's first lesson in life is that of the indignities of poverty. Those to whom her parents had been charitable drive her from their doors; the landlady of the garret in which she lives berates her for refusing to sell herself to a rich gentleman – does Justine think men are such fools as to give something for nothing to little girls like herself?. A woman on her own must learn to give men pleasure for that is the only way she can earn a living; but Justine cannot bring herself to put an exchange value on her body, only on her labour, and so obtains a post as maid of all work in the house of the usurer, du Harpin, where she must not dust the furniture for fear of wearing it out. This is her first experience of wage-labour and terminates when she refuses to rob a neighbour on du Harpin's instructions. He has her arrested on a false charge and, because she is poor, friendless and a woman, she cannot obtain a hearing and is condemned to death.

In prison, awaiting execution, she meets a woman who offers herself as a surrogate mother and instructress in the ways of the world, the brigand chieftainess, La Dubois, who has also been condemned to death. When La Dubois' confederates set fire to the prison, she and Justine escape together. La Dubois assures Justine that the practice of virtue will have her on the dung heap in no time. Like Bakunin, La Dubois suggests that the callousness of the rich justifies the crimes of the poor and asks Justine to join the robber band, but Justine, though almost persuaded by La Dubois' arguments, decides she will never fall from virtue. The robbers offer Justine a life that is not a form of slavery although, or because, it is that of the outlaw. The law itself has already shown Justine it will give her no protection but she cannot persuade herself to commit a transgression against the law. To live outside the law is to live in exile from the communities of humanity. She cannot do that because she is not inhuman, even though the law is not just. Her poverty, her weakness, her femaleness and her goodness put her on the wrong side of the law already but her dilemma is this; she has done nothing wrong.

Coeur-de-Fer, Heart-of-Iron, La Dubois' senior henchman, suggests that her virtue does not necessarily depend on the greater or lesser diameter of her vagina; at this stage, Justine is still a virgin. This is today a suggestion less radical than it was in the eighteenth century. But Justine refuses to sleep with him and takes the first opportunity that presents itself to flee the robber camp with a captive the band has just taken, Saint-Florent. For this desertion, La Dubois will later hound her like a fury, like a mother whose child has betrayed her – and La Dubois did indeed offer Justine a kind of mothering.

As soon as they reach the forest, Saint-Florent rapes Justine, robs her and leaves her alone and half-naked. Waking from a faint, she sees a valet buggering the Count de Bressac and overhears them plotting the death of de Bressac's rich aunt. They capture Justine, torture her and take her home, where de Bressac's aunt employs her as a chambermaid, out of charity. De Bressac threatens to murder Justine if she reveals his plot; she falls in love with him, in spite of his aversion to women. At last, he asks her to poison his aunt for him and at first she refuses, then pretends to agree, meanwhile informing his aunt. Discovering Justine's betrayal, de Bressac poisons his aunt himself, sets his dogs upon Justine and leaves her with the information that she is still wanted by the police for the robbery from du Harpin and also for causing the fire that released her from prison in the first place. He adds to her impressive if entirely fictitious criminal record the murder of his aunt, of which he has accused her.

Justine now takes refuge with an atheist surgeon, Rodin, and Rodin's daughter, Rosalie, whom her father had seduced when she was eleven years old. Rodin unsuccessfully attempts to seduce Justine, who consents to remain in the house as Rosalie's companion, with the secret plan of accomplishing Rosalie's conversion to Christianity. She succeeds in doing this shortly before Rodin locks his daughter up in the cellar as a preparation for her murder; he proposes to perform a scientific dissection upon her. Justine unlocks the cellar door but she and Rosalie are discovered before they can escape. Rodin is incensed Justine should try to abduct a daughter from her father's care and has her branded on the shoulder. This branding defines Justine as a common criminal. She wears her punishment on her skin, although she has not committed a single crime. Then he leaves her weeping in the forest.

She travels on until she sees the spire of the monastery of St Mary-in-the-Wood among the trees and decides to spend a few days there, tasting the solaces of religion.

The monastery of St Mary-in-the-Wood is the novel's largest set-piece, a microcosm in which a small group of privileged men operate a system of government by terror upon a seraglio of kidnapped women. As in all the Sadeian places of confinement, intimidation alone prevails and the only reward of virtue is to escape punishment, while virtue, as in the nursery, consists solely in observing an arbitrary set of rules. The monastery is utterly isolated; attached to the church is a secret pleasure pavilion, lavishly funded by the Benedictine order, whose notables have the right of residence here.

Brought here by force, their girls are released from the pavilion only by death. It is as if the place of terror and of privilege is a model of the world; we don't ask to come here and may leave it only once. Our entrance and our exit is alike violent and involuntary; choice has nothing to do with it. But our residence within this confinement is not upon equal terms.

The task of the girls is to minister to the pleasures of their masters, the monks. Complete submissiveness is their only lot. When a new girl is brought into the community, one of the residents is selected at random for 'retirement', that is, murder. The girls, all beautiful, all well-born, wear uniforms according to age groups; their lives are governed by a rigid system of regulations which exist primarily to provide the monks innumerable opportunities for punishment. Disordered hair, twenty strokes of the whip; getting up late in the morning, thirty strokes of the whip; pregnancy, a hundred strokes of the whip. The girls have no personal property. There is no privacy, except in the lavatory. For us, there is no hope at all. The monks rule their little world with the whim of oligarchs, of fate or of god. It is oddly like a British public school. It is like all hierarchical institutions.

With a pretty wit, the Benedictines have named their retreat after the Holy Virgin, and sited it deep in the heart of the forest, the place of rape. In this pleasure pavilion, the pleasure of a small minority of men devolves upon the pain of the majority, their serving women. Here, professional celibates extort unpaid sexual labour from sixteen well-trained women; these women are reduced entirely to their sexual function. Apart from that, they are nothing. There is a suggestion, made, rather touchingly, by the monk Clement, that these young and lovely women would never dream of performing such services for the ugly old men if they were not forced to do so. (Sade can never understand why women should wish to engage in sexual activity with ugly old men; he finds it perverse. They must do it from fear or for profit, he reasons. What *pleasure* can there be in it for them. It puzzles him very much.)

The sexual function of the women in the monastery is a thorough negation of their existence as human beings.

Justine is told she is as good as dead as soon as she enters the monastery. But Justine has a phenomenal resilience; shortly after her friend, Omphale, has been 'retired', Justine escapes by sawing through the bars on her dressing-room window and cutting through the thick hedge that surrounds the monastery. She prays to be forgiven the sins she has unwillingly committed at the hands of the monks and sets out on the road to Dijon.

She is immediately captured by the servants of the Count de Gernande and taken to his lonely chateau, to serve as his wife's maid. If the monastery was an oligarchy, then de Gernande's house is an absolute dictatorship. De Gernande metaphorically bleeds his tenants white; he is literally bleeding his wife to death, to satisfy his fetish for blood. To conceal this crime, he has told his wife's mother that the woman has gone mad and must not be visited. Gernande's life is all of a piece and self-consistent. Like a good vampire, it is the physical energy of the woman he extracts; he is a monstrously fat man, he has grown fat on the substance of his wives, for this is not the first woman he has killed in such a way.

Justine offers to take a letter to the Countess's mother and escapes from the house only to find herself in a walled garden. The count discovers her. She throws herself on his mercy and asks him to punish her. She fails to conceal the Countess's letter and he reads it. He imprisons Justine in a dungeon but, excited by the news his wife is now dying, he forgets to lock the door and Justine flees.

She takes the road to Grenoble, where she re-encounters Saint-Florent, who originally deflowered her. He offers her the post of his procuress, which she refuses, and continues south. A beggar asks for alms, as a ruse; Justine is once again robbed but, finding a man who has been robbed and also severely beaten, she cares for him, consoling herself with the reflection that his condition is worse than hers. When he recovers, he offers her a post as his sister's maid – charity disguised as servitude, again – and Justine goes off to the mountains with Roland the counterfeiter.

Roland exploits women primarily as labour but, like Justine's other masters, he enjoys the simple fact of mastery over her most of all. At his castle, with the secret torture chamber in its cellarage, she is lashed to a wheel with four other naked women; draws water; breaks stones; is beaten and forced to take part in Roland's cruel game of 'cut-the cord'.

The game of 'cut-the-cord' involves the hanging of a girl. The rope is cut, at the last moment, after Roland has enjoyed the spectacle of her terror, but, when Justine's friend, Suzanne, plays 'cut-the-cord', Roland does not cut the rope. Because Justine is so virtuous, Roland trusts her and invites her to cut the rope when he himself plays the game; he likes to play games with death himself, as well as watching them. She is tempted to let him hang but virtue asserts itself and she cuts the rope. He rewards her by suspending her in a pit filled with decomposing corpses. He departs for Italy, leaving the care of the castle in the hands of a kinder governor. In his absence, the castle is stormed by the police and those within it arrested. The kind caretaker will pay for the crimes of his master.

A magistrate interests himself in Justine's case and obtains her release. The rest are hung. In the inn where she lodges, she meets again the brigand chieftainness, La Dubois, who has become very rich by the practice of crime. La Dubois asks Justine to rob Dubreuil, a young man who has fallen in love with Justine. She prevents the robbery and accepts Dubreuil's offer of marriage, only to find that La Dubois has already poisoned him. He dies. La Dubois has already incriminated Justine for his death and left the town. A friend of Dubreuil's suggests Justine should run away too, and secures her a place travelling to the provinces with a Madame Bertrand and her child. Before they can set off, La Dubois, intent on vengeance, kidnaps Justine and delivers her to a local libertine but La Dubois and this cruel gentleman drink too much and fall asleep so Justine once again escapes.

She sets off with Madame Bertrand and the child but La Dubois, an avenging angel, sets fire to the hotel in which they spend the night and the child dies. La Dubois seizes Justine and is whisking her off for punishment when the police stop them and arrest Justine for an immense list of offences culminating in the burning of the hotel and the murder of the baby. La Dubois gladly gives Justine up to the law, which is as arbitrary and despotic as any of her other masters.

In prison, she begs aid from several of her former tormentors and all refuse, although Saint-Florent takes her out of the prison for an orgy, in which the judge also participates. Justine's reluctance ensures she will be found guilty at her trial.

She is on her way to her execution when she recounts this sad life to the rich lady and gentleman at the coach stop. The weeping and astonished lady now reveals herself as Justine's long-lost sister, Juliette, who, when their parents died, did not beg for charity at all but immediately apprenticed herself to a brothel and has done very well for herself. Her lover, a Councillor to the State, obtains Justine's release. She is taken to their sumptuous house and cared for while her name is cleared in the courts. A surgeon removes the brand from her shoulder; none of her tribulations has left her with a permanent stain. All goes well for Justine at last but she cannot believe the good times will last forever and, one stormy summer's evening, she is struck through the heart by a thunderbolt and so dies.

Juliette and her lover are overwhelmed with grief and remorse. Juliette enters a convent and devotes the rest of her life to good works. This devotional conclusion is amended in the sequel to this novel.

Justine's pilgrimage consists of the road; the forest; and the place of confinement. Nowhere is she safe from abuse. Upon her lovely and innocent head fall an endless stream of the ghastliest misfortunes and her virtue, the passive virtue of a good woman, ensures she can never escape them because the essence of her virtue is doing what she is told. Yet she is also trusting, endlessly trusting, ruled by ingenuousness, candour and guilelessness, a heroine out of Jean Jacques Rousseau; she possesses all the limpid innocence he admired in children and savages yet when she offers this innocence to others as shyly as if she were offering a bunch of flowers, it is trampled in the mud. She is a selfless heroine of Rousseau in the egocentric and cruel world of Hobbes.

It is a matter for discussion as to how far Justine's behaviour is innately that of a woman or how far she has adopted the stance of the cringe as a means of self-defence. She is not only a woman in a man's world; she is also a receptacle of feeling, a repository of the type of sensibility we call 'feminine'.

Her very first adventure is an emotional model for all the others. Justine is nothing if not self-conscious in her innocence and knows how to make a touching picture out of her misfortunes. She goes to seek help from the family priest, pale with mourning, tear-stained, in a little white dress, with that unshelled vulnerability of all literary orphans of whom she herself is both the apogee and the prototype. She presents herself emblematically in the passive mood, as an object of pity and as a suppliant. The priest tries to kiss her. She reprimands him; she is driven with blows and abuse from his door.

The question of her virtue is itself an interesting one. As the brigand, Coeur-de-Fer, says to her: why does such an intelligent girl so persistently locate virtue in the region of her genitals?

For Justine's conception of virtue is a specifically feminine one in that sexual abstinence plays a large part in it. In common speech, a 'bad boy' may be a thief, or a drunkard, or a liar, and not necessarily just a womaniser. But a 'bad girl' always contains the meaning of a sexually active girl and Justine knows she is good because she does not fuck. When, against her will, she *is* fucked, she knows she remains good because she does not feel pleasure. She implores La Dubois' brigands to spare her honour, that is, to refrain from deflowering her; a woman's honour, in the eighteenth century, is always a matter of her sexual reputation. Obeying the letter if not the spirit of her request, they strip her, sexually abuse her and ejaculate upon her body. 'They respected my honour, if not my modesty,' she congratulates herself. Her virginity has a metaphysical importance to her. Her unruptured hymen is a visible sign of her purity, even if her breasts and belly have been deluged in spunk.

Later, her virginity gone, she will tell herself that she has nothing to reproach herself with but a rape and, since that was involuntary, it was not a sin. She is less scrupulous than her literary progenitor, Richardson's Clarissa Harlowe, the first great suffering virgin in the history of literature, who, though she had been drugged into unconsciousness while the act took place, still believed herself in complicity with a rape of which she had known nothing. Justine is less scrupulous because her virtue is a female ruse that denies her own sexuality; nevertheless, though she may deplore the sexuality of incontinent men who think of rape the moment they see her, as all men do with Justine, she is sufficiently pragmatic to have deduced, from the fact that rape has patently not changed her, that Coeur-de-Fer was right and virtue does not depend exclusively on the state of her hymen. She concludes her virtue depends on her own reluctance.

Her sexual abstinence, her denial of her own sexuality, is what makes her important to herself. Her passionately held conviction that her morality is intimately connected with her genitalia makes it become so. Her honour does indeed reside in her vagina because she honestly believes it does so. She has seized on the only area she is certain of as a means of nourishing her own self-respect, even if it involves the cruellest repressions and a good deal of physical distress.

Repression is Justine's whole being – repression of sex, of

anger and of her own violence; the repressions demanded of Christian virtue, in fact. She cannot conceive of any pleasure at all in the responses of her own body to sexual activity, and so automatically precludes the possibility of accidentally experiencing pleasure.

Justine is the broken heart, the stabbed dove, the violated sepulchre, the persecuted maiden whose virginity is perpetually refreshed by rape. She will never feel one moment's gratification in any of her numerous, diverse and involuntary erotic encounters; she mimics sexual pleasure to ingratiate herself with the chief wardress of the girls at the monastery of St Mary-in-the-Wood but in reality assures us she felt nothing, as if, now she is no longer a virgin, her chastity can still exist in the form of frigidity. She seems almost a monster of the fear of sexuality. Since she herself denies the violence of her own desires, all her sexual encounters become for her a form of violence because she is not free to judge them. The fluids of *her* orgasm are the tears that are an implicit invitation to further rapes. For she does not fear rape at all; it is over in a moment and implies no relation with the aggressor. The violent but brief mastery of rape leaves her sense of self inviolate. A rape may be performed in the singular and denies the notion of consent. It is not rape but seduction she fears, and the loss of self in participating in her own seduction, for one must be willing or deluded, or, at least, willing to be deluded, in order to be seduced.

When she is offered seduction by the outlaws, she instinctively rejects it. It is not only that she senses the snare in this first seduction, that it will lead to her prostitution. But she cannot envisage a benign sexuality and, though her strength lies in her refusal to do so, nevertheless, the limitations of her sexuality are the limitations of her life. She sees herself only as the object of lust. She does not act, she is. She is the object of a thousand different passions, some of them very strange, but she is the subject of not a single one. She can indulge in her infatuation for the homosexual de Bressac because she knows in advance he will be indifferent to her. Later, she accepts Dubreuil's proposal of marriage solely because he has made it to her; it is not the exercise of a choice and, besides, her own sexual response does not enter into the contractual obligations of marriage.

But she has done nothing at all to deserve the pain inflicted upon her except to juxtapose the expectations of a well brought-up virgin, daughter of a rich banker, against the harsh cynicism of poverty. The rich can afford to be virtuous, the poor must shift as best they can. Justine's femininity is a mode of behaviour open only to those who can afford it and the price she has to pay for resolutely, indeed heroically maintaining her role of bourgeois virgin against all odds is a solitary confinement in the prison of her own femininity, a solitude alleviated only by the frequent visits of her torturers.

If her suffering itself becomes a kind of mastery, it is a masochistic mastery over herself. Like Patient Grizelda, as if Justine had been the good wife of an ungrateful world, her patience at last exhausts the ingenuity of her torturers, although it is a negative triumph, for though the world will not allow her to earn an honest living – in Sade's version of the world, there is no such thing as an honest living – it permits her to earn her death. In a final act of servitude, she is closing the windows for her sister to keep out the storm when the thunderbolt breaks through the glass and transfixes her.

Her life is dominated by chance, the chance enounters on the road, the chance escapes from prison, the chance thunderbolt. By chance, she passes from the cruel hands of one master to another and her innocence is so perfect that it precludes any advance knowledge of the strength and malice of her adversaries. Justine's life was doomed to disappointment before it began, like that of a woman who wishes for nothing better than a happy marriage. She pins her hopes always on those contingent to her, on the hypothetical benefactor who will protect her; but she meets only brigands, procuresses, woman-haters and rapists and, from these adventures, she learns not self-preservation but self-pity.

She is not in control of her life; her poverty and her femininity conspire to rob her of autonomy. She is always the dupe of an experience that she never experiences *as* experience; her innocence invalidates experience and turns it into events, things that happen to her but do not change her. This is the common experience of most women's lives, conducted always in the invisible presence of others who extract the meaning of her experience for themselves and thereby diminish all meaning, so that a seduction, or a birth, or a marriage, the central events in the lives of most women, the stages of a life, are marginal occurrences in the life of the seducer, the father or the husband.

And Justine's inability to be changed by experience is symbolised by her sterility. Her failure to conceive during ten years of enforced sexual activity is an aspect of her perennial virginity, but it is both a negative and a positive quality at the same time. Rape is unable to modify her intransigent singularity in any way. She is a free woman, in spite of herself.

But she has had her freedom thrust upon her, she has not seized it for herself. Her freedom is as involuntary as her punishment. Her freedom *is* her punishment, in the terms of the idealisation of femininity she represents. She is a caged and cherished bird all at once set free in the dangerous forest and it is a wonder she comes to no worse harm.

Justine's organ of perception is the heart that forbids her to engage in certain activities she feels to be immoral and her autobiography illustrates the moral limitations of a life conducted solely according to the virtuous promptings of the heart. This heart is an organ of sentiment, not of analysis, and it never prompts her to sacrifice herself for the principles by which she claims to live.

In the service of the vampiric Count de Gernande, she is

overcome with pity for the wife he tortures, Nevertheless, when the Count orders her to undress the unfortunate woman and bring her to him, Justine says: 'In spite of the loathing I sensed for all these horrors ... I had no choice but to submit with the most utmost resignation.' She has no choice because, if she does not do so, she herself will be punished and she cannot imagine how she might purchase Madame de Gernande a brief respite from pain at the price of undergoing a little pain herself.

Her heart is immoderate and if it does not allow her to put an exchange value on her flesh, neither does it allow her to put an exchange value on her suffering. It is a thing-in-itself, perceived as part of her condition. So Justine resolutely eschews the purchasing power of self-sacrifice; there *has* been a choice. Justine could have said 'no' to the Count de Gernande and refused to be his accomplice. But she does not do so. It does not occur to her to do so. She has no sense of identification with other people in pain.

The heart's egoism sees itself suffering when it sees another suffering and so it learns sympathy, because it can put itself in another's place; then the heart comes a little way out of its egoism and tentatively encounters the world. But, before the prospect of its own suffering, the heart melts completely and retreats into egoism, again, to protect itself.

In Gernande's house, Justine's sympathy only succeeds in worsening Madame de Gernande's plight, and her own. She runs away with a letter for Madame de Gernande's mother, whom the women hope will come and rescue them when she receives it. Gernande spies her early in the morning, as she escapes through the garden, just as God caught Adam in the garden on the morning of the primal transgression against authority. But Gernande thinks the girl is a ghost. Like all Sade's libertines, Gernande is a great coward; he is terrified, alone and helpless, and he would be entirely at Justine's mercy had she not quavered, even before he recognised her, 'O, master, punish me.' She demands punishment even before she has been accused. She does not even take advantage of Gernande's confusion to destroy the incriminating letters she carries.

As soon as she asks for punishment, Gernande is reassured. Now he knows who he is; she has told him so, she has told him he is her master. And she has told him what to do to her, to punish her. But he is still not quite sure why he should do it. He suspects Justine must be taking a plea for help to the outside world; he demands the evidence. 'I want to say I do not have it; but Gernande spies the fatal letter protruding above the kerchief at my breast, seizes it, reads it.' She makes no attempt to prevent him doing so. She adopts the humility of the cripple, she is always conciliatory. Her own punishment will be death; though, as she always does, she escapes it. But the punishment of the equally innocent woman she tried to help is an inescapable death. Justine's sympathy is always fatal to its object. Through its own unreason, the heart finds itself in complicity with the morality of cruelty it abhors.

In the castle of the counterfeiter, Roland, Justine is presented with several opportunities of murdering him. Indeed, on one occasion, she could kill him merely by strenuously exercising passivity. He wants her to play his favourite game of 'cut-the-cord'. He proposes to partially hang himself, in order to procure himself a particularly violent orgasm, and it is Justine who must cut the rope at the critical moment, at the point of emission, before death supervenes. He promises her he will set her free if she plays her part well but even Justine does not quite believe that. So Roland puts his life in the hands of a woman he has grievously abused and who has witnessed several of his own murders. Once again, she tells us she had no choice but to act out the part he assigned to her; he is her master and masters exist only in order to be obeyed. She does not even entertain the possibility of murdering him and that is the final limitation of her virtue; the unreason of the heart, the false logic of feeling, forbid her to exert mastery for even one moment and Sade achieves an immoral victory over the reader, who is bound to urge the spotless Justine, just this once, to soil her hands with crime.

Virtue has produced in Justine the same kind of apathy, of insensibility, that criminality has produced in Sade's libertines, who also never concern themselves with the nature of good and evil, who know intuitively what is wrong just as Justine knows intuitively what is right. She is incapable of anger or defiance because of her moral indifference; she feels no anger at the sufferings of her cell mates. She is as much a bourgeois individualist as Roland when she tells us how, during the first game of 'cut-the-cord', she feels an immense sense of happiness and peace when she realises that her companion, Suzanne, is to die and not Justine herself. Her virtue is egocentric, like the vice of the libertines. And it is entirely its own reward.

Indeed, Roland has chosen Justine as a playmate precisely because of the impeccable honesty that will not be seduced for even one treacherous moment by the idea of ridding the world of such a villain as he. He knows how to pick his accomplices. He relies on her native goodness when he puts her in charge of his life; she tells us she takes it into her hands only in order to restore it to him again. Singular generosity, singular magnanimity. If she wavered for a moment when she thought of the dead Suzanne, scarred with the marks of Roland's whips, or of the chain-gang of women who work in the castle, and then did not kill him, her refusal might be glorious; virtue humiliates vice. But Justine does not first judge him and then refuse to pass the death penalty. She exercises the female prerogative of mercy only because she is incapable of judgement and, in that sense, beyond good and evil, just as he is himself. She does not murder Roland only because he asks her not to. 'He is my master and I must obey him.'

Justine's virtue is not the continuous exercise of a moral faculty. It is a sentimental response to a world in which she always hopes her good behaviour will procure her some reward, some respite from the bleak and intransigent reality which surrounds her and to which she cannot accommodate herself. The virtuous, the interesting Justine, with her incompetence, her gullibility, her whining, her frigidity, her reluctance to take control of her own life, is a perfect woman. She always does what she is told. She is at the mercy of any master, because that is the nature of her own definition of goodness.

Her Christian virtues expose the praxis of the world. Her charity is always rewarded by theft; her piety leads her directly to the horrors of St Mary-in-theWood; when she converts the daughter of the surgeon, Rodin, to religion, she ensures the girl will die. Justine's virtue, in action, is the liberal lie in action, a good heart and an inadequate methodology.

In a world where women are commodities, a woman who refuses to sell herself will have the thing she refuses to sell taken away from her by force, The piety, the gentleness, the honesty, the sensitivity, all the qualities she has learned to admire in herself, are invitations to violence; all her life, she has been groomed for the slaughterhouse. And though she is virtuous, she does not know how to do good.

It is easy for a child to be good; a child's goodness is a negative quality. He is good if he does not do anything bad. A grown-up, however, cannot get away with this docile passivity. He must act out his virtue amongst an audience of others that includes himself. Doing good implies a social context of action, a whole system of social relations and Justine has been involuntarily deprived of this system. She does not even know it exists. She is a child who knows how to be good to please daddy; but the existence of daddy, her god, the abstract virtue to which she constantly refers, prevents her from acting for herself.

Nevertheless, her foolish and ignorant heart is never corrupted. The masters seek, always, not the submission of her body; that is easy for her to give, she always submits her flesh without any fuss – but they do not really want that. They want the submission of her heart and that she will never give. Good behaviour is always well chastised but never converted into its own opposite. The victim is always morally superior to the master; that is the victim's ambivalent triumph. That is why there have been so few notoriously wicked women in comparison to the number of notoriously wicked men; our victim status ensures that we rarely have the opportunity. Virtue is thrust upon us. If that is nothing, in itself, to be proud of, at least it is nothing of which to be ashamed.

So evil, the desire for dominance, gains a Pyrrhic victory over Justine, in the destruction but never the surrender of the object on which it vents its rage. 'The fool who persists in his folly becomes wise,' says Blake. In its fatal *single-mindedness*, Justine's negative capability for virtue becomes an involuntary affirmation of the humanism that the world in which she lives denies, even if not an affirmation of her own positive humanity, for that exists by accident.

Flight is Justine's salvation. She is woman as an escape artist, for whom only the self-defining life of the traveller, all of whose homes are aspects of a perpetual homelessness, offers freedom from the definitions of servitude that are all her female virtue is offered. And she must die an emotional, if not a physical virgin, like her literary granddaughters, Beth in *Little Women*, Eva in *Uncle Tom's Cabin*, the little girls who died in the angelic state of pre-pubescence and go straight to heaven, to daddy, because they are too good to live. This good little girl's martyrisation by the circumstances of adult life as a woman makes her the ancestress of a generation of women in popular fiction who find themselves in the same predicament, such as the heartstruck, tearful heroines of Jean Rhys, Edna O'Brien and Joan Didion who remain grumblingly acquiescent in a fate over which they belive they have no control. By some accident of literature, the unfortunate heroine of Judith Rossner's best-selling piece of didactic soft-core pornography, *Looking For Mr Goodbar*, even has the same name, Teresa, that Justine uses in disguise. There is presumably no direct literary influence from the eighteenth-century philosophical pornographer to these contemporary women novelists; but, in the character of Justine, Sade contrived to isolate the dilemma of an emergent type of woman. Justine, daughter of a banker, becomes the prototype of two centuries of women who find the world was not, as they had been promised, made for them and who do not have, because they have not been given, the existential tools to remake the world for themselves. These self-consciously blameless ones suffer and suffer until it becomes second nature; Justine marks the start of a kind of self-regarding female masochism, a woman with no place in the world, no status, the core of whose resistance has been eaten away by self-pity.

Justine's place in the aetiology of the female condition in the twentieth century is assured; she is the personification of the pornography of that condition.

She is obscene to the extent to which she is beautiful. Her beauty, her submissiveness and the false expectations that these qualities will do her some good are what make her obscene.

II THE BLONDE AS CLOWN

The real value of a sexually attractive woman in a world which regards good looks as a commodity depends on the degree to which she puts her looks to work for her. The lovely Justine, the sacred woman, denies her value in this world by refusing to sell herself on any terms and even refusing to accept the notion of the morality of contract. But her body is by far the most valuable thing she has to sell. She will never make a living out of the sale of her labour power, alone.

However, in a world organised by contractual obligations, the whore represents the only possible type of honest

woman. If the world in its present state is indeed a brothel –
and the moral difference between selling one's sexual labour
and one's manual labour is, in these terms, though never in
Justine's terms, an academic one – then every attempt the
individual makes to escape the conditions of sale will only
bring a girl back to the crib, again, in some form or another.
At least the girl who sells herself with her eyes open is not a
hypocrite and, in a world with a cash-sale ideology, that is a
positive, even a heroic virtue.

The whore has made of herself her own capital investment. Her product – her sexual activity, her fictitious
response – is worth precisely what the customer is willing to
pay for it, no more and no less, but that is only what is true
of all products. But the whore is depised by the hypocritical
world because she has made a realistic assessment of her
assets and does not have to rely on fraud to make a living.
In an area of human relations where fraud is regular practice
between the sexes, her honesty is regarded with a mocking
wonder. She sells herself; but she is a fair tradesman and her
explicit acceptance of contractual obligation implicit in all
sexual relations mocks the fraud of the 'honest' woman who
will give nothing at all in return for goods and money except
the intangible and hence unassessable perfume of her
presence. The honest whore is assured of her own immediate
value, not only in her own valuation but in the valuation of
her customers. So she can afford to ignore the opinion of the
rest of the world but she will not be respected for her integrity although, if she is successful enough, and her
business prospers, she may 'ruin' men, like any other
successful entrepreneur.

Justine's profane sister, Juliette, has 'ruined' a number of
rich men by the time she meets and succours her wretched
sister, even in the relatively decorous pages of the *Justine* of
1791. At this period, 'ruin', applied to a man, means
financial ruin, whereas, applied to a woman, it means only
that a woman has engaged in sexual activity, suggesting an
actual parallel between a bank balance and a body. A ruined

woman is one who has lost her capital assets, a virgin who has been deflowered and hence has nothing tangible to put on the market. Not a woman's face but her unruptured hymen is her fortune; however, if she regards her sexual activity as her capital, she may, once ruined, utilise her vagina to ruin others, as though, in fact, the opening of it allowed her access to a capital sum which had been frozen by virginity. No longer a virgin, she may put her capital to work for her.

A businessman in the same position as a successful whore would be applauded for his acumen and admired for his ruthlessness. The woman is censured for her immoral rapacity, although it is the same thing.

But the woman who makes no bones about selling herself will soon adopt the ideology of the small shopkeeper and identify her interests with the status quo. She will be a great upholder of marriage; doesn't the greater part of her trade come from married men? By accepting the contractual nature of sexual relations, even if on her own terms, she imprisons herself within them just as securely as a wife does, though she may retain a greater degree of individual independence. If marriage is legalised prostitution, then prostitution is itself a form of group marriage.

However, the whore may recoup some of the moral status she lost when she sold herself if she concludes her career by 'throwing herself away'. A woman who throws herself away is one who forms arbitrary sexual relations without any thought for their consequences. She will be regarded, not so much as pitiable, though she may condescendingly be pitied; rather, as feckless. The tart with a heart of gold, a mercantile image, is a tart who fecklessly gives away a substance that is as good as money. If physical generosity in a woman is reprehensible when used as a means of financial gain, it is clearly incomprehensible if it is spontaneous. 'Beauty too rich for use, for earth too dear'; a beautiful woman as such is so much bric-a-brac, and all her use value, that is, her sexual value, is denied her.

In the celluloid brothel of the cinema, where the merchandise may be eyed endlessly but never purchased, the tension between the beauty of women, which is admirable, and the denial of the sexuality which is the source of that beauty but is also immoral, reaches a perfect impasse. That is why Saint Justine became the patroness of the screen heroine.

The first attempt to get out of this predicament, that of the moral irreconcilability of physical attractiveness and sexuality, was the invention of the pre-sexual waif as heroine, a role Mary Pickford played until the brink of middle age. Sometimes this waif, as in Griffiths' *Broken Blossoms*, is as innocently erotic and as hideously martyrised as Justine herself, and, as a sexual icon, the abused waif allowed the customer to have his cake and glut himself upon it, too. She could be as enticing in her vulnerability and ringletted prettiness as she was able but the audience knew all the time that the lovely child before them was, in fact, a mature woman whom the fiction of her childishness made taboo. The taboo against acknowledging her sexuality created the convention that the child could not arouse desire; if she did so, it was denied. A sentimental transformation turned the denial of lust into a kitsch admiration of the 'cute'.

The taboo on the sexuality of the pre-pubescent child, who is tacitly assumed to be sexually inactive, also extends to the defusing of the potential menace of the sexuality of the middle-aged woman, whose sexual life may be assumed to be at an end. Mae West's sexuality, the most overt in the history of the cinema, could only be tolerated on the screen because she did not arrive in Hollywood until she had reached the age associated with menopause. This allowed her some of the anarchic freedom of the female impersonator, pantomime dame, who is licensed to make sexual innuendos because his masculinity renders them a form of male aggression upon the women he personates.

Mae West's joke upon her audience was, however, a

superior kind of double bluff. She was in reality a sexually free woman, economically independent, who wrote her own starring vehicles in her early days in the theatre and subsequently exercised an iron hand on her own Hollywood career. The words she spoke in her movies were the words she had written herself; the dramatised version of herself she presented to the world was based on the one she both invented and lived for herself. Age did not wither her but only increased her self-confidence until she could actually pretend to be a female impersonator, aided, not desexualised, by the maturity which frees women of the fecundity which is the most troubling aspect of their sexuality. If Mae West has a Sadeian avatar, it is neither Justine nor Juliette but the sterile, phallic mother who will succour not Justine but Juliette and teach Eugenie de Mistival the philosophy of the boudoir. Mae West's wit is castratory, if tender; and the part of her mind which is not scheming for libidinal gratification is adding up her bank accounts.

She selected theatrical and cinematic roles of women whose work entailed sexual self-display yet her ability to act out these roles on the screen was due solely to her middle-age, even if she was permitted to do so because she did not look middle-aged. She was forty when she made her first film in Hollywood, *Night after Night*, in 1932. The middle-aged woman, whose literary prototype is the nurse in *Romeo and Juliet*, may say what she pleases, wink at and nudge whomever she desires but we know it is all a joke upon her, for she is licenced to be free because she is so old and ugly that nobody will have her. Mae West relied on this freedom, even if she turned it on its head; universally desired, absolutely her own woman, she could pick and choose among her adorers with the cynical facility of the rake, inverting the myth of female masochism even in the titles of her movies – *She Done Him Wrong*, 1933. She made of her own predatoriness a joke that concealed its power, whilst simultaneously exploiting it. Yet she represents a sardonic disregard of convention rather than a heroic overthrow of taboo.

The European love-goddesses, Garbo and Dietrich, were another story. They brought their foreignness to Hollywood with them; to the country where girls learned the techniques of self-effacement from books called *Little Women* and *Good Wives*, they arrived fully fledged from Europe, the domain of adultery, where the fulfilled sexuality of women was culturally admitted and its socially disruptive quality acknowledged, even if it was always given a tragic resonance in the mythology of doomed adultery implicit in Flaubert's *Madame Bovary*, Tolstoy's *Anna Karenina*. If a tragic resonance to illicit fuckery is as silly as a straightforward denial that it exists, then at least it gives illicit fuckery a silly kind of dignity, and the adulteress can retain a little self-respect. Besides, the adulteress, if she plays her cards right, may evolve into the adventuress, whose status in life, if not in art, has always been that of a free woman.

Garbo and Dietrich both retained the air of the European adventuress. However discreetly they behaved in life – and both were models of discretion – it was obvious that their screen personalities had a stock-in-trade that consisted of more than an unruptured hymen. Besides, both often appeared in drag, which is always reassuring to men, since a woman who pretends to be a man has also cancelled out her reproductive system, like the post-menopausal woman, and may also freely function as a safety valve for homo-erotic fantasy.

The public sexual ideology of Hollywood finally formulated itself, in the nineteen forties, as a version of Justine's own. Female virtue was equated with frigidity and a woman's morality with her sexual practice. (These equations neatly deny women any access to questions of public morality.)

But, of course, it proved quite impossible to keep sexuality off the screen. It consistently reasserted itself, even when female virtue was equated with asexuality, because a pretty face and a provocative body remained the first pre-requisites of success for a woman in the movies. The movies celebrated allure in itself but either denied the attractions inherent in availability or treated availability itself as a poor joke.

The cultural product of this tension was the Good Bad Girl, the blonde, buxom and unfortunate sorority of Saint Justine, whose most notable martyr is Marilyn Monroe.

See how alike they look! Marilyn Monroe, the living image of Justine; both have huge, appealing, eloquent eyes, the open windows of the soul; their dazzling fair skins are of such a delicate texture that they look as if they will bruise at a touch, carrying the exciting stigmata of sexual violence for a long time, and that is why gentlemen prefer blondes. Marilyn/Justine has a childlike candour and trust and there is a faint touch of melancholy about her that has been produced by this trust, which is always absolute and always betrayed. This quality of trust is what the Sadeian libertines find most fascinating of all. Connoisseurs of the poetry of masochism that they are, they immediately recognise those girls who will look most beautiful when they are crying. Saint Fond, who employs Justine's wicked, brunette sister, Juliette, as his procuress, questions her anxiously about one of her finds: 'Does she weep? I love to see women weep; with me, they always do, all of them.'

The essence of the physicality of the most famous blonde in the world is a wholesome eroticism blurred a little round the edges by the fact that she herself is not quite sure what eroticism is. This gives her her tentative luminosity and makes her, somehow, always more like her own image in the mirror than she is like herself. To this, she owes her poetic ambiguity and her appearance of fragility. Marilyn Monroe's representative capacity for exquisite martyrdom is so extreme that Norman Mailer's life of her is composed entirely in mythic, rather than factual terms. His biography, *Marilyn*, is a contemporary version of the martyrdom of

Justine and, like a hagiography or dirty book, the text has
to be helped along with pictures before you can make sense
of it. You have to see her to know how she will look in extremis, which is, in your secret heart, the way you want to
see her – men; and women, too, who need to convince
themselves that the beauty they deny themselves will
always cause suffering to its unfortunate possessors. Mailer
endows his saint with all the tawdry rhetoric he can muster
up about the pathos inherent in prime, blonde flesh. And she
has all the dreadful innocence of lack of self-knowledge, too;
she is almost a holy fool. Mailer approvingly quotes Diana
Trilling:

> None but Marilyn Monroe could suggest such a purity of sexual
> delight. The boldness with which she could parade herself and
> yet never be gross, her sexual flamboyance and bravado which
> yet breathed an air of mystery and reticence, her voice which
> carried such ripe overtones of erotic excitement and yet was the
> voice of a tiny child – these complications were integral to her
> gift. And they described a young woman trapped in some
> never-never land of unawareness.

This is an apt anthem for Justine, always the unwitting
prey, who could have said, just as Monroe said to Groucho
Marx in *Monkey Business*: 'Men keep following me all the
time', without the least notion why they did so. If she had
had the self-confidence to be gross – because what is *wrong*
with being gross? – the story would have been quite different.

Marilyn's lonely death by barbiturates, nude, in bed, a
death adored and longed for by all necrophiles, is the contemporary death-by-lightning of the sweet, dumb blonde,
the blue-eyed lamb with the golden fleece led to slaughter on
the altar of the world. You can even see real scar-tissue
(from a gall-bladder operation; the female interior bearing
the marks of the intimate, cruel excavation of the scalpel) in
the nude pictures Bert Stern took of her the summer before
her death. Since a child, she had been steeped in the doc-
trines of Christian Science: 'Divine love has always met and

always will meet every human need', the pious Justine's own, unspoken maxim in a novel which is the pilgrimage of the soul in search of god written by an atheist.

Monroe was not born but became a blonde; blondeness is a state of ambivalent grace, to which anyone who wants it badly enough may aspire. According to Fred Lawrence Guiles' biography of her, *Norma Jean*, Monroe's agent told her, in 1946: 'I have a call for a light blonde, honey or platinum.' In this world, women may be ordered like steaks, well-done, medium rare, bloody. The identity of the blonde was the most commercially viable one available; cash betrayed her to sanctity and if she voluntarily took up blondehood, she always voluntarily took upon herself the entire apparatus of the orphan. Fatherless already through illegitimacy, she, heart-struck by the poignancy of her situation, invented for herself a true orphan's biography of hardship, a childhood spent in orphanages where she scrubbed floors, was beaten, accused of theft, bedded down in windowless cupboards and, inevitably, raped.

These misfortunes add the irresistible dew of suffering to her ripeness. 'I see your suffering,' says the hero of Arthur Miller's play, *After the Fall*, to a woman with a scandalous resemblance to Monroe. A visible capacity for suffering provokes further suffering. She is a past master at inspiring rage and at deflecting it from herself on to her entire sex; is she not a sex symbol, and hence the symbolic per-sonification of her entire sex? After *Some Like It Hot* was finished, the director, Billy Wilder, told an interviewer that it had been many weeks before he 'could look at my wife without wanting to hit her because she is a woman'. Mailer lovingly inserts this gossip-column nugget into the myth of 'Marilyn'.

The blonde's physical fragility is, of course, only ap-parent. She must have a robust constitution to survive the blows life deals her. Her fragility is almost the conscious disguise of masochism and masochism necessitates an infinite resilience. Nevertheless, the victim proclaims her vulnerability in every gesture, every word, every act; defining herself in the third person, the saint laments her lot in *Some Like It Hot:* 'Sugar always gets the fluffy end of the lollipop.' Her misfortunes are no fault of her own, she is quite certain of that; so it is not the demonstration of her innocence itself that makes her innocence real to us. Innocence is a transparent quality, difficult to see in full daylight. Her innocence is made real to us by the desecration of it; the white page is thrown into relief by the spattered mud.

This fatherless and bruisable child was never clever, was dumb; dumb like a fox is dumb, said one of Monroe's lovers. This dumbness is not stupidity but a naivety so perfect it is functionally no different from stupidity; it is only because she is innocent of her own strength that she thinks she will hurt easily. Because she is innocent of her exchange value, she thinks she is valueless.

Monroe, in her major movies, from *Gentlemen Prefer Blondes* to *The Misfits*, is a Good Bad Girl. The theory of the sentimental image of the Good Bad Girl is that she has all the appearance of a tart and an air of continuous availability but, when the chips are down, she would never stoop to sell herself. Less reprehensibly, indeed, almost commendably – and for a moment we are allowed to admire her misguided generosity – she gives it away for free. But her affairs always end badly, her generosity is always abused, she does not realise her flesh is sacred because it is as good as money. In short, she is the most risible and pathetic figure, the unsuccessful prostitute, living proof that crime does not pay and the wages of sin will be too small to pay the rent. Her poor show as a prostitute, as a business woman, is proof in itself that her heart is made of gold.

It is part of Saint Justine's baleful bequest that blonde Good Bad Girls always come to bad ends; brunettes and even redheads, Barbara Stanwyck, Joan Crawford, Shirley Maclaine, have acquired the toughness of Juliette and put their bodies to work actively for them. Indeed, Howard Hawkes' *Gentlemen Prefer Blondes* juxtaposes the deathly fragility of Monroe and the earthiness of Jane Russell almost like a benign version of Sade's diptych.

The mythic role of the Good Bad Girl is, however, directly at variance with the real facts of her life, as all mythic roles are apt to be. She pretends to be an unsuccessful prostitute but, in fact, she is a very successful prostitute indeed and, what is more, one who does not have to deliver the goods. She sells, not the reality of flesh, but its image and so she makes her living, a successful but imaginary prostitute. Yet, since she is not in control of her own marketing, her hypothetical allure and not her actual body is the commodity. She sells a perpetually unfulfilled promise of which the unfulfillment is a consolation rather than a regret. The reality of her could never live up to her publicity. So she retains her theoretical virginity, even if she is raped by a thousand eyes twice nightly.

The Good Bad Girl is celebrated for her allure but this allure is never allowed to overwhelm the spectator. Besides, she has not got enough self-confidence to overwhelm men. She has to rely on a childlike charm, she has more in common with Mary Pickford than with Mae West; she must make up to the paedophile in men, in order to reassure both men and herself that her own sexuality will not reveal to them their own inadequacy. And, like Justine, she cannot judge; her innocence is prelapsarian, she does not know the difference between good and evil, only that between nice and nasty.

Her innocence, furthermore, forbids her to solicit. Her innocence is her own excuse for her own object status; she cannot solicit because she does not know how to desire. She is always the prey, never the hunter, and 'The most innocent are tormented the most,' says the Sadeian libertine in *The Hundred and Twenty Days at Sodom*. But she does not understand that.

Above all, she discovers she must not take her own allure

seriously. She must laugh it off. The beautiful creature must become a comedienne. She will adopt the pathetic devices of the sexless clown as a means of protection from her pursuers. That a lovely woman is always, in essence, a comic figure, even in tragic art in the modern period, is curiously exemplified in Frank Wedekind's 'Lulu' plays, *Earth Spirit* and *Pandora's Box*. Throughout the action of both plays a conspicuous part of the decor is the portrait of the beautiful and sexually free Lulu dressed as Pierrot, the moonstruck clown of *Commedia del Arte*. This is surely a modern phenomenon, this downgrading of the physical value of the imperiously attractive woman; Shakespeare would scarcely have allowed the action of *Antony and Cleopatra* to be dominated by a portrait of his heroine dressed in the cap and bells of the court fool. But this one must make fun of herself because she can never admit she knows *why* she is pretty. Lulu herself certainly guesses why she is pretty; and Jack the Ripper must stab her to show her how her prettiness is itself the source of sin. In an attempt to avoid this unpleasant denouement, the pretty girl must voluntarily remove her boobs and buttocks from the armoury of the seductress. She must pretend she cannot understand how they got there, in the first place.

Soon they lose even the significance of the conventional attributes of the female; they become the signs of a denaturised being, as if there was an inherent freakishness about breasts and buttocks at the best of times, as if half the human race were not equipped with them. As if they were as surprising and unusual physical appurtenances to find on a woman as fins or wings.

The world breathes a sigh of relief; voluntary castration! She has desexed herself by acknowledging how comic her sexuality is; she is prepared to allow her tits and bum to turn into cues for raucous laughter, like a clown's red nose and baggy pants. They become no more than signs that provoke mirth. Groucho twitches his eyebrows and gnaws his moustache when Monroe can't think why she is being followed; he knows the joke is on her. Her ignorance of the erotic disturbance she creates is the product of her comic innocence and so she is denied even the possession of her self, just as that innocence shows how easy she will be to deceive. And she will not answer back; isn't she dumb, after all? She has torn herself off Lulu's crucifix of the tragic heroine to set herself up in the invisible pillory of the stand-up comic.

The milk bottle joke in Frank Tashlin's 'fifties movie, *The Girl Can't Help It*, illustrates perfectly this comic degradation. Jayne Mansfield clutches the milk bottles to her mammaries, a crude reminder as to the primary function of these glands – no, they are not orbs of delight; by no means that magic place where Freud, the romantic, thought that love and hunger met . . . they are farcical globes of fat and their function is more hygienically superseded by any dairy.

The Beautiful Blonde Clowns, Jean Harlow, Judy Holliday, Jayne Mansfield, a sisterhood of unfortunate J's, as if the name Justine lingered on as a race memory in the casting offices, all die young. All are Justine in her final degradation. Now she must endlessly apologise for the insulting lavishness of her physical equipment, which is a ceaseless embarrassment to her. But the laughter she invokes as a protection against the knowledge of her own sexuality is itself a form of the desecration she attempted to protect herself against by laughing at herself first of all.

She hopes to disarm, to endear by her ignorance of her own seductiveness, as Justine did when she went to see the priest in her little white dress and was – 'the men keep following me' – kissed for her trouble. But Sade had a tragic sense of life and did not find anything to laugh at in Justine's humiliation. The Beautiful Clown must endure laughter although she is comic only because she is ignorant of her power to compel, to attract, to receive voluntarily that submission from others which others force on her.

She has fostered her own innocence, her own stupidity, as

an insulation from the pain of her endless humiliations; therefore, exiled from her own allure, she does not know how much her allure deviates from the norm and, by doing so, suggests the inadequacy of the whole theory of the norm. She will not be loved, as she hopes to be, because she is so beautiful, such a perturbation, a challenge that continues to exist after it has been met; she will only be resented.

She intends the exhibition of her vulnerability will avert hostility and elicit cherishing. She thinks that if she says: 'See how much you have hurt me!' she will halt the punishment, but the punishment continues. It sharpens, since its object was the infliction of that pain her helpless protest has just confirmed.

She is not in control of the laughter and contempt she arouses. They are in control of her, modifying her opinion of herself, indignifying her.

In herself, this lovely ghost, this zombie, or woman who has never been completely born as a woman, only as a debased cultural idea of a woman, is appreciated only for her decorative value. Final condition of the imaginary prostitute: men would rather have slept with her than sleep with her. She is most arousing as a memory or as a masturbatory fantasy. If she perceives herself as something else, the contradictions of her situation will destroy her. This is the Monroe syndrome.

She has never perceived her appearance as a quality of herself but as something extraneous to her. She is afraid men only want her because she is beautiful so she is denied any use at all of her appearance, which exists for her only as a reflection in the eyes of spectators at a humiliation, at the spectacle of her distress, which gives the witnesses so much pleasure. She might be vain; she cannot be proud. And, because she is beautiful, she arouses concupiscence. Therefore she knows in her heart she must be bad. If she is bad, then it is right she should be punished. She is always ready for more suffering. She is always ready for more suffering because she is always ready to please. 'That's how

I like women!' exclaims Saint Fond in *Juliette*, when a girl
he is torturing bursts into tears.

Justine is the model for the nineteenth and early twentieth-century denial of femininity as praxis, the denial of
femininity as a positive mode of dealing with the world.
Worst of all, a cultural conspiracy has deluded Justine and
her sisters into a belief that their dear being is in itself
sufficient contribution to the world; so they present the
enigmatic image of irresistibility and powerlessness, forever
trapped in impotence.

III THE TOAD ON THE ROSE

Noirceuil, lover of Justine's sister, describes the perfect
object of the lust of the libertine, who acknowledges no law
except that of his senses' pleasure:

> Beauty, virtue, innocence, candour, misfortune – the object of
> our lust finds no protection in any of these qualities. On the
> contrary. Beauty arouses us further; virtue, innocence, candour
> enhance the object; misfortune puts it into our power, renders
> it amenable to us; so, all those qualities tend only to excite us
> still further and we should look on them all as simply fuel for
> our passions. These qualities also afford us the opportunity of
> violating another prohibition; I mean offer us the kind of
> pleasure we get from sacrilege, or the profanation of objects
> that expect our worship. That beautiful girl is an object of
> reverence only for fools; when I make her the target of my
> keenest and coarsest appetites, I experience the double
> pleasure of sacrificing to my appetites both a beautiful object
> and one before which the crowd bows down.

Sade's sexual metaphor is always ambiguous. Lin-
guistically, he mystifies the sexual attributes of the
female body; it is described in sacred terms, even in terms of
sacred architecture, as though it were a holy place. The
female orifice is a shrine, a place of worship. The surgeon,
Roland, apostrophises the cunt: 'temple of my long-loved
pleasures'. This ironic sacralisation of the female body is

used throughout Sade; even in its mortification, when it is spattered with blood and ordure, the altar retains its perfidious magic. Incense is burned at this altar; ejaculation is regularly 'the burning of incense', at the altars Nature intends for such homage. Orgasm itself is often described as the rendering of homage. This homage is itself equivocal, administered with such violence the recipient may regard it as sacrilege, the culmination of an act of pure hostility.

Now and then, Sade kitschifies the prick itself, calling it 'the first agent of love's pleasure', but, more often, it is a mechanical device, an engine or an instrument of warfare, a weapon. And, frequently, it is a snake. 'The snake emits its venom'; 'the serpent is about to discharge its venom.' When Justine sees Jerome, the licentious monk, insert his prick into the mouth of a young girl prisoner in the monastery of St Mary-in-the-Wood, she thinks of: 'the filthy reptile withering the rose'. Sexual approach is as much a defilement as a tribute, yet the very act of defilement reinforces the holiness of the temple. In a secular world, the notion of the impure is meaningless. Only a true believer can see the pure glamour of the blasphemy. In Sade's lengthiest piece of proscriptive Utopian writing: *Yet Another Effort, Frenchmen, If You Would Become Republicans*, the female sexual organs are referred to as 'common fountains'. It is impossible for such things to be defiled. But the egalitarian utopia of the republic is, as yet, unachieved; we must still deal with notions of dirt and transgression.

So it is necessary for the young girl, the virgin, the rose, the *rosa mundi* or Blessed Virgin, to be of exceptional beauty. Her beauty in itself excites abuse because it has helped to make her an object of reverence. Her expectation of reverence ensures her passivity and her weakness and also her horrid surprise when the state of grace in which she believes she exists is abruptly revoked.

Justine begins her miserable career with the idea she never quite rids herself of, that her beauty and virtue are in themselves qualities which demand respect. Beauty, youth and innocence in women give them an artificial ascendancy over a world that allots them love and admiration to precisely the extent a beautiful, young and innocent woman is deprived of the ability to act in the world. She is compensated for her defencelessness by a convention of respect which is largely false. Herself mystified by herself, narcissistically enamoured of the idea of herself as Blessed Virgin, she has no notion at all of who she is except in fantasy. To the extent that she has been made holy and thinks of herself as such, so she is capable of being desecrated. Purity is always in danger.

The girls imprisoned for the pleasure of the monks in the monastery of St Mary-in-the-Wood are all from well-to-do, 'distinguished' families. 'There is not one who cannot claim the highest rank, not one who is not treated with the greatest disrespect.' The libertines in *The Hundred and Twenty Days at Sodom* belong to a supper club when they are at home in Paris. There they hold four parties a week, one of which is especially reserved for the abuse and humiliation of girls of the upper classes. In addition they hold a regular weekly supper attended by four young women of the aristocracy who have been kidnapped from their parents' homes and are now prostituted. These girls are particularly vilely treated. When the libertines plan their holiday at the Chateau of Silling, they stipulate that the procuresses should find them victims from the most eminent families; for these services, the agents are paid thirty thousand francs a victim.

It is upon the women of the upper classes, whose beauty and chastity is a function of class and whom universal admiration has always acquitted of the need to be human, that the licentious wrath of the libertines falls most heavily. These girls are chastised because they expect to be admired and are raped because they have put too high a value on their own sexuality. Their sexual abstinence is a form, almost, of conspicuous consumption; it is an ostentatious luxury that is not available to women from a class that can achieve financial independence only through the practice of some form of prostitution. They overvalue their chastity in the way that certain modern women overvalue their orgasmic potential; both overvaluations are aspects of élitism.

However, the submissiveness the young ladies learned at their expensive boarding schools stands the libertines in good stead. The girls will not fight back. They do not know that it is possible for them to do so. The frigidity they had been taught to equate with virtue prevents them from achieving a sexual autonomy that would transform their passive humiliations into a form of action. Not only can they never feel pleasure in the embraces of their violators nor even admit it might be possible to do so, but, poor girls, they will always feel horror, revulsion and fear because they believe indifference to lust is as immoral as lust itself.

The princess of the fairy tale is reduced to the condition of the whore in the gutter; the fury of the libertines works this reversal. But, since the princess still retains her consciousness of herself as princess rather than acquiring the self-possession of a whore, she has been truly degraded.

The libertines show her that the qualities that made her precious can easily be stripped from her. They thrust her face-down on the bed and turn their attentions to her arse, that part of herself reverence has always particularly denied existed. They force her to publicly perform excretory activity she has always conducted furtively, in private, as if it were an activity that in itself degraded her, an activity too human, too common to be publicly acknowledged by such a rare creature as herself. (Swift exclaimed in horror: 'Celia shits!' How can it be possible such a precious being, all angel and no ape, should ever do such a thing? God must be very cruel, to shatter our illusions so.)

Her final humiliation is to realise that her value has never resided in herself but in the values of the open market; now the princess has a price tag thrust upon her. Like a common criminal, she has a price on her head. As if she were a cake, she is bought and sold.

Hitherto, like a porcelain figure, she had presented a glazed surface to the world. Her surfaces seemed too smooth, too impermeable to be fissured by any kind of feeling. But now, under the lash, splashed with excrement, deluged in spunk, she exhibits unmistakable evidence of common humanity. She screams, she pleads, she weeps. Pain, in triumph, has found a foothold on a carapace that had seemed too smooth to hold it. When she suffers, she exists. She will embrace her newly discovered masochism with all her heart because she has found a sense of being through suffering.

IV MORAL OF JUSTINE

Belmore, the immolator of small boys, suggests to his good friend, Juliette, Justine's sister, in the sequel to *Justine* that the origin of the unnatural reverence for women which finds its expression in the forms of romantic love derives from the professions of witchcraft and prophecy that women exercised in the antique past. To a man freed from ignorant superstition, says Belmore, women are no more than sexual receptacles, pieces of plumbing. All mystification stripped from her, Celia does not only shit; she becomes herself a commode.

Wives and mothers are sanctified by usage and convention; on them falls the greatest wrath. In the monastery of St Mary-in-the-Wood, pregnancy means a death sentence. Juliette tortures pregnant women during her holiday in Florence. The worst tortures of the Castle of Silling in *The Hundred and Twenty Days at Sodom* are reserved for the pregnant Constance. Madame de Mistival, wife and mother, the object of the fury of her daughter in *Philosophy in the Boudoir*, is utterly desanctified. Her motherliness is stripped from her in a ferocious rite of exorcism; her own daughter rapes her. In Sade's brothels, husbands prostitute wives; husbands force their wives to witness the prostitution of daughters.

The mother herself is taken from her shrine, the holy family, and turned over to the world, the public brothel, communalised, secularised, restored to a state of natural or original impurity from which her wifehood and mothering was a falling away. Clairwil, Juliette's accomplice, says: 'Libertinage in women used once to be venerated the world over; it had worshippers everywhere, even temples.' Not fucking but continence is the offence against nature. But the mother in her holiness does not understand that. She will accept punishment because it enhances her status in her own eyes but she will never tolerate the notion of pleasure, since pleasure robs procreation of its aspect of duty.

The ironic worshippers approach the temple and raze it to the ground. The libertines turn the Blessed Virgin over on her belly and sodomise her, transforming the hole nature intended for simple evacuation into an aperture for complex pleasure. Holy Mother says sex is sanctified only in the service of reproduction; nonsense! cry the libertines. The inversion of regular practice transforms the significance of the practice. A simple inversion then becomes a complex transformation. 'Love has pitched his palace in the place of excrement,' said Crazy Jane to the Bishop. The backside, the anus, the areas of the body the consecration of Beauty denies become desirable.

Once desired, they, too, become beautiful.

The libertines in *The One Hundred and Twenty Days at Sodom* take four hideous and aged crones with them on their holiday at the castle. The sexual enthusiasm they exhibit for the wrinkled and ulcerated old monsters is an ironic reversal of the veneration of physical beauty; human ugliness at its most extreme is as extraordinary a phenomenon as beauty and a phenomenon of the same kind, one of excess. So why may it not, too, be appetising? And, like the beautiful girls and boys, the monstrous old women are tortured and killed; they must pay the high price of their own desirability as soon as they are desired.

To be the *object* of desire is to be defined in the passive case.

To exist in the passive case is to die in the passive case – that is, to be killed.

This is the moral of the fairy tale about the perfect woman.

Paradoxically, Justine's only triumph is her refusal to treat herself as a thing, although everybody she meets does. Since this awareness of herself is not shared by anybody else, it remains a victory in a void. She is the bourgeois individualist in its tragic aspect; her sister, Juliette, offers its heroic side. Both are women whose identities have been defined exclusively by men.

three

SEXUALITY AS TERRORISM:
THE LIFE OF JULIETTE

> Time is a man, space is a woman, and her masculine
> portion is death.
>
> *Vision of the Last Judgement*, William Blake

I MAKING IT

The life of Juliette exists in a dialectical relationship to that
of her sister. The vision of the inevitable prosperity of vice,
as shown in her triumphant career, and the vision of the
inevitable misfortunes of virtue that Justine's life offers do
not cancel one another out; rather, they mutually reflect and
complement one another, like a pair of mirrors. Each story
has the same moral, offered at many levels, which may be
summed up as: the comfort of one class depends on the
misery of another class. There is no room in Sade's impeccable logic for the well-upholstered wishful thinking that
would like the poor to have more money if that did not mean
we ourselves had less. To be a woman is to be automatically
at a disadvantage in a man's world, just like being poor, but
to be a woman is a more easily remedied condition. If she
abandons the praxis of femininity, then it is easy enough to

enter the class of the rich, the men, provided one enters it on the terms of that class.

The life of Juliette proposes a method of profane mastery of the instruments of power. She is a woman who acts according to the precepts and also the practice of a man's world and so she does not suffer. Instead, she causes suffering.

'It was no accident that the Marquis de Sade chose heroines and not heroes,' said Guillaume Apollinaire. 'Justine is woman as she has been until now, enslaved, miserable and less than human; her opposite, Juliette, represents the woman whose advent he anticipated, a figure of whom minds have as yet no conception, who is rising out of mankind, who will have wings and who will renew the world.' Seventy years ago, Apollinaire could equate Juliette with the New Woman; it is not so easy to do so today, although Juliette remains a model for women, in some ways. She is rationality personified and leaves no single cell of her brain unused. She will never obey the fallacious promptings of her heart. Her mind functions like a computer programmed to produce two results for herself – financial profit and libidinal gratification. By the use of her reason, an intellectual apparatus women themselves are still inclined to undervalue, she rids herself of some of the more crippling aspects of femininity; but she is a New Woman in the mode of irony.

She is, just as her sister is, a description of a type of female behaviour rather than a model of female behaviour and her triumph is just as ambivalent as is Justine's disaster. Justine is the thesis, Juliette the antithesis; both are without hope and neither pays any heed to a future in which might lie the possibility of a synthesis of their modes of being, neither submissive nor aggressive, capable of both thought and feeling.

If Justine is a pawn because she is a woman, Juliette transforms herself from pawn to queen in a single move and henceforward goes wherever she pleases on the chess board.

Nevertheless, there remains the question of the presence of the king, who remains the lord of the game.

Like *The Misfortunes of Virtue*, *The Prosperities of Vice* is also a black fairy tale; but it is Justine-through-the-looking glass, an inversion of an inversion, so that it has a happy ending in which true lovers are united and good fortune smiles on everyone. The immense, picaresque narrative relates with precision every detail of Juliette's career. Juliette performs all the crimes of which Justine is falsely accused, and is never punished for them; instead she is rewarded because she does not submit to the law at all. She does not need to submit to the law; she is in complicity with the law and it is adjusted, if not made, for her benefit. She sleeps with the makers of the laws and caters to their picturesque sexual needs; she knows their weak spots, and indulges them, and so she has their Mafia-like protection. Further, the pain inflicted on Justine is transformed into Juliette's pleasure, by the force of Juliette's will and desire for self-mastery and heightened extremes of experience. Juliette has learned to take pleasure from pain and herself demands that delicious excitation of the nerves; and nothing will scar the thick skin of this well-fleshed brunette, who knows how to do her own soliciting and is never the sexual prey, except for the sake of a ruse or a game.

Juliette's life is like the reign of Tamburlaine the Great, an arithmetical progression of atrocities. If we admire the campaigns of a great general, is it hypocrisy to refuse to admire Juliette's? If her life is also, as is Justine's life, a pilgrimage towards death – for even Juliette must die – in a world governed by god, the king and the law, the trifold masculine symbolism of authority, then Juliette knows better than her sister how useless it is to rebel against fate. She is so much in control of herself she may not even do this unconsciously.

The story of Juliette begins, not where the version of *Justine* of 1791 ends, with a repentant Juliette entering a convent, but at the beginning of Juliette's own

autobiography after a rather more extravagant version of
the life of Justine herself. We return to Juliette's boudoir
and Justine herself is there to listen to Juliette's story. The
novel will end with another, profane, version of the death of
Justine.

Juliette's story-telling function is itself part of her
whoreishness. She is a perfect whore, like the whores in *The
Hundred and Twenty Days at Sodom*. In that book, four
libertines take four of the most brilliant and distinguished
prostitutes in Paris off for a holiday to the remote and
isolated Castle of Silling, besides a numerous complement of
wives, servants and victims. These four women survive the
ensuing holocaust; they will all return home safe and sound,
not only because they are consummately wicked, but
because, like Scheherazade, they know how to utilise the
power of the word, of narrative, to save their lives. The
continuity of their narratives protects them from the
discontinuity of death. These women, like Juliette, tell the
stories of their lives. Their sexual anecdotes determine the
form of the orgies in the castle and so they can ensure they
themselves will not be sacrificed during any of them.
Juliette, the personfication of the whore as story-teller,
often breaks off her narrative for sexual encounters with her
listeners, who are all old friends and occasionally appear as
actual actors in it. She leaves a pornographic hole in the text
on purpose for them.

For Justine, an unwilling listener, her sister's autobiography and her own involuntary participation in the
rituals accompanying it, are another form of martyrdom,
the martyrdom of unwilling exposure to pornography.

Juliette's education begins in the convent where she and
her sister spent their childhoods. If Justine learned piety
and submission there, Juliette learned pleasure and reason.
The abbess, Delbène, has been sent to the convent against
her will, to spare her parents the expense of a dowry, and
she spends her ample leisure inculcating in those young girls
in her charge in whom she spies a natural propensity for vice

the elements of sexual expertise, the relativity of ethics, militant feminism and doctrinaire atheism. The notion of a natural propensity for vice is essential to Sadeian psychology; vice is innate, as is virtue, if social conditions are unalterable. This straitjacket psychology relates his fiction directly to the black and white ethical world of fairy tale and fable; it is in conflict with his frequently expounded general theory of moral relativity, that good and evil are not the same thing at all times and in all places. So his characters represent moral absolutes in a world where no moral absolutes exist. This is the major contradiction inherent in his fiction, which he never resolves.

Like all Sade's rational women, Delbène prefers her own sex. Juliette is an eager pupil; she gains information, not only from Delbène, but from a friend who runs away to work in a brothel. Juliette makes friends easily, unlike her sister; solitude is not her quality, even when she is alone, and she is as incapable of introspection as she is incapable of melancholy. Not only has she no inner life; she would deny the existence of such a thing.

For Juliette, the convent is a school of love. Her initiation is completed by a murder, for the convent is also a Sadeian place of privilege where everything is permissible. The Abbess Delbène adopts a mothering relation to Juliette. She is the first and welcomed fairy godmother in Juliette's history, the type of the mature libertine woman who has sharpened her reason and her sex into a weapon. She is an aristocratic and cultured version of the brigand, La Dubois, whose protection Justine refused in the early days of her career. Unlike La Dubois, Delbène has had the means and the opportunity to cultivate her intellect; she reads Spinoza and lectures Juliette on the nature of justice and on the sexual autonomy of women. She has a cold heart, and she murders for pleasure.

The voice of reason, always subversive, must issue from a monster; Sade must censor Delbène, as he creates her. She is rational, therefore wicked.

In Delbène's arms, Juliette nourishes her own special qualities of transgression and sacrilege. From Delbène, she learns a stoicism that serves her well when Delbène turns her out of the convent the moment Juliette's father loses all his money. Delbène is not interested in poor girls. Juliette parts company with the grief-stricken Justine when she sees Justine will not accompany her to the brothel where her friend preceded her. But Juliette herself is eager to learn a trade with which to support herself.

This brothel is an earthly paradise where all the pleasures of the flesh are available, but nothing is free. It is a Sadeian place of privilege; like all brothels in Sade, it is an evil Eden that might, at any moment, turn into hell. It operates with the wholehearted support and approval of the police. In an absolute privacy purchased for cash, all sexual tastes are permissible but it is as if a *cordon sanitaire* surrounds these places. The Sadeian paradise is a model of the world, in its cash-sale structure; and also it is a place of exile from the world, a place of imaginary liberty where the ritual perversions of the libertines contain no element of a taboo freely broken but come to dominate their lives, like the rigid rituals of the Catholic church. Privilege has a negative aspect. It is like the freedom of the outlaw, which only exists in relation to the law itself. Privilege is in itself a denial of common experiences. The brothel presents a closed system, encapsulated from the reality it both mimics and denies. Women rule in the brothel, as in the nursery, which it somewhat resembles; but the economic power lies in the hands of the customers, who can always take their cash elsewhere, or even refuse to pay. So the whores resort to theft.

Theft represents the morality of the outlaw. Duval, the master thief, lectures the girls: 'If you trace the right of property back to its source, you always arrive at usurpation.' Theft, therefore, is a moral imperative; it is a means of redistributing property. Theft, deceit and cunning are the revenges of the weak upon the strong, of the poor upon the rich. One of Juliette's colleagues encourages her to steal for the sake of the principle of human equality; where equality has not been established by chance or fate, it is up to the poor to ensure it by their ingenuity.

The brothel is also a place of lies, of false appearances. Juliette's virginity is sold successively to fifty buyers and, for each customer, she must act out a part – that she is starving and forced to sell herself; that it was her mother who sold her to the brothel. And so on, a series of flattering charades designed to persuade the customers they are not dealing with simple business-women, that the weeping creatures who reluctantly bend themselves to their superior will are, in fact, so many innocent Justines.

Juliette concludes her apprenticeship of flesh by selling her anus to an archbishop. She has already a well-developed taste for anal intercourse; she is proud of her superb arse and the outrageous, unnatural uses to which she puts it. Not only is it a crime, according to the morality of her century, it is also an excellent contraceptive measure, and motherhood, as yet, has no part in her plans.

Now, the last of her virginities gone, she is fully equipped to enter upon a wider stage than that of her first brothel, Madame Duvergier's establishment.

She meets a man of power, the statesman, Noirceuil, who teaches her how Nature made the weak to be the slaves of the strong. She learns her lesson at once; to escape slavery, she must embrace tyranny. All living creatures are born and die in isolation, says Noirceuil; in the cultivation and practice of egoism and self-interest alone may be found true happiness. Juliette is immediately drawn to this credo of bourgeois individualism.

When Noirceuil tells Juliette that he murdered her father, she declares that she loves him and is soon installed in his house as his mistress, with special instructions to torment his wife, whom he designates as a 'mere pleasure machine'. Noirceuil has also instructed her in the rare pleasures of avarice. She returns to Duvergier's brothel, to earn more money in her spare time, for the richer she becomes, the more money she must have.

Duvergier, the madame, is another fairy godmother, although she is not a diabolic one. The most wicked act that she performs is an attempt to foist a syphilitic upon Juliette and she apologises when Juliette angrily rejects him, and goes off to find a substitute harlot, because the syphilitic pays well so she cannot turn him away. If Juliette did indeed accept Duvergier's proffered mother, she might have led the quiet and unexemplary life of a fairly honest whore, in time the mistress of her own establishment. But Juliette has ambitions far beyond this.

The brothel is a place of appearances and lies; it is also a place where paradoxical truths are put into the mouths of those we expect to lie, so you may accept them or not, as you please. If the whores and the thieves have advanced a libertarian—communist theory of the ownership of property, then Duvergier offers a rational distinction between love and fancy. Love, she says, need not cohabit with fidelity; she shows Juliette a room filled with respectably married women all waiting for illicit lovers. Yet not one of these women does not adore nor is not adored by the man with whom she lives. And there is nothing odd about that opines Duvergier cosily! Love is a moral and intellectual passion based on respect and comradeship; the fancies of the flesh are of a different order of experience, not to be despised because they give us so much pleasure but in no way trespassing on the integrity of the heart's affections.

Juliette rewards Duvergier for her good advice and cherishing by, later, poisoning her.

Juliette is well-paid by Noirceuil. She steals. She sells herself on the side. She prospers, until she falls foul of a certain Duke whom she has robbed and he has her thrown in prison. Noirceuil rescues her on condition she incriminates an innocent girl for the crime; the unfortunate are the playthings of the rich.

By this act of false witness, Juliette puts herself firmly in the camp of the masters. Like her sister, she feels no natural bond between herself and other women; why should she? Her circumstances are not those of most women. She has no sense of women as a class; it is difficult to ascertain whether Sade does so himself. Sade regularly subsumes women to the general class of the weak and therefore the exploited, and so he sees femininity as a mode of experience that transcends gender. Feminine impotence is a quality of the poor, regardless of sex. Juliette is an exception; by the force of her will, she will become a Nietzschian superwoman, which is to say, a woman who has transcended her gender but not the contradictions inherent in it.

After this brush with justice, Juliette is ready to be introduced to the representatives of the law. Noirceuil invites her to a dinner party to meet Saint Fond, one of whose activities is the distribution of warrants for arbitrary arrest. Another guest is D'Albert, chief justice of the Parlement de Paris, who promises Juliette a life-long immunity from punishment under the law. Saint Fond makes Juliette lick his arse, after dinner: 'Kneel and face it; consider the honour I do you in permitting you to do my arse the homage an entire nation, no, the whole world aspires to give it!' Sade occasionally, if confusingly, sometimes says exactly what he means. The interminable arse-licking his characters engage in is nothing more than metaphor made concrete.

Coprophagy is one of the rarest sexual variations but it plays a large part in Sade's lexicon of sexual activity. Juliette soon accustoms herself to eating the shit of the great. In *The Hundred and Twenty Days at Sodom*, the four libertines who rule the castle always take a victim or two with them to the privy, to clean their arses for them. This is the way to court the favour of the great, to gently cleanse their maculated assholes with a cunning tongue. If you do it long enough, it becomes second nature; you hardly notice the taste. Not the pursuit of erotic pleasure but enlightened self-interest has overcome the barrier of disgust.

For the libertines themselves, it is a different matter.

They, too, gladly eat shit but they control its production. An elaborate bureaucracy is established to govern the production and distribution of faecal matter in *The Hundred and Twenty Days at Sodom.* The victims are placed on special diets, to ensure the quality and flavour of the turds. Saint Fond will put Juliette on a similar diet, for the same reason, and instruct her how to take care of her health to safeguard his own. The libertines become veritable connoisseurs of the turd, comparing vintages and bouquets with the mincing pedantry of the wine snob.

But the excremental activity of the victims who produce these comestibles is governed by rigid sanctions. In the Castle of Silling, the victims may shit only at certain times of the day and then only with permission of the masters, who may refuse at whim. The involuntary production of shit is severely punished.

The nature of production-consumption relation of shit in Sade is illuminated by a psychoanalytic interpretation. The faeces are the child's first gift. He can give them or withhold them at whim; utilising his excremental production, he can cause his mother delight or distress since, by producing them, he expresses active compliance with his environment and, by retaining them, disaffection. With his shit, he expresses obedience or disobedience. Before he can speak, his excretions are the child's means of expression – shit and tears; in this, he is just like the victims in the castle. He is, however, more in control of his shit than he is of his weepings. Excretion is his first concrete production and, through it, the child gains his first experience of labour relations. He may reserve the right to go on excremental strike or to engage in a form of faecal offensive. The excremental faculty is a manipulative device and to be baulked of the free control of it is to be deprived of the first, most elementary, expression of autonomy. The victims of the libertines may not shit when and as they please; they are under the severest restraints in this particular. But the masters are perfectly free to roll at will in their own ordure, to be as clean or as filthy as they please, to exercise total excremental liberty. This is a sign of their mastery, to return, as adults, freely, to a condition of infantilism.

The libertines acknowledge the turd as gift. 'Let me eat her gift,' says a coprophagic customer of the prostitute-narrator, Duclos, in *The Hundred and Twenty Days at Sodom*. But these gifts are always extorted. The gifts are brutally ravished from the owners, produced on order according to contract in the brothel and by Juliette, or in fear of force in the castle. The libertines usurp the primary physical freedom of the body. They monopolise the elementary productions of the bodies of others and arbitrarily regulate involuntary physical functions.

The coprophagic passions of the libertines reflect their exhaustive greed. The anal Juliette has an appropriately anal passion for capital accumulation. There is more to coprophagy than a particularly exotic perversion that requires an extraordinary degree of mastery of disgust to be able to indulge in it; the coprophage's taste asserts the function of flesh as a pure means of production in itself. His economic sense, alert even in the grip of passion, insists that even the waste products of the flesh must not be wasted. All must be consumed.

The coprophiliac Saint Fond, who demands that even his own waste products should be treated with reverence, employs Juliette as his procuress and his poisoner at a fabulous salary. Her first task in this position is to poison Noirceuil's wife; her next, to poison Saint Fond's father. Her relation with Noirceuil contains a great deal of the affection characteristic of Sadeian comrades in crime; that with Saint Fond is based more on self-interest tinged with fear. But now she makes her first truly significant relationship; she becomes the friend of the beautiful and terrible Madame de Clairwil, who prides herself upon never having shed a tear.

Her relation with Clairwil is, at first, not quite one of equals although Juliette never adopts a subservient role to her. Juliette is more beautiful than she; she does not frighten men so much and this gives her a tactical advantage over her friend but there is no element of rivalry between them, for Clairwil is a great aristocrat, born to power of her own. She does not need men to validate her power, as Juliette does. But she is less resilient than Juliette because she is less flexible. Juliette, child of a banker and hence a daughter of the bourgeoisie, is the representative of a rising class, the class that will dominate the coming century, and Clairwil's aristocratic ascendancy is on the wane. The ease with which Juliette robs princes and, later, with which she disposes of the Princess Borghese when she gets tired of her, also suggests the aristocracy no longer have the power that the politicians, Noirceuil and Saint Fond wield.

Nevertheless, she and Clairwil have enough in common to feel themselves sisters. Later, they will pose as sisters. Both belong to the same maenad and violent sisterhood of female libertines and so form a terrible alliance, like avenging angels who are always in complicity with the seat of power; they remain angels of the lord. Having acceded, as women, to the world of men, their mastery of that world reveals its monomaniac inhumanity to the full, just as Justine's incompetence trapped in the circumstances of her life as a woman, also did. Their liberation from the limitations of femininity is a personal one, for themselves only. They gratify themselves fully but it is a liberation without enlightenment and so becomes an instrument for the oppression of others, both women and men. One of Sade's cruellest lessons is that tyranny is implicit in all privilege. My freedom makes you more unfree, if it does not acknowledge your freedom, also.

Clairwil's monstrous lusts encompass murder and she hates men far more than Juliette does. It is men she loves to murder: 'I adore avenging my sex for the horrors men subject us to when the monsters have the upper hand.' Her beauty is the cruel beauty of the Medusa; she overwhelms and dominates whereas Juliette, more cunning, is content to seduce. Clairwil's rationality is allied with wit and her atheism has a kind of wild glory about it. Her castratory rage is intellectually qualified; she has always felt herself debased by the mere sight of men. Only men arouse her to serious cruelties. She is an 'enragée', like some of the furious women of the French Revolution, but her rage extends only to her own nymphomaniac passions, that reduce the men upon whom she inflicts her vengeance to disembodied phalli. She has no other use for them. She is dedicated to sexual warfare and will, as the sequel to an orgy in a Carmelite monastery during which she and Juliette have exhausted every single one of the inmates, shear off the handsome prick of a young friar, embalm it and use it for a dildo.

Clairwil's enthusiasm for the depersonalised prick, the sublime penis, is boundless. After she dies, she claims, a dissection will find a penis growing in her brain; her desire is so great that she has incorporated the desired object in herself, but, unassimilated, it still retains its own form. This is one of the contradictions of Sade's female libertines, that they ingest but do not integrate within themselves the signs of maleness.

Juliette is now obscenely rich and lives with obscene opulence. During a famine, she finds herself unable to give charity to the starving because of the expenses she has incurred in a project for building mirrored boudoirs in her park, in the purchase of statues for her garden, in improving her lawns. It gives her great pleasure to deny charity; if it gives her so much pleasure *not* to do good, she reasons, must it not give her still greater pleasure to do evil? As soon as the decision is made, she moves firmly from the passive to the active, to gratuitous crime, and Clairwil puts her up for membership of a unique club, the Sodality of the Friends of Crime.

The Sodality is an institution of the highest privilege. It is a model of a society entirely devoted to libidinous gratification, like the Castle of Silling in *The Hundred and Twenty Days at Sodom* and the monastery of St Mary-in-the-Wood and so it is like a nursery as it might be if the children themselves had the sole running of it, and it is also like a concentration camp from the point of view of the guards. It is itself a secularised monastery; indeed, it is a post-humanist, ironic version of Rabelais' Abbey of Thélème, which had as its only rule the exhortation: 'Do what thou wilt.' This is certainly the motto of the Sodality. But Rabelais believed no rules were required 'because men that are free, well-born, well-bred and conversant in honest companies, have naturally an instinct and spurre that prompteth them unto vertuous actions, and withdraws them from vice.' No such considerations apply here. Like all Utopias, its literary and political origin is the Republic of Plato, which the Sodality curiously resembles in its inflexibility and elitism; a parodic Good Society, supported by wealth, power and immunity from the law.

The luxuriously appointed premises of the Sodality are fitted up with seraglios, printshops and torture chambers; it runs its own kitchens and its own cab-ranks, self-feeding and self-transporting. It is a society in miniature in which nobody engages in productive labour nor wears any clothes except the ritual uniform of nakedness which is a mark of the members' elite status. Even their skins have become signs of rank. Here, the price of pleasure is death but not the death of any of the initiates. The Sodality is divided into three classes: the libertines; their victims; and their servants, the cooks, harem keepers, torturers and nurses who are immune from harm because they are useful. Their serviceability precludes their victimisation. Unlike Plato, however, Sade allows a token handful of artists to enter this sacrosanct domain, at a cheap rate. This is like a little prefiguration of Marcuse's theory of repressive sublimation; if artists are allowed a taste of some of the wild joys of privilege, they will throw their lots in with the masters immediately. If art is indeed, as Sade defined it, 'the perpetual immoral subversion of the existing order', the artist is emasculated the moment he enters, with the complimentary ticket he has accepted with such humiliating eagerness and gratitude, the brothels of the ruling class. This might also apply to Juliette herself.

The Sodality is dedicated to atheism and its members acknowledge none of the familial and marital bonds that they have outside its doors. All dissolve on entering the Sodality's premises. Its privilege extends to all areas of sexual taboo. Expulsion is guaranteed for good works. The president and all the officers are elected by secret ballot; in a community of equals, the libertines observe egalitarian relations with one another. Any woman or any man may be elected president, even if the rules for women members of the Sodality state categorically that women 'are created for the pleasure of man'. The egalitarianism of the Sodality extends only to the members of the class of masters, however. The Sodality, with its rules, its system, its free ballots, its torture chambers, its acknowledgement of the diabolism of privacy, its mutual regard among its members, is the most systematic and depraved of Sade's inverted Edens. Even the Castle of Silling allows more humanity to its victims.

Juliette is now visited by her father, who, it turns out, never died at all, although her mother did; he was ruined and forced into hiding. He reappears with all the unexpectedness of picaresque fiction, a good and virtuous man moved to tears to meet his daughter again. She easily seduces him, is impregnated by him, murders him and subsequently aborts his child; so she rids herself of the spectre of his paternal authority over her by a systematic series of ritual transgressions. She absorbs his essence and then excretes it. Justine weeps to hear all this. Juliette's patricidal embrace and the infanticide which is the completion of the banishment of the father from her life seems the completion of some form of apprenticeship; she is now ready to enter the ranks of the sexual instructresses and Noirceuil entrusts her with the education of his new wife,

Saint Fond's daughter. But the girl does not show herself an apt pupil. She will not join Juliette and Clairwil in the camaraderie of libertine superwomen. Instead, she will be sexually martyrised for her husband's pleasure, just as all his other wives have been.

Now Juliette is ready to meet the poisoner, Durand, who has used the formal methods of reason to become a witch. Durand's primal powers are precisely those of enlightenment and reason, put at the service of nihilism. She quotes Archimedes; 'give me a lever big enough and I will move the world', but, for herself, it is a herb that might poison the world she wants. She is a biochemist and her area of study is natural poison. Her profession is the sale of death.

Durand has mastered this world so well that she can foretell the future and she forecasts the death of Clairwil. She is the greatest, most monstrous, most potent of all Sade's cruel godmothers. Her habits are those of the wicked stepmother of fairy tale, the ogre queens who devour babies, and her sexual ambivalence is hermaphroditic. Though she is well past the age of child-bearing, she is extraordinarily beautiful and she is prepared to adopt Juliette as her daughter. The crimes and libertinage of Durand will become the protection and the pleasures of her beloved. But not yet; having introduced herself to the two women, she vanishes, with the suddenness of magic.

Saint Fond now takes Juliette into his complete confidence, and outlines a scheme for the devastation of France which will result in immense profits for himself. He will raze the schools and poorhouses to the ground; send the country to war, the most profitable of all speculations; and produce a famine by his monopoly of the supply of corn. He suggests that Juliette assist him. When she hears his proposals, she shudders and, for this involuntary show of horror, she is doomed. Saint Fond sees her shudder and decides to kill her. Her friend, Noirceuil, warns her; she runs away at once, abandoning her mansions, her safes filled with money, her bank accounts. Her flights, her peregrinations are as involuntary as her sister's but her life does not have the form of a pilgrimage, more of a battle campaign, and now she beats a strategic retreat. However much money she leaves behind, ever forethoughtful, she always manages to conceal a little around her person, that person which is in itself her capital.

She opens a gambling house at Angers and prospers. Soon, she marries the virtuous Count de Lorsanges, cuckolds him, bears him a daughter, poisons him, inherits all and, rich once again, abandons her child to travel to Italy, posing as a rich courtesan. Now she aspires to the highest style. Her friends and clients are kings and princes, all persons of unspeakable wickedness. Her whoreishness is her preservation since she acts as a kind of Figaro of vice, the servant who maintains the instruments of control whilst adopting the attitudes of submission. Control, method, system are Juliette's qualities.

Yet Juliette has a passion for volcanoes, which seem to her the image of the strength and indifference of nature. Whilst gazing into the crater of a volcano, she and her companions – for, unlike Justine, she is never without a faithful entourage – are captured by the cannibal giant, Minski, who lives in a castle in the middle of a lake, a place of privilege with a strong symbolic resemblance to the great original of all places of privilege, the womb. Minski's castle is furnished with girls – chairs, tables, sideboards all formed of the living flesh of captive women. He has reduced women to their final use function, 'thingified' them into sofas, tables and candelabras. His wealth is a guarantee he will live on in this fashion undisturbed. Juliette drugs him and escapes with her friends and his treasure, assuring the castle full of victims they have released from their dungeons that Minski is dead. The victims rejoice; when he wakes up from his drugged sleep, he will kill them all. How Juliette and her maids laugh to think of this dénouement.

Now she travels to Florence, opens a brothel, grows infinitely rich, robs her customers as if theft were a form of

sexuality or sexuality of theft, commits many murders and
moves on to Rome, the holy city.

Rome is significant for Juliette for two reasons. First, she
makes another bosom friend, the wicked and beautiful
Princess Olympe de Borghese. If Clairwil, the man-hater
who has absorbed the phallus, the sign of maleness, into her
own brain, is savagery and lucidity, then the velvet, in-
dolent Borghese is a pure voluptuary; her crimes are part of
her vicious sensuality and are not the fruit of a steely
process of self-discipline. She is a princess and wickedness is
as natural to her as breathing. She is a glutton for pleasure,
like a huge, cruel cat and cruel as a cat is sleepily cruel, by
nature. She lives for sensual excess and pain is a judicious
sharpening of her senses. Her tastes tend towards the
rococo, the decorative; her orgies require the presence of
menageries of animals and the deformed, dwarves,
geriatrics, hermaphrodites.

She loves to keep captives and would like to enslave entire
nations but, also, she would like to be a public whore, the
butt, the plaything, the victim of libertines, desiring at the
same time to enslave and be herself enslaved. A certain
hysteria characterises her. Like the Italy in which she lives,
she is so ripe that she is rotten.

Juliette's second acquaintance in Rome is the Pope
himself. This Pope, like many of his predecessors, is a
profligate atheist. His coprophilia is a statement of his
apostasy: 'I worship shit.' Juliette participates in an orgy at
the altar of St Peter's, a venue of, simultaneously, privilege
and sacrilege. There are further murderous orgies in the
Sistine Chapel; these are the most fitting shrines for crime,
opines Sade. After robbing the Pope of a vast sum of money,
Juliette sets out for fresh infamies in Naples. Once more,
she is captured on the way; again, her capture is a fortunate
one. The brigand chief, Brisatesta, takes her to his moated
castle at the peak of a mountain but his wife, the sister with
whom he lives, gives a cry of joy when she sees Juliette;
there will be no tortures for this captive, for Brisatesta's

incestuous wife is none other than Clairwil. The two women
fall into one another's arms. By a happy accident, the next
wayfarer brought captive to the castle proves to be
Juliette's new friend, Borghese, and she, too, is reprieved
and feasted.

Brisatesta now tells his life story. This is interesting
because of its account of a comprehensive Sadeian
education. He and Clairwil were grounded thoroughly in
libertinage at the hands of their father and his mistress,
their governess. Their mother took part in the anatomy
lessons only under duress; at one point, Brisatesta bit off
her nipple and, finally, at his father's request, murdered her.
Next, inspired by greed for his inheritance, he murdered his
father and set out on his travels – Europe, the Netherlands,
Sweden and at last Russia, growing richer and more wicked
with every crime along the way. In Russia, he met Catherine
the Great, a Sadeian malefic despot, the Messalina of all the
Russias, and became her lover but, when he bungled the
poisoning of the Tsarevitch, she sent Brisatesta to Siberia.
He escaped to Turkey and an eventual reunion with his
beloved sister; she has abandoned Paris for him and they
now devote themselves to domesticity, brigandage and
orgiastic recreations in their mountain fastness. A marriage
of true minds, they are a model Sadeian couple.

But Clairwil's love for Juliette overcomes that for her
brother. The three women decide to travel on together,
posing as sisters, and arrive in Naples, where they engage in
atrocious infamies with the king and queen, utilising, as
Juliette does more and more frequently, ingenious
mechanical contrivances that arithmetically multiply the
humiliation and the suffering of her victims. Her passions
now require an increasingly technological gratification.
Flesh itself is no longer enough.

The girls soon grow bored with Borghese and toss her into
the crater of Vesuvius; then they leave Naples, taking with
them half the contents of King Ferdinand's treasury, after
framing his queen for the theft. But Clairwil's time is

running out. It is not that Juliette is growing bored with her too; their affinity is too strong to be eroded by boredom. But the date that the crystal-gazing fortune teller, Durand, forecast for her death is approaching and they meet Durand again, in Ancona, famous for its shrine. Consumed by passion for Juliette, Durand tricks her into poisoning Clairwil and Juliette admits that she, too, is in love with Durand. The two women form a pact of trust, affection and obligation that, henceforward, neither will break.

The form of marriage contract they make between them is an interesting one. Both are murderesses by temperament; they will not even promise that they will not kill one another, however, for such a denial would, in itself, imply a lack of trust. Durand, for all her infinite knowledge and power, is a suppliant for Juliette; she is the more in love and she asks Juliette for only one thing – that she, Durand, will always be the mistress of Juliette's heart and, as to her body, she may do with it what she pleases. Juliette, struck by this combination of rationality and sentiment, swears this will be so. They also make complicated arrangements about their shared finances and their travelling plans. Their first adventure together is a spree with a group of sailors to whom they also sell a great quantity of poisons; in the hands of these two women, Eros is not at war with death but in complicity with it. Their second joint venture is a profitable robbery. Then they set out for Venice, where they open a combined brothel and poison dispensary, with Durand posing as Juliette's mother.

In Venice, Durand experiences her unique but potentially fatal moment of weakness. Representatives of the Serene Republic ask her to spread a plague throughout the city and, stunned by the enormity of the crime, she refuses. As soon as the words are out of her mouth, she knows she is lost. She warns Juliette to run away, and herself vanishes, with that magic speed and conclusiveness characteristic of her. Juliette assumes Durand has been murdered. Once again, Juliette leaves great wealth behind her but, since

Saint Fond is now dead, she is able to return to France,
where she is welcomed by Noirceuil and establishes herself
once again in Paris. All the money she abandoned there is
restored to her. Her travels are at an end; home life can
begin again. She sends for her infant daughter from Angers;
it is time that the child's education began, she has reached
the age of seven. They all leave for the country, to educate
her in the privacy of Noirceuil's country house.

Noirceuil announces that he wishes to indulge in a curious
fancy.

> I should like to get married, not once, but twice on the same
> day. At ten o clock in the morning, I wish to dress as a woman
> and marry a man; at noon, wearing male dress, I wish to marry
> a female role homosexual dressed as my bride . . . I wish,
> furthermore, to have a woman do the same as I do, and what
> other woman but you, Juliette, could take part in this game?
> You, dressed as a woman, must marry a woman dressed as a
> man at the same ceremony where I, dressed as a woman,
> become the wife of a man. Next, dressed as a man, you will
> marry another woman wearing female attire at the same time
> that I go to the altar to be united in holy wedlock with a
> catamite disguised as a girl.

Her own daughter will marry Juliette when Juliette is
dressed as a man; Noirceuil will marry a son and then a
daughter of his own. The ceremonies are carried out. They
are followed by the slaughter of all the children; these sterile
marriages produce, not births, but infanticide.

This charade of sexual anarchy, this gross parody of
marriage, this demonstration of the relative mutability of
gender, with its culmination in child-murder carried out in a
maenad frenzy, is Juliette's annihilation of her residual
'femaleness'; it is, psychologically and emotionally, the
climax of her career. Although the narrative continues for a
few pages more after this extraordinary episode, she herself
has reached her apogee and become the type of criminal
female libertine who has cauterised the wounds of her own
castration and become a source of pure power. Justine's life
was a pilgrimage; Juliette's is a battle campaign with, as its

final victory, the conquest of all disgust, horror, superstition, prejudice – and finally, humanity.

When she hurls her daughter into the fire, as she does, she
is, at last, absolutely free from any lingering traces of the
human responses that can only be learned through the
society of others who are not accomplices, who are not
aspects of the self that confirm the omnipotence of the self.
She has indeed attained the lonely freedom of the libertine,
which is the freedom of the outlaw, a tautological condition
that exists only for itself and is without any meaning in the
general context of human life. Sade's irony suggests that
only those who make the laws may inherit this freedom; the
moral of Juliette's life suggests the paradox of the hangman
– in a country where the hangman rules, only the hangman
escapes punishment for his crimes.

Juliette lives in a country where the hangman rules. The
hangman is god, the king and the law itself; the hangman is
the representative of a patriarchal order which is unjust not
because such an order specifically oppresses women but
because it is oppressive in itself, since it confines power to a
single dominant class. Juliette survives and prospers in this
country because she has identified all her interests with
those of the hangman.

For Noirceuil and not she has been the instigator of this
extraordinary game of dressing up and gender transformation, and he is careful to omit certain elaborations
that would truly suggest an anarchy of the sexes – that, for
example, Juliette, as a man, should marry he himself, as a
woman; not for one moment, even in fantasy, could he allow
Juliette to act out that kind of class dominance over himself. For all her aggression, in spite of her dominance over
others, Juliette remains a contingent being in relation to
Noirceuil, her protector. She depends on his approval; she
does as he bids, and her final act of defeminisation is
prompted and approved by him.

But now she and Noirceuil proceed to dizzying crimes;
they poison a well, and spread devastation throughout the

province. They are comrades. They exult in their power of distributing death. As a result of throwing in her lot with the hangman, Juliette has become the hangman herself.

Her autobiography in her own words concludes here. Now the narrative reverts to the third person, in order to report the second version of the death of Justine in an objective style. Justine is to die, again, in an atrocious fashion.

A storm rages outside. The company turns its attention to Juliette's weeping sister; she is thrust out into the tempest and at once a thunderbolt enters her mouth and bursts out through her vagina. She is dead. Juliette and her companions laugh to see how the thunderbolt has ravaged her and commit derisory necrophilies upon her corpse. After a few aphorisms on the negative rewards of virtue, they leave her in the rain and return to the house. Nature has killed Justine in a parody of the act of giving birth.

A coach now arrives at the mansion and from it descends, wonder of wonders, Durand, alive and well and, besides, bringing with her all the revenues that Juliette had abandoned in Venice. She escaped death by acceding to the request of the Republic and infecting the city with plague; she stifled her reluctance and asked for Juliette's funds as a bonus payment. The two women embrace; to the joys of wealth they add those of friendship and of passionate attachment.

Now good news rains in from all sides. A courtier arrives from Versailles; Noirceuil has been made Prime Minister and shares his good fortune with his friends, distributing money and offices with a lordly hand. All ends in a splendid banquet and orgy. They return to Paris, to rule the country.

Juliette will continue her glittering career; until, at about the time of her climacteric, she will die, suddenly, like a meteor that is suddenly extinguished.

II DEATH OF THE GODDESS

Justine is the holy virgin; Juliette is the profane whore. If Juliette has notably fewer spiritual great-granddaughters than her sister in the imaginary brothel where ideas of women are sold, then perhaps it serves to show how much in love with the idea of the blameless suffering of women we all are, men and women both. Juliette never pretends to be blameless. On the contrary, she glories in her crimes, especially in their gratuitousness, and eschews guilt as if it were her victims who should be guilty at their stupidity in falling into her clutches. Since she specialises in *realpolitik*, it is not surprising that she is more like a real woman than Justine could ever be, and bequeathed only a now outmoded model – that of the vamp – to the image industry. Her appearances as Miss Stern, or Dolores, Lady of Pain, are role-playing; Miss Stern existed before Juliette and, as a sexually specialised fantasy, is never either more or less with us.

And, shorn of her menacing apparatus of flagellatory machines, poisons and cunt-cracking dildos that suggest men are supererogatory, Juliette stands for the good old virtues of self-reliance and self-help; 'looking after Number One', as we say in Britain. She is an advertisement of the advantages of free enterprise and her successes in business – her gambling houses, brothels and dispensaries thrive, her investments always yield fruitful returns – are so many examples of the benefits of a free market economy. And not only does she illustrate the advantages of self-help but also of mutual aid. Self-reliant as she is, where would Juliette be without the friends who advise her investments, protect her from the law and warn her when the time comes, as it must come sooner or later in the life of every entrepreneur, to cut her losses and flee to the anonymous securities of her Swiss bank account?

Her satiric function, then, is obvious. The prosperity of crime depends on the fiscal morality of a market-place red in tooth and claw. Juliette is equally criminal in all her dealings, financial as well as sexual. She exploits everyone; no one escapes. The methods of her exploitation are the conventional ones. If Justine's image gave birth to several generations of mythically suffering blondes, Juliette's image lies behind the less numinous prospect of a boardroom full of glamorous and sexy lady executives.

Juliette is of the world, worldly. The main chance is her *modus vivendi*. Her sexual affairs are engaged in either for profit or for fun; she is contemptuous, embarrassed by professions of love. When I think of Juliette, when I try to imagine what she might look like in a restaurant or a night club in late twentieth-century London or New York, when I put her behind a red leather desk high up in one of the corporate palaces of multinational corporations, tetchily telephoning her stockbroker or, most strikingly, interviewing a secretary, male or female, eyeing the applicant with the canny eye of a farmer in the beast market, I see no more resonant image than that of the *Cosmopolitan* girl – hard, bright, dazzling, meretricious. She plays to win, this one; she knows the score. Her femininity is part of the armoury of self-interest.

Juliette's image has less poetic resonance than that of her sister because its heiresses have inherited a modicum of the power available in the world now. She is the token woman in person. Noirceuil told her how it must be so: '. . . intellect, talents, wealth and influence raise some of the weak from the class into which Nature placed them; as soon as these exceptions enter the class of the strong, they acquire all the rights of the strong. Now tyranny, oppression, impunity from the law and the liberal exercise of every crime are fully permitted to them.'

However, Juliette is also something more than this. The suffering sisterhood of imitation Justines all lack the most singular quality of their progenitor, one it is easy to lose sight of among the misfortunes. Fate rains on Justine. For Justine is extraordinarily single-minded. This single-mindedness makes her a rebel against that Fate that mistreats her; she is in revolt, even, against human nature itself, or, rather, against a view of human nature as irredeemably corrupt. Justine would say, as all good revolutionaries have said: 'Even if it *is* so, then it should not be so', and, though she is too pusillanimous to do anything about it, she never deviates from her frail and lonely stand, from the idea that men and women need not necessarily be wicked. And to think of Juliette perfectly at home in the twentieth century, telephoning call-girls for her company's clients, is to purposely overlook the same single-mindedness that gives the girls their curious family resemblance.

Juliette is single-mindedly destructive. Her careerist efficiency is a mask for her true subversiveness: her enthusiasm for systems, organisation and self-control conceals her intuition for entropy, for the reinstitution of a primal chaos, her passion for volcanoes. The sisters exist in a complex dialectic with one another; the experience of one makes plain the experience of the other. The innocent Justine is punished by a law she believes is just; the crime-soiled Juliette is rewarded because she undermines the notion of justice on which the law is allegedly based.

If Juliette is ruthless with her creditors, her clients and those who foolishly seek charity from her, she is also ruthless with herself. She desecrates everything, including herself. She overcomes all barriers of fear, shame and guilt in the business of her life, of her career of self-enhancement. She is the embodiment of that merciless excess, that overreaching will to absolute power that carries within it the seeds of its own destruction because in this world, unhappily, there are no absolutes. *Justine* is a pilgrimage of the soul in search of God written by an atheist; *Juliette* is a version of Faust written by a man who believed that, if man exists, we do not need to invent the devil.

Juliette, Delbène, Clairwil, Borghese, Charlotte of Naples and the unhistoric Catherine the Great who appears in Brisatesta's narrative are exceptional women, so exceptional it is easy to mistake them for female impersonators. Mary Wollstonecraft remarked that she had been 'led to imagine that the few extraordinary women who have rushed in eccentrical directions out of the orbit prescribed to their sex were *male* spirits, confined by mistake in female frames.' The virility of these demonic whores – they use the word, 'whore', as a term of endearment for one another almost as often as they affectionately call one another 'buggeress' – suggests male appetites; but, since the avidity of the male appetite is a social fiction, their very insatiability is a mark of their feminity. Clairwil, the man-hater, can exhaust the combined pricks of all the inhabitants of the monastery of the Carmelites, since this insatiability has in itself a castratory function. Male sexuality exhausts itself in its exertion; Clairwil unmans men by fucking them and then retires to the inexhaustible arms of her female lovers.

For these women, the living prick and the manufactured dildo are interchangeable. Both are simply sources of pleasure; the body itself, to which the prick is or has been attached, is no more than a machine for the production of sensation. The world of Juliette is a mechanistic one, even if she and her friends are machine-minders rather than machines themselves, although they define their own pleasure in mechanical terms, so much friction, so many concussions of the nerves. They are the recipients of a technological approach to biology which ensures that Juliette herself is living proof that biology is not destiny, since biology may be so easily emended.

Yet Juliette is more technically a woman than her sister because she bears a child. Justine's inability to conceive is evidence of her invulnerable virginity and she never gives a thought to her reproductive function. Juliette, on the contrary, is fertile. The contraceptive techniques of her time, the sponges inserted in the vagina, the suppositories, the evasion of vaginal penetration, are incorporated into her hygiene. If she should prove unlucky, there is the midwife with her long needle and concoctions of juniper. She aborts an inconvenient foetus; but is prepared to bring to term the child who will ensure her inheritance from the Count de Lorsanges, although she abandons and eventually murders this daughter. Neglect and infanticide are the formal imperfections of Juliette's mothering. They render her mothering invalid.

Her acknowledgement of her fecundity and her refusal to conceive transforms both the form and the content of the act of love itself, just as her refusal to act as a mother changes the nature of the fact that she has given birth. Anal intercourse was, at that time, a capital crime in France because it robbed sexuality of its reproductive aspect; therefore Juliette's enthusiasm for buggery is a subversive use of her own reproductive organs. She is happy to ignore them in the pursuit of pleasure, and, to the pleasure of the flesh, she adds the moral pleasure of a sin against God. Each time she offers her backside to a new lover, she commits an irreligious sacrilege.

Sacrilege is essential to these Sadeian women. The Abbess Delbène loves to get herself fucked upon a coffin in a crypt. In the chapel of the Carmelites, Juliette and Clairwil shit upon crucifixes after the wafer and the wine have been inserted in their fundaments, a comprehensive and ingenious blasphemy. In Rome, Braschi, the Pope, buggers Juliette with a consecrated wafer which has been placed on the tip of his prick. Juliette accomplishes a long-cherished ambition in the Vatican; she has desecrated the holiest sanctum of the Roman church and had an instrumental part in buggering the Host Himself, with all the verb's connotations of contempt, violence and anger. She is a little blasphemous guerilla of demystification in the Chapel.

She uses sex as an instrument of terror; death is more frequently the result of it than birth. She lobs her sex at men and women as if it were a hand grenade; it will always blow up in their faces. She is a token woman in high places; she is engaged in destroying those high places all the time that she is enjoying the pastimes they offer. She engages in murderous orgies with the Pope and then robs him. She will turn on her friend, Borghese, and toss her into the crater of a volcano. When something better offers itself, she views the death of her beloved Clairwil without regret. And, all the time, she is never in less than full control of her physical self and she has chosen infertility as a way of life because she has chosen sexuality as terrorism as a way of life.

Juliette's infertility is not modified by the fact of giving birth because, under her veneer of acquiescence with the law, she subverts that patriarchal and hereditary institution by denying it her use value, that is, her womb, and the nourishment provided by her breasts.

There is a world of difference between a helplessly barren woman and a purposely infertile one. A woman who remains childless in spite of her own wishes may feel herself bereft and uncompleted, a sub-standard product of the assembly line of nature, who is only a passenger in the world because she has been denied a fertility she feels is part and parcel of her own nature. Rack her brains as she might, she cannot think of any other use for a women except as a breeder; if she cannot breed, what is she to do? She may think fertility is her birthright, the sign of a theoretical womanhood that gives her a hypothetical pre-eminence over men who may seed the human race but cannot, in themselves, nourish it. This theory of maternal superiority is one of the most damaging of all consolatory fictions and women themselves cannot leave it alone, although it springs from the timeless, placeless, fantasy land of archetypes where all the embodiments of biological supremacy live. It puts those women who wholeheartedly subscribe to it in voluntary exile from the historic world, this world, in its historic time that is counted out minute by minute, in which no event or circumstance of life exists for itself but is determined by an interlocking web of circumstances, where actions achieve effects and my fertility is governed by my diet, the age at which I reached puberty, my bodily juices, my decisions –

not by any benevolent magics.

Because she is the channel of life, woman as mythic mother lives at one remove from life. A woman who defines herself through her fertility has no other option. So a woman who feels she has been deprived of motherhood is trebly deprived – of children; of the value of herself as mother; and of her own self, as autonomous being.

But a woman who has chosen infertility does not feel this deprivation. All the same, she is not a surrogate man. By no means. All of her, her breasts, her cunt, her innards, are perfectly female – perhaps more perfectly so, from the point of view of aesthetics, than those of a woman who has borne children. But the significance of these things is completely altered.

We are living in a period where this alteration of significance is under debate in a variety of ways. Techniques of contraception and surgically safe abortion have given women the choice to be sexually active yet intentionally infertile for more of their lives than was possible at any time in history until now. This phenomenon is most apparent in those industrialised countries where the social position of women has been a subject of dissension since the late eighteenth century and the beginning of the industrial revolution; indeed, the introduction of contraception is part of the change in the position of women over the last two centuries. But all this speculation does not seem to have lessened the shock of the psychic impact of the division between the female body and the fact of child-bearing. It ought to seem self-evident that this body need not necessarily bear children but the trace-effects of several millenia during which this fact was not self-evident at all, since it was continually obscured by enforced pregnancies, have clothed the female body almost inpenetrably with a kind of mystification, of kitschification, that removes it almost from the real or physiological fact.

Consider the womb, the 'inner productive space', as Erik Erikson calls it, the extensible realm sited in the penetrable flesh, most potent matrix of all mysteries. The great, good place; domain of futurity in which the embryo forms itself from the flesh and blood of its mother; the unguessable reaches of the sea are a symbol of it, and so are caves, those dark, sequestered places where initiation and revelation take place. Men long for it and fear it; the womb, that comfortably elastic organ, is a fleshly link between past and future, the physical location of an everlasting present tense that can usefully serve as a symbol of eternity, a concept that has always presented some difficulties in visualisation. The hypothetical dream-time of the foetus seems to be the best that we can do.

For men, to fuck is to have some arcane commerce with this place of ultimate privilege, where, during his lengthy but unremembered stay, he was nourished, protected, lulled to sleep by the beating of his mother's heart and not expected to do a stroke of work, a repose, of course, not unlike that of a corpse, except that a foetus's future lies before it. And the curious resemblance between the womb and the grave lies at the roots of all human ambivalence towards both the womb and its bearer; we mediate our experience through imagination and dream but sometimes the dream gets in the way of the experience, and obscures it completely – the womb is the First and Last Place, earth, the greatest mother of them all, from whom we come, to whom we go. (Unless we more hygienically decide to resolve ourselves to fire – imagery, however, from a different religious structure than that of Western European culture and difficult to reconcile with it. It will be a long time before the idea of the crematorium transcends its pedestrian function, that of burning corpses, and becomes as numinous as the graveyard.

The womb is the earth and also the grave of being; it is the warm, moist, dark, inward, secret, forbidden, fleshly core of the unknowable labyrinth of our experience. Curiously, it is the same for both men and women, because the foetus is either male or female, though sometimes both; but only men

are supposed to feel a holy dread before its hairy portals.
Only men are privileged to return, even if only partially and
intermittently, to this place of fleshly extinction; and that is
why they have a better grasp of eternity and abstract
concepts than we do.

They want it for themselves, of course. But not, of course,
a real one, with all the mess and inconvenience that goes
with it. The womb is an imaginative locale and has an
imaginative location far away from my belly, beyond my
flesh, beyond my house, beyond this city, this society,
this economic structure – it lies in an area of psychic
metaphysiology suggesting such an anterior primacy of the
womb that our poor dissecting tools of reason blunt on its
magnitude before they can even start on the job. This inner
space must have been there before any of the outer places; in
the beginning was the womb and its periodic and haphazard
bleedings are so many signs that it has a life of its own,
unknowable to us. This is the most sacred of all places.
Women are sacred because they possess it. That, as Justine
would have known if she had thought about it, is why they
are treated so badly for nothing can defile the sacred.

Sade's invention of Juliette is an emphatic denial of this
entrancing rhetoric. For rhetoric it is, compounded out of
several millenia of guesses and fantasies about the nature of
the world. The truth of the womb is, that it is an organ like
any other organ, more useful than the appendix, less useful
than the colon but not much use to you at all if you do not
wish to utilise its sole function, that of bearing children. At
the best of times, it is apt to malfunction and cause
sickness, pain and inconvenience. The assertion of this
elementary fact through the means of a fictional woman
involves an entire process of demystification and denial, in
which far more than the demystification, the secularisation
of women is involved.

To deny the bankrupt enchantments of the womb is to
pare a good deal of the fraudulent magic from the idea of
women, to reveal us as we are, simple creatures of flesh and

blood whose expectations deviate from biological necessity sufficiently to force us to abandon, perhaps regretfully, perhaps with relief, the deluded priesthood of a holy reproductive function. This demystification extends to the biological iconography of women.

The breasts remain, but must be encountered, now, as breasts, not as the balcony of the goddess from whence she magisterially addresses her devotees in a metalanguage of self-adulation. They are no longer the general rendezvous of love and hunger, inspiring a Pavlovian response of need, but the specific breasts of a specific woman. One must not generalise about any breasts any more. To generalise is to lose the woman to whom they belong. They may remind both men and women of their own mother's breasts but these were also the lactatory glands of a specific woman and in her specificness alone resides their significance. Inside the belly, the womb, the ovaries and the Fallopian tubes remain; however, the ovaries and the Fallopian tubes have never, for some reason, been enriched with such a queasy burden of overvaluation as the womb, although child-bearing would be impossible without them. All this apparatus remains; but a voluntary sterility, freely chosen, makes them of as little and as great significance as any other part of the human body without which it is possible to survive.

The goddess is dead.

And, with the imaginary construct of the goddess, dies the notion of eternity, whose place on this earth was her womb. If the goddess is dead, there is nowhere for eternity to hide. The last resort of homecoming is denied us. We are confronted with mortality, as if for the first time.

There is no way out of time. We must learn to live in this world, to take it with sufficient seriousness, because it is the only world that we will ever know.

I think this is why so many people find the idea of the emancipation of women frightening. It represents the final secularisation of mankind. The old joke of the early sixties –

the astronaut, returning from heaven, describes God: 'This may come as a bit of a shock, but *she's black* – was a last queasy attempt to put something transcendental, at least up there, even if the Supreme Being was doubly devalued, by virtue of Her sex and Her race. With the death of the goddess go the last shreds of the supernatural. With apologies to Appollinaire, I do not think I want Juliette to renew my world; but, her work of destruction complete, she will, with her own death, have removed a repressive and authoritarian superstructure that has prevented a good deal of the work of renewal. For Juliette, secularised as she is, is in the service of the goddess, too, even if of the goddess in her demonic aspect, the goddess as antithesis.

III THE PHALLIC MOTHER

Durand is in her late forties. She has arrived at post-menopausal sterility and exists purely as a being of flesh and reason. She cannot reproduce, even if she wanted to. This is also the condition of the four brilliant whores who survive the holocaust at the Castle of Silling in *The Hundred and Twenty Days at Sodom*, women whose intellectual rapacity and sexual omnivorousness is the equal of that of Juliette and her friends. All these women are well past the age of child-bearing and child-bearing has never been a major factor in their lives. For preference, the whores, Madame Champville, Madame Martaine, Madame Duclos and Madame Desgranges, utilise the anus, the unisexual orifice; that of Madame Desgranges, in particular, has become extremely capacious through use. Sin and contraception aside, anal intercourse has an egalitarian lure for Sade. If sexual relations are implicitly political in Sade, the sexual act, among equals, is one of mutual if sequential dominance. Now the woman, now the man, penetrates and is penetrated in turn; gender itself can become interchangeable, as in the sexual charade that concludes

Juliette's career. The homosexual de Bressac told Justine how much he enjoyed becoming a woman for the purposes of sex; Dolmance, the erotic tutor in *Philosophy in the Boudoir*, enjoys experiencing his anus as a vagina. The female libertines, as Zarathustra recommended, never forget their whips when visiting; but they never leave behind their dildos, either.

And the four whores in *The Hundred and Twenty Days at Sodom* are more virile, in many respects, than the libertines who employ them. Durcet, the banker, with his vestigial tits and soft buttocks, is a singularly equivocal figure. But Madame Champville has a clitoris capable of erecting itself three inches, the extent of Durcet's own erection. This flexible clitoris-cum-prick is in ironic contrast to some of the pricks of the male sexual slaves at the Castle, which are of such a size that they cannot penetrate a woman at all, and are so many meaningless appendages, signs of a masculinity so gross it exceeds its own purpose.

Erectile clitorida are a feature of Sade's tribades; they are reminiscent in this respect of certain African tribeswomen whose labia minora and clitorida are artificially elongated until they resemble male genitals. Volmar, an inhabitant of the convent where Juliette was educated, is equipped with a three inch-long clitoris that enables her to penetrate other women both vaginally and anally; of voracious sexual appetites, she must either be a nymphomaniac or a sodomite or else cease to fuck at all. By exercising a Sadeian right to fuck, she automatically flies in the face of Nature whatever she does.

Durand is the queen of all these androgynes. She is 'the most remarkable libertine of her century'. She is handsome, with superb breasts, an enormous clitoris and an obstruction of the vagina which has prevented her from ever engaging in orthodox heterosexual intercourse in all her life. The way to her womb is blocked.

Though she cannot make babies, she can make corpses. 'She takes a box out of her pocket and sprinkles the

cemetery with the powder the box contained' relates
Juliette. 'All at once, the ground was scattered with
corpses.' These magical performances suggest that
Durand is beginning to approach the strangeness of an anti-
myth of mothering. In the place of a reproductive function,
she has acquired an absolute mastery of the physical world.
She has exchanged motherhood for domination. 'All Nature
obeys my orders, because she always submits herself to the
will of those who uncover her secrets,' she tells Juliette. She
is a scientist; it is the discipline of the scientific method that
has brought her to this pitch.

If she could but lay her hands on the one poison plant she
knows would do the trick, she has the ability to destroy the
entire earth; she is the ecological crisis in person. She can
propagate epidemics; poison wells; slaughter cattle; destroy
villages; infect the Republic of Venice with a fatal plague.
She has invented an entire pharmacopoeia of poisons and, if
she procures a handsome profit from their sale, she is also
moved in her research by an impulse of pure misanthropy.
She would like, she confides to Juliette, to destroy
everything.

In her house, the rich immolate the poor with the aid of
baroque machinery, amongst picturesque decors similar to
those of the ballets of the period. She is a choreographer of
life and death. And, although she works her macabre
miracles with the aid of science, she has about her a
theatrical whiff of black magic. Her laboratory and her
garden of venomous plants are those of the medieval
alchemist and the witch-herbalist. She calls up sylphs and
spirits with incantatory formulae. She practises divination,
the antique practice of woman as oracle and seer; a mother-
figure is reproduced in the form of a goddess of destiny in
Jean Thenaud's sixteenth century *Traité de la Cabale*, yet
Durand derives much of her style from the fashionable
necromancy of the late eighteenth century. She is both a
cabalistic enigma and *diabolism à la mode*.

Juliette falls in love with her at first sight when she meets her in Paris; but, the next time Juliette visits Durand's house, the windows are shuttered, it is deserted. No matter how hard she tries, she cannot find out what has become of the sorceress, who has vanished with a magic and complete precipitation, to reappear again just as mysteriously in Italy. Even though she has been condemned to death, Durand will magically resurrect herself to crown Juliette's final good fortune; her capacity for appearance and disappearance exceeds even the generous limits of the picaresque novel so that, for all her invocations of science, her outlines are subtly blurred with the supernatural even if the god she invokes for Juliette and Clairwil turns out to be a mortal phallus.

She treats science as if it were magic. She uses her discoveries for personal gratification and for financial profit, just as Dr Faustus in Marlowe's play did with the powers for which he exchanged his soul. She has made, of forbidden knowledge, a service industry.

However, the more one examines this ambivalent and terrifying woman, the more unreal she becomes, the more like a reformulation of the goddess in the terms of a different reading of her iconography. Durand comes to resemble a mother indeed, but not the adult sentimentalization of the memory of the protective mother; rather, she is the omnipotent mother of early childhood who gave and withheld love and nourishment at whim, as it seemed to us. The cruel mother, huge as a giantess, the punishment giver, the one who makes you cry.

But Durand, final terror, is not only infertile but also unapproachable; she may not be entered by the antechamber of the womb. She is therefore unappeasable.

It is as if the milk from her superb breasts had been transformed into poisons when Nature imperiously denied access to her interior. The ambiguous affirmation of Durand's breasts recalls the fantasies of the small boys described by Bruno Bettelheim, who believed that women could suckle themselves. These boys were envious of breasts independently of lactation, says Bettelheim; they viewed them as sources of strength and power in themselves.

This power is perilous. Durand is like a version of the Terrible Mother, the Hindu goddess, Kali, who stands for both birth and death, and not only destruction but Nature's cruel indifference to suffering. Clairwil and Juliette, like Tantric devotees of Kali, engage in sexual rituals in a graveyard, at Durand's instigation. Kali herself dances upon severed heads, juggles with limbs, wears necklaces of skulls and copulates with corpses. Snakes issue from her vulva.

Durand is as destructive as Kali, a sumptuous infecundity whose masterpieces are plagues.

In Durand, the Enlightenment returns to pure mythology. Reason overreaches itself and turns into the opposite of reason. Scientific order, ruthlessly applied, reduces the world to chaos. Durand, the rational biochemist, is the very mythic terror that reason fears most.

But her mothering passion for Juliette serves to reassure us that her ambivalence is inconsistent and, though she has an infinite capacity for destruction, she will not use her poisons and magics against us, whom she loves. If Durand's penetrable vagina, the road back to the solace of the womb, is inaccessible, that is because it has been turned inside out, has become the clitoris that Juliette, when she first sees it, at once begins to suck, as though it were a teat.

Durand is a virile and non-productive mother, who chooses her own children and seduces them, too. She is a mother with a phallus; she can rape even nature itself. The dead goddess resurrects herself in the form of her antithesis, not as cherishing and nourishment but absence and hunger. Or, rather, as cherishing for some and absence for others.

But Juliette has Durand's promise this mother will never desert her. Unlike Justine, Juliette is not an orphan in the world. She is intimately related to the origins of chaos and so she will be protected from it, until it repossesses her.

four

THE SCHOOL OF LOVE: THE EDUCATION OF A FEMALE OEDIPUS

> The aggressive impulses of little girls leave nothing to
> be desired in the way of abundance and violence.
>
> *New Introductory Lectures in Psychoanalysis, No. Three:*
> *'Femininity', Sigmund Freud*

I MOTHERS AND DAUGHTERS

Philosophy in the Boudoir is not a picaresque epic novel. It is a dramatic interlude, on a very much smaller scale than the novels and very much less cluttered and repetitious in style. Its manner is intimate and domestic, its setting a boudoir as elegant and civilised as those in the pictures of Watteau and Fragonard. The characters, with the exception of a gardener, are all of Sade's own class and the atmosphere of the piece has the elegant depravity of Laclos' *Les Liaisons Dangereuses*. If, outside, they are selling pamphlets on the steps of the Palace of Equality, inside, in the privileged boudoir, the ladies and gentlemen still pleasure themselves at leisure.

At the conclusion of *Philosophy in the Boudoir*, a young

girl, Eugénie de Mistival, commits a gross sexual assault upon her mother. Though it is performed with obscene relish, this monstrous act is primarily occasioned by vengeance, rather than lust. The girl rapes her mother because the woman has attempted to curtail Eugénie's sexual experience. The woman who does not wish to permit others to engage in sexual activity for the sake of pleasure must herself have sex inflicted on her as retribution, as a form of punishment uniquely fitted for her crime against pleasure.

Eugénie, however, goes much further than a simple rape. She first rapes her and then sews up her mother's genital orifice with needle and thread, as though she must effectively annihilate her mother's sexuality before she herself can be free. It would seem that, in some sense, her mother's sexuality menaces her own. The mother wishes Eugénie to behave as if her sexual organs were sealed and therefore Eugénie seals up her mother, to remove the possibility of rivalry, the only reason her mother might possibly have to wish to repress her daughter's sexuality.

King Oedipus' transgressions were mother-incest and parricide; when he found out what he had done, he blinded himself, that is, underwent a symbolic castration. Eugénie, unlike Oedipus, acts in the knowledge she is committing a crime. Her crime is the culmination of her search for knowledge. She fucks her mother out of vengeance and so finds herself in the position of a female Oedipus but she is not blinded, she is enlightened; then, in spite and rage, she seals up the organs of generation that bore her and so ensures that her mother will not fuck again with anyone.

Philosophy in the Boudoir is a detailed account of the erotic education of a Sadeian heroine. The basis of the plot is Eugénie's relation to her mother and her final ambivalent triumph over the female principle as typified in the reproductive function. The mother has burst angrily into the profane academy, the school of love, during her daughter's initiation in order to rescue her daughter from sexual experience; her punishment is rape, infection and infibulation.

The narrative, composed in a series of seven dialogues in dramatic form, begins when Eugénie, fifteen years old, arrives at the boudoir of Madame de Saint-Ange, her libertine father's mistress, eager for instruction. Innocence is not her quality. She is already engaged in a lesbian affair with Saint-Ange. But she is ignorant and has come to the older woman to be instructed, with her father's knowledge, against her mother's wishes. Saint-Ange intends to spare nothing to 'pervert her, degrade her, demolish in her all the false ethical notions with which they (her mother's friends) have been able to dull her.'

The voluptuous Saint-Ange, a widow of twenty-six, has employed as fellow tutors her brother, the Chevalier de Mirvel, and the libertine Dolmancé. Dolmancé, a lover of the Chevalier, has succumbed to Saint-Ange's invitation only in order to take the opportunity of sodomising her; he refuses to approach women by any other orifice than the unnatural one. He will preside over Saint-Ange's little academy. The course will encompass both theory and practice. Saint-Ange intends her brother to depucelate Eugénie's frontal orifice, Dolmancé to deal with her anus. These deflorations are duly performed, to Eugénie's delight.

Saint-Ange and the cynical Dolmancé share that sensual rapacity which is the mark of the Sadeian libertine. The Chevalier, though equally adroit sexually, yet retains a sense of the injustice of their voluptuous privilege, and, curiously enough, is not punished for announcing this, although his sermon is ignored. It is he who will introduce politics into the lessons. But the purpose of the gathering is primarily this: to strip Eugénie of all her socialised virtues and to restore her to the primal and vicious state of nature. Her education has regression rather than maturation as its goal.

She is given an anatomy lesson in which Saint-Ange's body serves as a blackboard. She is instructed in the func-

tion of the clitoris and told that all a woman's powers of
sensation lie there. Dolmancé's prick and balls are
demonstrated to her and she is taught how to masturbate
him. The physiology of sex, however, takes up very little of
their time. The strenuous and protracted orgies, conducted
with military precision and clockwork timing, are punc-
tuated by philosophical sermons on the family, on marriage,
contraception, abortion, prostitution, cruelty and love. The
virile and handsome gardener joins them for some of the
sexual activity but he is prudently ordered out of the room
while Chevalier reads aloud the political pamphlet: *Yet
Another Effort, Frenchmen, if you Would Become
Republican*. This pamphlet occupies between a third and a
half of the text of the entire piece. During the revolution of
1848, it was extracted from its pornographic context and
republished by the followers of the Utopian, Saint-Simon.

The opinions expressed in it are republican and atheist;
they are the blueprints for a society where the laws are 'so
mild, so few, that all men, whatever their character, can
easily keep them'. In this society, women are held in
common; but also hold men in common.

> If we admit . . . that all women should submit to our desires,
> surely we ought also to allow them to fully satisfy their
> own . . . Charming sex, you will be free; just as men do, you
> shall enjoy all the pleasures that Nature makes your duty, do
> not withhold yourselves from one. Must the diviner part of
> mankind be kept in chains by the other? Ah, break those bonds;
> nature wills it. Have no other curb than your tastes, no other
> laws than those of your own desires, no more morality than
> that of Nature herself. Languish no more under those bar-
> barous prejudices that wither your charms and imprison the
> divine impulses of your heart; you are as free as we are and the
> career of the battles of Venus as open to you as to us.

Sade does not concern himself with problems of capital
investment or economic organisation in the hypothetical
republic; those are not his areas of concern. He is concerned
to forge a libertarian sexuality and the libertines listen with
approval. Eugénie's education will take this lesson into

account; if it does not leave her in possession of the liberty the pamphlet attempts to describe, then she will go out into the world in possession of a certain qualified freedom, the most the historical circumstances of the time can offer. This qualified freedom may not be attained without a process similar to an initiation. Almost as soon as she arrives in the boudoir, she gives us a clue as to who it is who must be sacrificed before her initiation is complete.

EUGÉNIE: . . . every day I see before me an abominable creature I've wanted in her grave for years.

SAINT-ANGE: I think I can guess who that might be.

EUGÉNIE: Who do you suspect?

SAINT-ANGE: Your mother?

EUGÉNIE: Oh, let me hide my blushes in your bosom!

Eugénie's tutors apply rational science to the discussion of this antipathy. Since rationality is also relative, the science to which they refer is, in fact, incorrect. Saint-Ange opines that, because 'the foetus owes its existence only to the man's sperm', filial tenderness is naturally reserved entirely for the father. This theory was general scientific currency of the period. The animalculists, or spermists, who believed the spermatozoa were of more significance than the ova in the process of conception, had returned to the classical theory of Aeschylus: the parent is the male, the mother only 'the nurse of the young life that is sown within her'. This devaluation of the actual biological status of women indicates how far prejudice can invalidate certain scientific theorising before it even begins. On this biological misinterpretation, Sade builds an edifice of mother-hatred.

DOLMANCÉ: I am not yet consoled for my father's death; when I lost my mother, I lit a perfect bonfire for joy . . . formed uniquely out of the blood of our fathers, we owe nothing at all to our mothers. All they did was to co-operate in the act which our fathers urged them to. So, it was the father who desired our birth; the mother only consents to it.

There is no virtue in the accidental creativity of the mother since fecundity itself is not a necessary part of the natural scheme of things, says Sade. Nature does not urge procreation but merely tolerates it; Saint-Ange urges Eugénie to avoid conception by whatever means she can. However, once the homunculus has been deposited within a woman, she herself is in sole charge of it. Now she may exercise a free choice as to what she intends to do with it. 'We are always mistress of what we carry in our womb,' says Saint-Ange. She must not dread the idea of abortion, if that is what she so wishes. (Attempted abortion and infanticide were both capital crimes in France at the time, also.)

Sade is content to deny any significance to the activity of the physical mother beyond the fact of the ripening of the embryo in her body. Since he seeks a complete divorce between sexuality and reproduction, he does not see any value in physical mothering at all. Moral mothering, the care and education of children, is a different matter and should be left to those who have shown themselves competent at it; besides, if the sexual liberty he wishes to see in the Republic is put into practice, legitimacy will cease to be a legal fact and the nuclear family itself will wither away. Further, one must take into account the child, whose existence is Mother's sole claim to distinction in the world. The existence of the child is essential to the notion of motherhood but the child has had even less choice in the matter than its mother has. In this enforced and involuntary relationship, how can mother and child be anything but enemies? Especially when a girl child grasps the fact of her mother's passive acquiescence in her conception, and, in Freudian terms, realises that her mother is castrated?

Let Eugénie, then, savagely restore to her mother the phallus she lacks, mocking her mother's gratuitous fecundity with a mechanical implement that will not fecundate her. Eugénie will fuck her with a cunt-cracking dildo. 'Come, dear lovely Mama, come, let me treat you like a husband.' Eugénie takes on the sexual aggressiveness of her father by mimicking her father; she exhibits a naive triumph at the speed and completeness with which she has superseded the condition of female passivity to which she had been trained.

As Dolmancé penetrates her anally while she inflicts the artificial penis with which he has equipped her upon her mother, Eugénie cries: 'Here I am, at one stroke incestuous, adultress, sodomite and all that in a girl who has only lost her virginity today!' The act of profanation and sacrilege she has performed, a fugue of sexual and familial misconduct, is a Sadeian *rite de passage* into complete sexual being. The violence of Eugénie's reaction is some indication of the degree of repression from which she has suffered. It is also a characteristic piece of Sadeian black humour.

Then the libertines invalidate Madame de Mistival's long-cherished and hypocritical chastity by introducing into the gathering a syphilitic who inoculates her with the pox in both orifices, forcing her to suffer the very punishment specially reserved by natural justice for the pleasures she has always denied herself. Finally, Eugénie seizes needle and thread and sews her securely up. Then, to complete the exemplary humiliation, we will assure her we have her husband's, our father's, full approval of all the infamies we have committed and drive her from our bedroom, the abode of unrepressed sexuality, an inverted Eden beyond the knowledge of good and evil, a dark Beulah where contrarities exist together, with abuse and blows.

DOLMANCÉ: Let this example serve to remind you that your daughter is old enough to do what she wants; that she loves to fuck, that she was born to fuck, and that, if you do not wish to be fucked yourself, at least you can leave her alone.

But before the mother goes, she must beg her daughter's pardon for attempting to repress her. Eugénie's delirious transgression has ensured her own sexual freedom at the cost of the violent cessation of the possibility of her mother's own sexual life. Her triumph over her mother is complete.

The relation between Eugénie and her mother is an extreme and melodramatised, indeed, pornographised description of the antipathy between mothers and daughters which suggests that women, also, retain elements of the early erotic relation with the mother that has been more fully explored and documented in men. Indeed, *Philosophy in the Boudoir* in many ways precedes Freud's essay on femininity, and should be seen in the same Western European context of competition and rivalry between women that devalues women as they act them out in the dramas of sexual life. But Sade is not engaged in the exposition of fact but of fantasy, of symbolic sexual interaction, and his version of the conflict between mother and daughter may be interpreted like this: the mother wishes to repress her growing daughter's sexuality because she herself is growing old and social custom is removing her from the arena of sexual life. She sees her daughter, the living memory of herself as a young woman, as both an immediate rival and a poignant reminder of what she herself is losing. The daughter, on the other hand, sees the mother, not as an ageing rival but as a mature woman and one in permanent possession of her father, who is the most immediately present object on which she may focus her desire. Not only is the mother the rival of the daughter but her position as wife of the father is impregnable. Sexual hostility is therefore the inevitable relation between mother and daughter, as long as the mother regards sexuality as synonymous with reproduction and hence sanctified activity in which only the Holy Mother, herself, may indulge. Saint-Ange, as instructress, adopts another kind of maternal role towards Eugénie, as Durand does towards Juliette. But no natural mother in Sade is capable of this, because she is a shrine of reproductive sexuality. She is herself the embodiment of the repression of sexual pleasure; how, then, can she not attempt to repress sexuality in her daughter?

Mother is in herself a concrete denial of the idea of sexual pleasure since her sexuality has been placed at the service of reproductive function alone. She is the perpetually violated passive principle; her autonomy has been sufficiently eroded by the presence within her of the embryo she brought to term. Her unthinking ability to reproduce, which is her pride, is, since it is beyond choice, not a specific virtue of her own. The daughter may achieve autonomy only through destroying the mother, who represents her own reproductive function, also, who is both her own mother and the potential mother within herself.

If the daughter is a mocking memory to the mother – 'As I am, so you once were' – then the mother is a horrid warning to her daughter. 'As I am, so you will be.' Mother seeks to ensure the continuance of her own repression, and her hypocritical solicitude for the younger woman's moral, that is, sexual welfare masks a desire to reduce her daughter to the same state of contingent passivity she herself inhabits, a state honoured by custom and hedged by taboo.

Vengeance. Transgression. Glory! Eugénie de Mistival offers her arse to her mother and invites her to kiss it. Her seizure of her own autonomy necessitates the rupture of all the taboos she can apprehend. She will take her mother to wife and symbolically kill her, too; and the conflict is solely between women. Father, though continually invoked, is absent from this malign fiesta, just as he is absent from every child's primary experience, the birth and the breast, the first bed and the first table. Eugénie and her companions, her playmates, are alone with Eugénie's first beloved and first seducer and may wreak upon her a suitable vengeance for her betrayal.

Baby is hermaphrodite. It is polysexual. It is all the sexes in one and first of all it will love the thing that feeds and caresses it, out of necessity. During this period, father is only a troublesome rival for the attention of the mother. Freud suggests that the relation with the mother regularly structures a woman's relation with her father. Adult women with particularly strong attachments to their fathers had usually, he suggests, transferred a peculiarly strong first passion for the mother to the father in all its entirety and intensity. This primal passion has necessarily been libidinal and will have passed through all the oral, sadistic, and phallic phases of infantile sexuality; it will be essentially ambivalent, now affectionate, now hostile. There will be fantasies of making the mother pregnant and of becoming pregnant by the mother. Mother and daughter live as each one the other's image.

In the Freudian orchestration, now father enters the nursery and interposes his phallic presence between his daughter and her mother; his arrival in the psychic theatre, bearing his irreplaceable prick before him like a wand of office, a conductor's baton, a sword of severance, signifies the end of the mother's role as seducer and as beloved. 'The turning away from the mother is accompanied by hostility; the attachment to the mother ends in hate,' hypothesises Freud in his essay on femininity in the *New Introductory Lectures in Psychoanalysis*. The primary passion was incapable of the consummation of a child. The girl now turns to the father in the expectation he will give her the object that he possesses which she lacks, the phallus that is a substitute child and also makes children, that weapon which is a symbol of authority, of power, and will pierce the opacity of the world. Freud's account of this process has such extraordinary poetic force that, however false it might be, it remains important as an account of what seemed, at one point in history, a possible progression. It retains a cultural importance analagous, though less far-reaching, to the myth of the crime of Eve in the Old Testament.

Now Eugénie obeys the Freudian scenario as if she were one of his patients. She seeks the aid of a man, even if Saint-Ange, her surrogate mother, has adequately endowed her with aggression and competently seduced her, too. But Dolmancé, the ambiguous schoolmaster, the Tiresias who loves to play the woman and scrupulously avoids cunts, presses into Eugénie's hand a false limb, a dildo, and suggests a parodic accomplishment of the first desire of all, an act of sexual aggression that will exorcise the desire for good and all. So Eugénie 'plays the husband' to her lovely Mama, acts out upon the mirror image of her own flesh a charade of domination and possession.

In the terms of a theory of sexuality that denies any significance to reproduction, such as Sade's, the castrate is the human norm. If Eugénie, a typically Freudian girl, suffers a typically Freudian penis-envy, then it is amply compensated for by the acquisition of a mechanical device that is just as good a phallus as a real one could ever be. When Clairwil in *Juliette* masturbates with a mummified penis, the penis becomes an object, dissociated from any human context. It is no longer a symbol of malehood. It is 'the sceptre of Venus', 'the primary agent of love's pleasure', and may be wielded by whomsoever chooses to do so, regardless of the bearer's gender.

Eugénie penetrates her mother. Madame de Mistival faints. Eugénie hopes she has not died because she had already planned her summer wardrobe; what a bore it would be to have to abandon all her pretty frocks and put on mourning instead! Even her tutors are taken aback at that; she has already surpassed her masters in the art of hardening her heart. Then Dolmancé whips the woman awake with freshly gathered thorns while his companions perform a sprightly erotic tableau and achieve orgasm in well-choreographed unison. Each actor then pronounces judgement upon the vanquished mother. Eugénie, most vicious since most in love, would like to drive whips tipped with sulphur into her mother's body and set fire to them. But Dolmancé, the most cerebral, has a better idea; it is he who introduces the syphilitic, who will inject his poison into Madame de Mistival's vagina and anus 'with this consequence: that so long as this cruel disease's impressions shall last, the whore will remember not to trouble her daughter when Eugénie has herself fucked.'

Everyone applauds the scheme. It is carried out immediately, while the others vigorously whip one another. Then Saint-Ange, the surrogate or adoptive mother, suggests Eugénie sew her natural mother up, to prevent the infection leaking out of her.

EUGÉNIE: Excellent idea! Quickly, quickly, fetch me needle and thread! . . . Spread your thighs, Mama, so I can stitch you together – so that you'll give me no more little brothers and sisters.

The child ceases to love Mother when the arrival of siblings puts its nose out of joint for good. Eugénie's delirium is now in a fugal flood where innumerable themes play together; but jealousy and the desire for revenge are uppermost. Mother must be punished because her passivity invites action; humiliated, because of her pride; raped, in order violently to restore to her the penis which she lacks; infected, to mock her chastity; rendered incapable of reproduction, because she has sanctified her fecundity.

And all these villainies must be heaped upon her unwilling but helplessly compliant body because it could not accommodate the impossible demands for absolute love that the child, her everlastingly unrequited suitor, made upon it. So Mama leaves the School of Love and the Chevalier, who takes her home, is warned to keep his hands off her, since she has the pox. She has learned that her daughter is old enough to do as she pleases, that her attempts at sexual restraint have proved worse than useless, have provoked the most violent reaction, have destroyed her.

And perhaps Mama has been enlightened; but not so far enlightened that Sade will let her stay to join in the fun.

'Mothers,' thunders Sade in the preface of the first edition, 'prescribe this book to your daughters!' In the second edition, however, he changes his tune. He vacillates. He warns: 'Mothers, proscribe this book to your daughters.' But perhaps this is a printing error; by the time the second edition was printed, Sade had been interred in the asylum at Charenton and had no control over the proofs. Nevertheless, the vowels slip into and out of one another. Prescribe. Proscribe. What to do, what to do.

He acknowledges to the full the mutual antagonism between mother and daughter. But should the mother or the daughter be enlightened as to the nature and extent of this antagonism? Which one of them should have the benefit of the lesson? Or should they both?

Eugénie's libido thrusts her towards an attack upon the female orifice itself, which is an implicit attack upon her own biological function. But it is an attack, a rape, not a ravishment. She never contemplates a seduction, even though she eroticises her mother when she fucks her. She opens her up for pleasure with the massive dildo. 'I believe, dear Mother, you are coming . . . Dolmancé, look at her eyes! She comes, it's certain.' At this point, Madame de Mistival decides to lose consciousness and so censor her own situation. In other words, Sade has scared himself so badly by the obvious resolution of the psychodrama that he has set his creators to act out that he decides to censor her response. It frightens him. So Madame de Mistival must deny responsibility even for her own responses. She will experience sexuality like a theft from herself.

Neither she, nor Eugénie, nor Dolmancé, nor even Saint-Ange, nor, especially, Sade, can tolerate the implication of her orgasm. 'She comes, it's certain!' But this is Eugénie's vicious mockery; Mother must never be allowed to come, and so to come alive. She cannot be corrupted into the experience of sexual pleasure and so set free. She is locked forever in the fortress of her flesh, a sleeping beauty whose lapse of being is absolute and eternal. If she were allowed to taste one single moment's pleasure in the abuses that are heaped upon her, abuses that would glut Saint-Ange or her own daughter with joy, that would overthrow the whole scheme.

Vice and virtue, that is, energy and passivity, that is, evil and good, would then be states to which one could accede. As it is, in the model of the world that Sade has made, a man or a woman is naturally vicious or naturally virtuous; Eugénie is already corrupt when she arrives at Saint-Ange's boudoir, Juliette was already wicked when she registered at Delbène's academy. Sade's manicheistic dualism sees the world as irredeemably evil; vice must always prosper, virtue always despair. There is no hope for us as we are now. The Republic in which the laws 'are as mild as the people they govern' is as much a fantasy as Saint-Ange's voluptuous boudoir. Sade's vision is utterly without transcendence. But, if he could have allowed himself to violate the last taboo of all, and allow wretched and abused Madame de Mistival to experience pleasure, then the terms of his vision would be disrupted. Transcendence would have crept in. He might even have to make room for hope.

Being would cease to be a state-in-itself; it would then be possible to move between modes of being in a moral and not a sexual sense. By denying the possibility of corruption, Sade denies the possibility of regeneration.

The possibility of the redemption from virtue would suggest the reciprocal possibility of a fall from vice.

But Madame de Mistival, if she does indeed feel the first faint prick of pleasure, faints to avoid the consciousness of it. They rouse her from the faint only to sew her up. Then she is infected and now she is impregnable. She no longer co-exists with even the possibility of pleasure. She is better than dead.

Now we are beginning to approach the central paradox of all Sade's pornography, which is inherent in the paradox of his own sexuality.

Sade, contemplating the phallus, real or artificial, dithers. Let us prescribe it to our daughters, by all means. But he cannot finally decide whether it is an instrument of pleasure, pure and simple, as it might be in the Republic, where women are 'common fountains of pleasure', or a weapon of admonition, pure and simple, as it is for Eugénie, for Clairwil and his male libertines.

He himself has always wanted one. He wanted his mother's phallus but it transpired she had none to give him; if Freud is correct and boy children regularly endow all the other beings in the world with the appendage they themselves possess, the shock and grief of the discovery that the mother lacks one must be profound. The mother is also his dearest beloved and his mirror, just as she is for the girl child.

He wanted his mother's imaginary phallus but found he had deceived himself; she possessed, instead, a dark, secret place of which he was so afraid that he had hastily to seal it up before it engulfed him. But the existence of this unstoppable hole makes him perpetually dissatisfied with his own equipment. He wants a bigger, a yet bigger one and rummages around in the chest in which he keeps his dildos, a chest like the one Saint-Ange keeps in her boudoir filled with dildos of every size, he searches to find one that will be big enough to console him for his fear of castration, a phallus of the size with which he adorns his heroes and also his heroines.

But, the more immense the organ with which he equips himself, the greater grows the abyss into which it must plunge. In order to fuck his mother, he needs the most massive dildo in the world; and still it will not satisfy her. Still she will not die of it. Still she will not come; for, when the anatomy lesson, the misanthropy lesson, the lesson in politics, in rage, in terror, is over, we must send her back to her husband, to Father, to whom she belongs.

Home again, home again, fast as you can.

So Mother is exile in perpetuity from this world in the locked, rotting castle of her flesh. We may not fully enjoy her. Exhaustion will always intervene. 'It's finished . . . over . . . oh, why must weakness succeed passions so alive?' There is no solace for the libertine's insatiability because access to the object of love is always denied him. Eugénie's transgression initially disrupts but finally restores the status quo. Mother has not been eroticised. Eugénie has destroyed, spoiled what she could not possess, exorcised the ghost of her first love and now she can exist freely in this world.

Has she not her father's permission to do so?

Home again, home again, fast as you can, my lovely Mama, to the husband who has prepared this instructive afternoon for you.

For Eugénie's transgression is authorised. It is her graduation exercise at the school of love in which her father has enrolled her. Her mother arrives at the academy in order to remove her from it shortly after the delivery of a letter from the licentious de Mistival himself, authorising his wife's martyrisation. When they strip her, they discover her husband has just roundly whipped her. They may do with her whatever they please; Father has told them so. The boudoir, the temple of vice, is a Garden of Eden in which God has permitted the consumption of the fruit of the tree of the knowledge of good and evil.

So, finally, the violation of the mother is no more than a performance, a show; it demonstrates and creates Eugénie's autonomy but also the limits of her autonomy, for her freedom is well policed by the faceless authority beyond the nursery, outside the mirror, the father who knows all, sees all and permits almost everything, except absolute freedom.

The boudoir is a privileged place where these dangerous experiments in synthesising freedom may be conducted in safety. Eugénie does not place herself at real risk by her experiments, nor does she put her companions at risk by aspiring, with her new-found independence, to acts which would put them in jeopardy. She attacks only that part of herself, her reproductive function, she can afford to lose. The taboo against the mother is truly broken once and once only and that is when Eugénie penetrates her mother with the dildo.

Were Madame de Mistival to have come, then all the dykes would be breached at once and chaos and universal night instantly descend; pleasure would have asserted itself triumphantly over pain and the necessity for the existence of repression as a sexual stimulant would have ceased to exist. There would arise the possibility of a world in which

the concept of taboo is meaningless and pornography itself
would cease to exist. Sade, the prisoner who created
freedom in the model of his prison, would have put himself
out of business; he is as much afraid of freedom as the next
man. So he makes her faint.

He makes her faint because he can only conceive of
freedom as existing in opposition, freedom as defined by
tyranny. So, on the very edge of an extraordinary discovery
about the nature of the relation between mothers and
daughters, at the climax of his pioneering exploration of
this most obscure of psychic areas, he gives in to a principle
of safety. Instead of constructing a machine for liberation,
he substitutes instead a masturbatory device. He is on the
point of becoming a revolutionary pornography; but he,
finally, lacks the courage.

He reverts, now, to being a simple pornographer.

Moreover, the old lag is always imprisoned, even when he
is out of his cell, by his own perversion. His perversion, that
is an unnatural obsession with pain, is almost like a magic
circle which he has constructed around himself to preserve
himself from the terrible freedom to which his ideas might
lay him open. If 'art is the perpetual immoral subversion of
the established order', then why, having gone so far, why
not now let Madame de Mistival be overcome by the
passions which surround her? Could not the object of
genital hatred become the object of genital love? Why does
this notion upset him so?

But the taboo against the mother has been violated only
to be immediately and hideously restored. The obscenities
and profanations never quite fulfil the subversion implicit in
them. Shall we prescribe or proscribe this book to our
daughters? Sade dithers.

Father must know all, authorise all, or else Eugénie might
truly take possession of her autonomy and, say, sheer off
Dolmancé's prick, transform him forever to the condition to
which he aspires when he spreads out beneath the handsome
virility of the Chevalier, and so truly exercise for herself the

phallic mastery at which Sade, Dolmancé himself and her own father assure her she has just arrived.

She savages her mother in order to achieve sexual autonomy, according to the rules of the academy; to attack Father or his substitutes in order to achieve existential autonomy is against the rules. Eugénie's sexual egoism must be sanctioned by the group in which she participates; it must be observed. It must be contained by their observation or else it might threaten the rules of the school itself.

The Sadeian woman, then, subverts only her own socially conditioned role in the world of god, the king and the law. She does not subvert her society, except incidentally, as a storm trooper of the individual consciousness. She remains in the area of privilege created by her class, just as Sade remains in the philosophic framework of his time.

Nevertheless, Sade suggests a type of Oedipal conflict in relation to the mother which is not restricted by gender. Eugénie enacts the crime of Oedipus in a richly psychotic trance; she both copulates with her mother and effectively murders her. In this bewildering dream, Mother becomes the essential primal object, subsuming both parents to herself, as Durand, the phallic and non-reproductive mother, also did.

And, perhaps, in spite of the instructions he sends by his messenger, Father is always absent from this scenario because, in fact, he does not exist.

II KLEINIAN APPENDIX: LIBERTY, MISANTHROPY AND THE BREAST

The struggle between life and death instincts and the ensuing threat of annihilation of the self and of the object by destructive impulses are fundamental factors in the infant's initial relation to his mother. For his desires imply that the breast and soon the mother should do away with these destructive impulses and the pain of persecutory anxiety.

Envy and Gratitude, Melanie Klein

Eugénie's transgression is an exemplary vengeance upon
the very idea of the good, a vengeance upon the primal
'good' object, the body of the mother. In the terms of the
analysis of Melanie Klein, 'good breast' is the prototype of
the fountain of all nourishment; the breast that Sade's
libertines take such delight in whipping, upon which they
take such derisive glee in wiping their arses, is, as Freud
says, 'the place where love and hunger meet', a moving
symbol of the existence and the satisfaction of the most
basic of all human needs. The body of the mother is the
great, good place, the concretisation of the earthly paradise;
these fantasies, according to Klein, enrich the primal object,
the first thing we meet when we come out of the womb, the
great, good place in which we lived without knowing it. The
experience of the primal object becomes the foundation for
trust, hope and a belief in the existence of good.

Sade/Eugénie profanes the primal object in the conviction
that hope, trust and the good are delusions.

'Envy contributes to the infant's difficulties in building
up a good object, for he feels that the gratification of which
he was deprived has been kept for himself by the breast
that frustrated him,' says Melanie Klein. This envy may
manifest itself in violent attacks on the mother's body.
Envy, jealousy and greed are the vices of early childhood. If
envy implies the subject's relation with one other person only and a desire to rob that person of a desirable
possession, or, if robbing is impossible, at least to spoil it, so
that nobody else may benefit from it, then jealousy implies a
more peopled landscape and a relation to at least two people.
Envy and greed are our first negative emotions; we envy the
breast its abundance and greedily wish to drink it dry.
Jealousy implies a degree of maturing; we now perceive
something other than the breast and ourselves, we perceive
a third. The experience of jealousy marks the point at which
the solipsistic accord between child and mother ceases. Life
as a social being begins.

We are jealous because we feel there is only a limited

amount of love available and somebody else may secure it all. Eugénie sews up her mother so that she will not be able to produce any little brothers and sisters; Madame de Mistival must undergo this ordeal in order to remove the desolating notion of the arrival of rivals who will jostle Eugénie for attention for themselves and deprive her of unique nourishment. But Madame de Mistival is already possessed by Eugénie's own father; she bears the marks of his possession on her body, he has beaten her until her buttocks look like watered silk, to show how absolute is his right to the use of her flesh and the degree to which her flesh affects him by its insubornable separateness from him. Eugénie's rage is no different at source from her father's rage. The libertine frenzy of father and daughter in Sade's parable spring from greed, envy and jealousy, a helpless rage at the organs of generation that bore us into a world of pain where the enjoyment of the senses is all that can alleviate the daily horror of living. In the introduction to *Philosophy in the Boudoir*, Sade writes: 'It is only by sacrificing everything to sensual pleasure that this being known as Man, cast into the world in spite of himself, may succeed in sowing a few roses on the thorns of life.'

Sade's quarrel, therefore, is not only with the mother, who can deprive him of love and sustenance at will; it is the very fact of generation that he finds intolerable. In the short story, *Eugénie de Franval*, Franval denies his daughter's right to marry and have children: 'Then you think the human race should be allowed to die out?' his wife asks him. 'Why not?' he replies. 'A planet whose only product is poison cannot be rooted out too quickly.'

The Sadeian libertine cannot forgive the mother, not for what she is, but for what she has done – for having thoughtlessly, needlessly inflicted life upon him. Therefore he conducts his irreconcileable existence entirely upon a metaphysical plane; his whole life is a violent protest against an irreversible condition because, though it is easy to stop living, it is impossible to erase the fact of one's birth.

One may not remove oneself from history, though Sade tried to do it. His will directs he should be buried in a ditch, and 'the ditch, once covered over, about it acorns shall be strewn, in order that the spot become green again, and the copse grown back thick over it, the traces of my grave may disappear from the face of the earth, as I trust the memory of me shall fade out of the minds of all men.'

Rage and despair of this quality has a heroic monumentality; but, in his work, Sade is finally ambivalent. Eugénie seals up her mother to keep the dangerous infection of fecundity from spilling into the world but she does not, dare not, excise the womb where the child is produced. Let us quarantine the fecund woman; let us keep her out of sexual circulation, so she does not allow a fallen race to continue to perpetuate its miseries. But we will not go quite so far as to sterilise her completely – because Sade is still in complicity with the authority which he hates.

five

SPECULATIVE FINALE:
THE FUNCTION OF FLESH

> ... the process of human cultural development, in which
> sexuality remains the weak spot.
>
> *Three Essays on the Theory of Sexuality*,
> Sigmund Freud

The word 'fleisch', in German, provokes me to an involuntary shudder. In the English language, we make a fine
distinction between flesh, which is usually alive and,
typically, human; and meat, which is dead, inert, animal and
intended for consumption. Substitute the word 'flesh' in the
Anglican service of Holy Communion; 'Take, eat, this is my
meat which was given for you . . .' and the sacred comestible
becomes the offering of something less than, rather than
more than, human. 'Flesh' in English carries with it a whole
system of human connotations and the flesh of the Son of
Man cannot be animalised into meat without an inhar-
monious confusion of meaning. But, because it is human,
flesh is also ambiguous; we are adjured to shun the world,
the flesh and the Devil. Fleshly delights are lewd distrac-
tions from the contemplation of higher, that is, of spiritual,
things; the pleasures of the flesh are vulgar and unrefined,

even with an element of beastliness about them, although flesh tints have the sumptuous succulence of peaches because flesh plus skin equals sensuality.

But, if flesh plus skin equals sensuality, then flesh minus skin equals meat. The skin has turned into rind, or crackling; the garden of fleshly delights becomes a butcher's shop, or Sweeney Todd's kitchen. My flesh encounters your taste for meat. So much the worse for me.

What are the butcherly delights of meat? These are not sensual but analytical. The satisfaction of scientific curiosity in dissection. A clinical pleasure in the precision with which the process of reducing the living, moving, vivid object to the dead status of thing is accomplished. The pleasure of watching the spectacle of the slaughter that derives from the knowledge one is dissociated from the spectacle; the bloody excitation of the audience in the abattoir, who watch the dramatic transformation act, from living flesh to dead meat, derives from the knowledge they are safe from the knife themselves. There is the technical pleasure of carving and the anticipatory pleasure of the prospect of eating the meat, of the assimilation of the dead stuff, after which it will be humanly transformed into flesh.

Flesh has specific orifices to contain the prick that penetrates it but meat's relation to the knife is more random and a thrust anywhere will do. Sade explores the inhuman sexual possibilities of meat; it is a mistake to think that the substance of which his actors are made is flesh. There is nothing alive or sensual about them. Sade is a great puritan and will disinfect of sensuality anything he can lay his hands on; therefore he writes about sexual relations in terms of butchery and meat.

The murderous attacks on the victims demonstrate the abyss between the parties to the crime, an abyss of incomprehension that cannot be bridged. The lamb does not understand why it is lead to the slaughter and so it goes willingly, because it is in ignorance. Even when it dawns on the lamb that it is going to be killed, the lamb only struggles because it does not understand that it cannot escape; and, besides, it is hampered by the natural ignorance of the herbivore, who does not even know it is possible to eat meat. The lamb could understand easily enough how mint sauce might be delicious but it does not have the mental apparatus to appreciate that its own hindquarters are also nourishing food if suitably cooked, for those with different tastes. Which is why we prefer to eat the herbivores. Because, under no circumstances, could they eat us.

The relations between men and women are often distorted by the reluctance of both parties to acknowledge that the function of flesh is meat to the carnivore but not grass to the herbivore.

The ignorance of one party as to the intentions of the other makes the victim so defenceless against predation that it can seem as if a treacherous complicity finally unites them; as though, in some sense, the victim wills a victim's fate. But, if any of the Sadeian victims seem to incite their masters to their violence by tacitly accepting their right to administer it, let us not make too much of this apparent complicity. There is no defence at all against absolute tyranny.

Constance, most abused of all the wives in *The Hundred and Twenty Days at Sodom*, seeing she has no choice, cleans out her husband's arsehole with her tongue. 'And the poor creature, only too accustomed to these horrors, carried them out as a dutiful, a thoughtful wife, should; ah, great God! what will not dread and thralldom produce.' Absolute tyranny is, by definition, absolute; once the victims, seized by force, enter the impregnable castle, they are already as good as dead. Minski, the cannibal giant, tells Juliette that she and her companions are in his power, to do with as he pleases, as soon as they enter his island fortress. Don Clement warns Justine that any resistance to the masters in the church of St Mary-in-the-Wood is useless. The Chateau of Silling, the imitation Sodom, is utterly impregnable and the paths that brought the victims there have been destroyed behind them. The victims have been erased from the world and now live, their own ghosts although they are not yet dead, only awaiting death, in a world where the function of their own flesh is to reveal to them the gratuitous inevitability of pain, to demonstrate the shocking tragedy of mortality itself, that all flesh may be transformed, at any moment, to meat.

Necrophagy is the exposition of the meatiness of human flesh. Necrophagy parodies the sacramental meal by making its assumptions real. The fifteen-year-old boy roasted for dinner at Minski's house is served up without ceremony; for Minski, he is nothing more nor less than a good meal. Minski claims he owes his health, strength, youthful appearance and abundant seminal secretions to his habitual diet of other people. Cannibalism, the most elementary act of exploitation, that of turning the other directly into a comestible; of seeing the other in the most primitive terms of use.

The strong abuse, exploit and meatify the weak, says Sade. They must and will devour their natural prey. The primal condition of man cannot be modified in any way; it is, eat or be eaten. Eat, assimilate; but the process doesn't stop there. Defaecate, assimilate again. How greedily the coprophile consumes the physical surplus of the act of eating.

Only the most violent of all transformations, that of the transformation of the Kingdom of God into a secular republic will overthrow these relations. In the Kingdom of God, man is made in the image of God and therefore a ravenous, cannibalistic, vicious, egocentric tyrant. Since God does not exist, man must make of himself something a great deal better; that God must be *shown* not to exist, and only corrupts our institutions as a baleful shadow, is the source of Sade's passionate and continual atheism. The Kingdom of God and the secular Republic are notions that transcend monarchy, religion and democracy; they are to do with authoritarianism and libertarianism.

In this world, which was made by God, sexuality is inhuman. In other words, in a society which still ascribes an illusory metaphysic to matters which are in reality solely to do with the relations between human beings, the expression of the sexual nature of men and women is not seen as part of human nature. Sexuality, in this estranged form, becomes a denial of a basis of mutuality, of the acknowledgement of equal rights to exist in the world, from which any durable form of human intercourse can spring.

Sexuality, stripped of the idea of free exchange, is not in any way humane; it is nothing but pure cruelty. Carnal knowledge is the infernal knowledge of the flesh as meat. The fruit of the tree of the knowledge of good and evil is cooked up and served for breakfast in Minski's house in the form of testicle patties and virgin's blood sausages.

So flesh becomes meat by a magical transition about which there is nothing natural. Nobody in Sade's pornography dies of natural causes, of old age or sickness. Death is always a violent infliction by another, or even by Nature itself. Or perhaps, rather, death is always 'natural' since Nature itself is a murderer. When the thunderbolt strikes down Justine, Nature has murdered the girl as effectively as the libertines could have done. In Sade, Nature is a version of the Cruel God of the Old Testament.

Death, in Sade, is always the sudden, violent metamorphosis of the vivid into the inert. Death is always such an outrage, such a crime, such an impiety that Sade must have found it as hard to reconcile himself to the fact of mortality as he did to the fact of birth.

The act of predation – the butcher's job of rendering the flesh of the victim into meat for the table, which Minski himself performs in an exemplary fashion by the violence of his very act of copulation – is the assertion of the abyss between master and victim. There is no question of reciprocal sensation; the idea of it is abhorrent to the Sadeian libertine, except under certain special circumstances where *two of a kind* meet and perform rituals of which both understand the significance. In these cases, violence is a form of play. Otherwise, the dichotomy between active and passive, evil and good, is absolute, and, what is more, perceived as unchanging, an immutable division between classes.

Reciprocity of sensation is not possible because to share is to be robbed.

Dom Clement the monk outlines an economic theory of the nature of sexual pleasure to Justine during her stay in his establishment. Just as Juliette was so rich that she could not afford to give alms, so Clement argues that there is not enough pleasure to go round and he must have it all. If I give anybody else any of my pleasure, I will diminish my own, just as, if I give you half my apple, then I shall only have half left for myself. Pleasure may never be shared, or it will be diminished. A shared pleasure is a betrayal of the self, a seeping away of some of the subject's precious egotism. To share is to be stolen from, says Clement; when a woman pilfers her sexual pleasure from a man, she patently reduces his own and to witness her pleasure can do nothing more for him than to flatter his vanity.

Since gratified vanity is a pleasure of sentimental affect only and therefore inferior to the real pleasure of the senses, it is to be despised. Besides, a man's vanity may be flattered in a far more piquant manner by harshly denying a woman any pleasure at all and forcing her to minister only to the man's pleasure, at the cost of her visible pain. 'In one word, is not he who imposes much more surely the master than he who shares?' The nature of Clement's pleasure is by no means a sensual one; his pleasure is a cerebral one, even an intellectual one – that of the enhancement of the ego. When pleasure is violently denied the partner, the self's pleasure is enhanced in direct relation to the visible unpleasure of the victim. And so the self knows it exists.

Sexual pleasure, therefore, consists primarily in the submission of the partner; but that is not enough. The annihilation of the partner is the only sufficient proof of the triumph of the ego. Dolmancé declares that an erection is sufficient in itself to make a man a despot; pride, says Dolmancé, causes a man 'to wish to be the only one in the world capable of experiencing what he feels; the idea of seeing another enjoy as he enjoys reduces him to a kind of equality with that other which impairs the unspeakable charm *despotism* inspires in him.'

The uniquely unselfing experience of orgasm may be enjoyed to the full only when it is experienced uniquely; perhaps only when there is nobody to observe the loss of self in the orgasm. Dolmancé prefers to take women from behind, in a position where he cannot see or be seen.

Now the sexual act becomes a matter of extreme privacy, in which only the nervous agitation of the partner who experiences the strongest sensation during intercourse has any significance. The despot inflicts sex on the slave and he is perfectly justified in doing so. Dolmancé opines that nature intends man to feel superior, to be a despot, and that is why man is physically stronger than woman. Further, the orgasm is experienced as a fury because nature intends that 'behaviour during copulation should be the same as behaviour in anger'.

Wreaking an impotent fury on an object that may not respond because it has been stunned into submission, he gnaws, bites and soils the loved and hated flesh. All men want to molest women during sexual activity, says Dolmancé; that is the sign of their natural superiority to them.

Remember that this lecture is given to an audience of women; Saint-Ange and Eugénie listen and applaud; since he is good enough to class them with the masters, they, too, will be permitted to tyrannise as much as they please. Libido, since it is sex itself, is genderless; vessels of undiluted libido, these superwomen are included amongst the agressors, the unique individuals who follow the desolating logic of the imagination to that lonely pitch of phallic supremacy up above the world in as awesome and rigorous a

puritanism as Simeon Stylites on his pole. This is a conspiracy of carnivores. 'We, you, Madame, and I, those like
ourselves – we are the only people who deserve to be listened
to!'

Dolmancé, however, has so greatly excited himself with
his own discourse that he is forced to break off and bugger
Augustin, the gardener. All present execute another
geometric exercise and ejaculate in unison. But the presence
of his fellow-conspirators in the group games does not
alleviate the solitude of the libertine; rather, it enhances it.
The libertine's sovereign orgasm is not shared with his
fellow libertines; it simply occurs at the same time. The
parallel if simultaneous orgasms of the libertines cannot
intersect with one another. There is no fusion to confuse, to
interfere with the unique experience.

In Sade, sexual pleasure is an entirely inward experience.
Roles may be changed about and women become men, men
women; the whipper will be whipped in his turn. But the
territoriality of the subject's pleasure cannot be invaded
because sexual pleasure is nothing but a private and individual shock of the nerves. Noirceuil defines pleasure:
'What is pleasure? Simply this: that which occurs when
voluptuous atoms, or atoms emanated from voluptuous
objects, clash with and fire the electrical particles cir-
culating in the hollow of our nerve fibres. To complete the
pleasure the clash must be as violent as possible.' This is a
form of exacerbated auto-eroticism. Sexual pleasure is not
experienced *as* experience; it does not modify the subject.
An entirely externally induced phenomenon, its sensation is
absolutely personal, just as it does not hurt the knife if you
cut yourself with it.

Yet, curiously enough, Sade himself is the lamb led to
slaughter as well as the butcher with the insensible knife. In
the well-documented events of a certain morning in 1772 in
a bedroom in Marseilles, the hired girl flogged Sade with a
heather broom; he marked the number of blows with his
knife in the mantlepiece. Then, while he coupled with the

girl, his valet buggered him. Throughout the Cytherean morning, the girl stated, he addressed his servant as 'Monsieur le Marquis', elementary transformation of pain and pleasure, aristocrat and servant. Dolmancé gasps to Saint-Ange's brother: 'Deign, Oh my love, to serve me as a woman after having been my lover.' He presents Eugénie de Mistival with her weapon; an indiarubber dildo, with which to bugger him. When he whips her, he consoles Eugénie with the assertion of a dialectic of mutual aggression: 'Now victim for a moment, my lovely angel, soon you'll persecute me in your turn.'

These violent transformations of appearance are the only ways in which Sade can envisage reciprocity. Mutual aggression can never take place at the same time but only in a serial fashion, now me, now you, and the cock, the phallus, the sceptre of a virility which is not a state-in-itself, in fact, however phallocentric the notion of sexuality implicit in Sade's pornography might be, but a modality, is passed from man to woman, woman to man, man to man, woman to woman, back and forth, as in a parlour game.

We must not confuse these parlour games with those kinds of real relations that change you. Sexual activity in these Sadeian communities of equals is a social exploit, a communal activity, an infertility festival, with a choric quality. It has certain relations to kinetic art. The libertines assemble themselves in architectonic configurations, fuck furiously, discharge all together – all fall down. They have arranged themselves as for a group photograph, and it is the most complicated mechanics that must set the erotic engine in motion, mouth against cunt, cock in anus, tongue on testicles, finger on clitoris (whose sexual function is not a discovery of the twentieth century). Like a good housewife organising her store cupboard, Sade wants a place for everything and everything in its place in the regimented pursuit of pleasure.

Suitably garbed for these pornographic occasions in kitsch uniforms of gauze, assembled in voluptuous boudoirs or arranged like sacrilegious offerings upon the altars of churches, the libertines perform extraordinary tableaux with well-drilled precision. Among this well-populated activity, there is as little room for intimacy as there is upon the football field.

The bed is now as public as the dinner table and governed by the same rules of formal confrontation. Flesh has lost its common factor; that it is the substance of which we are all made and yet that differentiates us. It has acquired, instead, the function of confusing kind and gender, man and beast, woman and fowl. The subject itself becomes an *objet de luxe* in these elaborately choreographed masques of abstraction, of alienation.

The libertine goes to the orgy to enhance his notion of his unique and supreme self; but, only in the group, among his peers, is the self truly lost. Where desire is a function of the act rather than the act a function of desire, desire loses its troubling otherness; it ceases to be a movement outwards from the self. The arrows of desire are turned back on the heart, and pierce it.

For the libertine chooses to surround himself, not with lovers or partners, but with accomplices, The libertine would not trust a partner, who would rob him of pleasure by causing him to feel rather than to experience.

The presence of his accomplices preserves his ego from the singular confrontation with the object of a reciprocal desire which is, in itself, both passive object and active subject. Such a partner acts on us as we act on it; both partners are changed by the exchange and, if submission is mutual, then aggression is mutual. Such a partner might prove to the libertine that sexuality is an aspect of being, rather than a crime against being; but the libertine doesn't, after all, want to know that. If the evidence of Sade's ingrained puritanism is that he believes sex in itself to be a crime, and associates its expression with violent crime, the libertine's entire pleasure is the cerebral, not sensual one, of knowing he is engaging in forbidden activity. It is the presence of his

accomplices, all engaged on the same project, that convinces
him he commits a crime. The knowledge that sexuality is
criminal preserves him from the onslaught of love.

If he were not criminal, he would be forced to abdicate
from his position as the lord of creation, made in the image
of God; his criminality is his excuse, the source of his pride,
and of his denial of love.

The libertine's perversions are the actings-out of his
denial of love. Yet Freud suggests the 'mental factor' plays
a large part in accomplishing the transformation of the
instinctual desire for simple sensual pleasure in the case of
necrophily, coprophily and bestiality. The Sadeian libertine
is proudly conscious of such activities as 'perversions', even
as he strenuously denies the actual concept of perversion;
that to eat shit and screw corpses and dogs are not the
pastimes of the common man is part of his pride in doing so
himself. Yet this transformation of the appetite in favour of
the initially unappetising is human work, not criminal work.
Freud says: 'It is impossible to deny that . . . a piece of work
has been performed which, in spite of its horrifying result, is
the equivalent of an idealisation of the instinct. The omnipotence of love is perhaps never more strongly proved
than in such of its aberrations as these.'

The excremental enthusiasm of the libertines transforms
the ordure in which they roll to a bed of roses. The pleasure
of the libertine philosophers derives in a great part from the
knowledge they have overcome their initial disgust. By the
exercise of the will, they have overcome repugnance and so,
in one sense, are liberated from the intransigence of reality.
This liberation from reality is their notion of freedom; the
way to freedom lies through the privy. But the conquest of
morality and aesthetics, of shame, disgust and fear, the
pursuit of greater and greater sexual sophistication in terms
of private sensation lead them directly to the satisfactions
of the child; transgression becomes regression and, like a
baby, they play with their own excrement.

Even the pursuit of the vilest of all passions, the murderous passions, lead them back to the cradle in the end; they have not acquired these tastes in the process of maturing. They had only forgotten them. Now, freed from all adult restraint, they remember them again. 'It may be assumed that the impulse of cruelty arises from the instinct for mastery and appears at a period of sexual life at which the genitals have not yet taken over their later role,' suggests Freud. The shamelessness and violence of the libertines is that of little children who are easily cruel because they have not learned the capacity for pity which the libertines dismiss as 'childish' because the libertines themselves have not yet grown up enough to acknowledge the presence of others in their solipsistic world.

Juliette, as Theodor Adorno and Max Horkheimer say, embodies 'intellectual pleasure in regression'. She attacks civilisation with its own weapons. She exercises rigorously rational thought; she creates systems; she exhibits an iron self-control. Her will triumphs over the barriers of pain, shame, disgust and morality until her behaviour reverts to the polymorphous perversity of the child, who has not yet learnt the human objections to cruelty because, in a social sense, no child is yet fully human. Her destination has always been her commencement. The triumph of the will recreates, as its Utopia, the world of early childhood, and that is a world of nightmare, impotence and fear, in which the child fantasises, out of its own powerlessness, an absolute supremacy.

Yet the adult world of work may not be evaded; but it, too, is transformed. Sexual satisfaction may be obtained only at the cost of enormous expenditures of energy. Pleasure is a hard task-master. *The Hundred and Twenty Days at Sodom* offers a black version of the Protestant ethic but the profit, the orgasm obtained with so much effort, the product of so much pain and endeavour – the pursuit of this profit leads directly to hell. To a perfectly material hell. The final murderous passion recounted by Desgranges is called the 'hell-game'. The libertine, assisted by torturers disguised as demons, himself pretends to be the devil; Juliette similarly dresses Saint Fond as a demon during an orgy. If we once needed the notion of a hell in order to console ourselves that something exists worse than this world, we no longer need it now.

The elaboration of pleasure will change its quality; the simple passions of the libertines in Duclos' accounts in the first book will elaborate insensibly, will become the complex atrocities of the third book.

To obtain his precious orgasm, the libertine must now hunt it down single-mindedly through seas of blood and excrement. But, the more earnestly he strives, the further the goal recedes from him. He is forced to invest more and more energy in the pursuit of orgasm; all the same, it grows harder and harder for him to come. His rituals become more elaborate, his needs more abstract. The structure of his own invented reality hardens around him and imprisons him. The passions he thought would free him from the cage of being become the very bars of the cage that traps him; he himself cannot escape the theatrical decor he has created around himself in order to give himself the confidence to immolate his victims. During the hell-game, the libertine is himself as much in hell as his victims are and they can at least escape from it by dying. He cannot.

Sade's eroticism, with its tragic style, its displays, its cortèges, its sacrifices, its masks and costumes, preserves something of the demonology of primitive man. The libertines are indeed like men possessed by demons. Their orgasms are like the visitation of the gods of Voodoo, annihilating, appalling. Minski's orgasm, that kills his partners, is announced by a ringing yell. Catherine the Great screams and blasphemes. Durand emits dreadful screams and her limbs twitch and thresh; she seems to have succumbed to a fit. Saint Fond's shrieks, his contortions, his blasphemies are appalling and he half faints at the climax. These descriptions are those of torture; this is 'the precious climax, which characterises the enjoyment as good or bad.'

The return to the self after such a crisis must be a lowering passage. Orgasm has possessed the libertine; during the irreducible timelessness of the moment of orgasm, the hole in the world through which we fall, he has been as a god, but this state is as fearful as it is pleasurable and, besides, is lost as soon as it is attained. He has burst into the Utopia of desire, in which only the self exists; he has not negotiated the terms of his arrival there, as gentle lovers do, but taken Utopia by force. See, the conquering hero comes. And, just as immediately, he has been expelled from it, a fall like Lucifer's, from heaven to hell.

The annihilation of the self and the resurrection of the body, to die in pain and to painfully return from death, is the sacred drama of the Sadeian orgasm. In this drama, flesh is used instrumentally, to provoke these spasmodic visitations of dreadful pleasure. In this flesh, nothing human remains; it aspires to the condition of the sacramental meal. It is never the instrument of love.

In his diabolic solitude, only the possibility of love could awake the libertine to perfect, immaculate terror. It is in this holy terror of love that we find, in both men and women themselves, the source of all opposition to the emancipation of women.

POSTSCRIPT:
RED EMMA REPLIES
TO THE MADMAN OF CHARENTON

History tells us that every oppressed class gained
true liberation from its masters through its own efforts.
It is necessary that woman learn that lesson, that she
realise that her freedom will reach as far as her power to
achieve her freedom reaches. It is, therefore, far more
important for her to begin with her inner regeneration,
to cut loose from the weight of prejudices, traditions,
and customs. The demand for equal rights in every
vocation of life is just and fair; but, after all, the most
vital right is the right to love and be loved. Indeed, if
partial emancipation is to become a complete and true
emancipation of woman, it will have to do away with the
ridiculous notion that to be loved, to be sweetheart and
mother, is synonymous with being slave or subordinate.
It will have to do away with the absurd notion of the
dualism of the sexes, or that man and woman represent
two antagonistic worlds.

Pettiness separates, breadth unites. Let us be broad
and big. Let us not overlook vital things because of the
bulk of trifles confronting us. A true conception of the
relation of the sexes will not admit of conqueror and
conquered; it knows of but one great thing: to give of
one's self boundlessly, in order to find one's self richer,
deeper, better. That alone can fill the emptiness, and
transform the tragedy of woman's emancipation into
joy, limitless joy.

The Tragedy of Woman's Emancipation,
Emma Goldman

BIBLIOGRAPHY

SADE'S WORK

Oeuvres complètes, 16 vols. (Cercle du Livre Precieux, Paris, 1966-7)

Translations

The Complete Justine, Philosophy in the Bedroom and other writings tr. Richard Seaver and Austryn Wainhouse (Grove Press, New York, New York, 1965)

The Hundred and Twenty Days at Sodom (Grove Press, New York, 1966)

Juliette (Grove Press, New York, 1968)

OTHER SOURCES

The Dialectics of Enlightenment, Theodor Adorno and Max Horkheimer, tr. John Cumming (Allen Lane, London, 1973)

Sade/Fourier/Loyola, Roland Barthes, tr. Richard Miller (Jonathan Cape, London, 1977)

L'Erotisme, Georges Bataille (Editions de Minuit, Paris, 1957)

Must we Burn Sade?, Simone de Beauvoir, with selections from his writings chosen by Paul Dinnage (John Calder, London, 1962)

Anthologie de l'Humeur Noir, ed. André Breton, Jean Jacques Pauvert (Paris, 1966)

Symbolic Wounds, Bruno Bettelheim (Thames and Hudson, London, 1955)

Life against Death: the Psychoanalytical Meaning of History, Norman O. Brown (Routledge & Kegan Paul, London, 1959)

Black Skin White Masks, Frantz Fanon, (MacGibbon & Kee, London, 1968)

Love and Death in the American Novel, Leslie Fiedler (Jonathan Cape, London, 1967)

Madness and Civilisation: a History of Insanity in the Age of Reason, Michel Foucault, tr. Richard Howard (Tavistock Publications, London, 1965)

Introductory Lectures on Psychoanalysis, Sigmund Freud, tr. James Strachey (Hogarth Press, London, revised edition of 1962)

New Introductory Lectures on Psychoanalysis, Sigmund Freud, tr. James Strachey (Hogarth Press, London, revised edition of 1962)

Beyond the Pleasure Principle, Sigmund Freud, tr. James Strachey (Hogarth Press, London, edition of 1961)

Three Essays on the Theory of Sexuality, Sigmund Freud, tr. James Strachey (Hogarth Press, London, revised edition of 1962)

The Life and Ideas of the Marquis de Sade, Geoffrey Gorer (Panther, London, 1964)

Norma Jean: the story of Marilyn Monroe, Fred Lawrence Guiles (W. H. Allen, London, 1969)

Leviathan, Thomas Hobbes, edited by C. B. Macpherson (Penguin, London, 1968)

Envy and Gratitude, Melanie Klein (Tavistock Publications, London, 1957)

'Kant avec Sade', Jacques Lacan, essay in *Ecrits II* (Editions de Seuil, Paris, 1971)

Marquis de Sade, Gilbert Lely, tr. Alec Brown (Paul Elek, London, 1961)

Psychoanalysis and Feminism, Juliet Mitchell (Allen Lane, London, 1974)

Marilyn, Norman Mailer (Hodder and Stoughton, London, 1973)

Not in God's Image, Julia O'Faolain and Lauro Martines (Temple Smith, London, 1973)

Art and Pornography, Morse Peckham (Basic Books, New York, 1969)

The Complete Works of François Rabelais, tr. Sir Thomas Urquhart and Peter Motteux (Bodley Head, London, 1933)

The Marquis de Sade, Donald Thomas (Weidenfeld and Nicholson, London, 1977)

Earth Spirit, and Pandora's Box, Frank Wedekind, tr. Stephen Spender (Calder and Boyars, London, 1972)

Anarchism and Other Essays, Emma Goldman, with a new introduction by Richard Drinnon (Dover Publications, New York, 1969)